MERSEY FERRIES

Volume 2
The Wallasey Ferries

An artist's impression of Egremont ferry in 1878. The terminal building surmounted by the clock survived many changes until demolished long after the closure of the ferry. The building with the tall chimney to the right housed the machinery for hauling in the running-out stage while the buildings to the left were used as the ferry workshops for many years.

M. Jenkins collection

MERSEY FERRIES

Volume 2

The Wallasey Ferries

by

T. B. MAUND, FCIT, FILT
and
MARTIN JENKINS, BA

Black Dwarf Publications

Copyright: T. B. Maund, Martin Jenkins and Black Dwarf Publications, 2003
Designed by Ian Pope

British Library Cataloguing-in-Publication Data. A catalogue
record for this book is available from the British Library
ISBN 1 903599 08 3

Black Dwarf Publications is an imprint of Black Dwarf Lightmoor
80 Tutnalls Street, Lydney, Gloucestershire GL15 5PQ
website: www.lightmoor.co.uk

Printed by The Alden Press, Oxford

CONTENTS

INTRODUCTION

Volume 1, published in 1992, described the seven ferries crossing the River Mersey from Woodside, Birkenhead, up river to Eastham and this volume completes the story with a description of the three ferries between Seacombe and the mouth of the river at New Brighton.

There are sharp contrasts between the histories of the two groups. Both commenced as a result of private initiatives but whilst the southern group started to diminish in numbers as early as 1870 and private enterprise persisted until 1904, the three ferries in the northern group were unified under municipal ownership as early as 1861. Municipal councils and their actions dominate both stories and a significant factor was the mutual antipathy of the councils of the two major towns, Birkenhead and Wallasey, to collaboration where their ferry undertakings were concerned yet, with hindsight, it is obvious that a Joint Committee or some such statutory undertaking, would have had enormous economic benefits to both towns. While both towns' ferries experienced seasonal peaks, Birkenhead's could easily be absorbed by the basic service at relatively little cost while Wallasey's summer traffic was so heavy that considerable additional infrastructure was needed to cope with it.

Over the years, Birkenhead's council showed a very pragmatic approach to ferry management and when the first Mersey Tunnel scheme threatened to affect the stability of the ferries, quickly came to terms with the situation and shrewdly allowed the Tunnel authority to take control of the ferry undertaking to the extent that it was indemnified against financial loss for forty years. By contrast, Wallasey took up an isolationist position which succeeded only in eliminating it from the Tunnel scheme and burdening its ratepayers with enormous losses.

This is a story of misguided municipal pride and the squandering of enormous sums of money on grandiose schemes which had no hope of giving a return on the capital employed and of a failure of both councillors (and in some cases also of managers) to grasp the economic realities of the undertaking.

The glory days of the Mersey Ferries have long past and the present day rump is treated as a leisure service rather than a part of the region's transport network. But in the past, ferry crossings were integral parts of the daily journey to work for over 40% of Wallasey's workforce. Their rise and fall present a fascinating story of social changes over two centuries.

It is unfortunate that far fewer records of the Wallasey Ferries have survived compared with Birkenhead where very comprehensive archives had been carefully preserved. The authors have tried to do the best with what is available and realise that the statistical records cannot be compared with those in Volume 1.

ACKNOWLEDGEMENTS

The authors acknowledge with grateful thanks the invaluable assistance given by J. N. Barlow, C. Bidston, A.S. Clayton, J. B. Horne, Jean Jenkins, R. T. McMahon, E. J. McWatt, T. Morgan, E. Moxey, G. Parry, Janice Taylor (Wirral Archive Service), David Thompson and T. G. Turner.

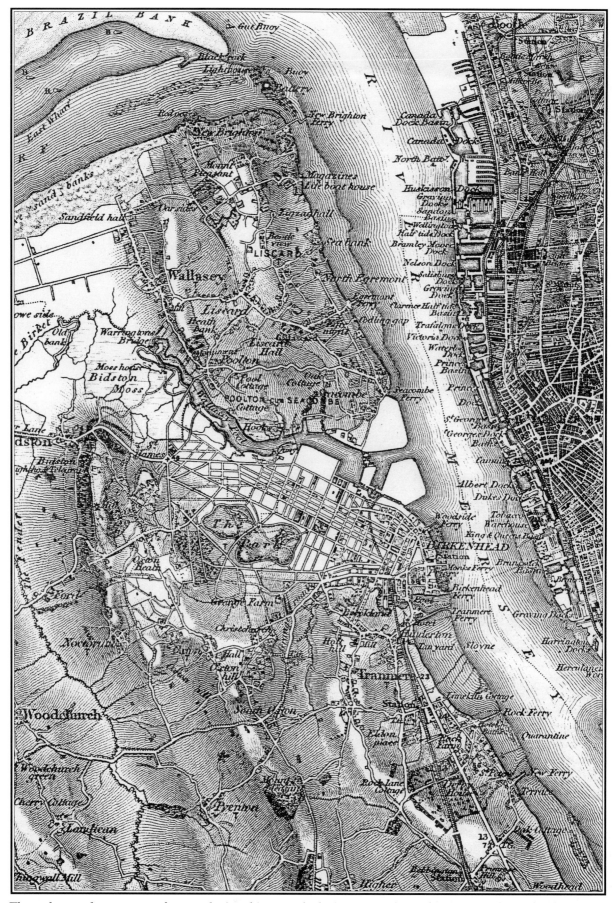

The authors make no excuses for reproducing this map which also appeared in Volume 1 as it shows the locations of the various ferries and also the reclaimed land between Seacombe and Woodside which altered the Wirral coastline for all time.

Ordnance Survey, Crown Copyright Reserved

1 EARLY TIMES

AFTER the Norman Conquest, Wallasey (Walea) formed part of the territory administered by the Norman knight, Robert de Rodelent and is listed in the Domesday Survey of 1087, published one year before his death. De Rodelent's estates included lands on both sides of the Mersey so it is reasonably safe to assume that he either created a new 'right of passage' or confiscated an existing ancient passage, perhaps controlled by the deposed Saxon landlord of Walea, Untred. As de Rodelent controlled the Cheshire coast from Neston on the Dee – at least as far as the southern tip of Wallasey Pool on the Mersey – and possibly further, encompassing Tranmere Pool as well, it is equally likely that he established rights of passage to, from and across the Wallasey Pool. As he died without issue in 1088, his lands were divided between other Norman families but no powerful single family emerged. In fact, the district was so inhospitable and inaccessible that the Normans may well have left their affairs in the hands of the local Saxons who, according to Domesday, numbered 35 in Walea. To protect themselves, they combined together to administer the various 'rights of passage' on behalf of the community. However, in 1150, they found these communal interests threatened by the decision of Hamo de Mascy to finance the building of a Benedictine Monastery on Birchen Head.

The Monastic Period

De Mascy chose the location for the priory carefully; it was the spiritual home of 16 Benedictines of the Order of Black Monks who were enjoined by their Founder to provide hospitality to strangers, as they would to Christ himself, at major road and river crossings. Woodside, situated on a narrow rocky foreshore, commanded the shortest and safest of the Mersey crossings passable at most states of the tide. Of the others, Seacombe was only of local interest and Tranmere, the use of which involved a shorter journey from Chester, then the primary source of traffic, was 500 ft from the water's edge at low tide. To support the Priory, de Mascy endowed it with lands at Moreton, Saughall Massie, Bidston, Tranmere, Higher Bebington, Claughton and Wallasey. The monks rented out some of the endowments to tenant farmers who, in the movement of produce to market, were frequently obliged to cross the Wallasey or Tranmere Pools.

Until the first decade of the 13th century Chester, still a thriving port, exercised considerable influence over the area. However, in a determined bid to undermine its political importance, King John, attracted by the safe anchorage of the Liver Pool, elevated the unknown hamlet (which was not even mentioned in the Domesday Book) to the status of a Royal Borough and started to fortify it in 1207. A weekly market, a three-day Martinmas Fair, a castle, court house and mill were established together with a 'right of passage' across the river to the Cheshire shore.

During the early years of the 14th century, the Birkenhead monks were in dispute with neighbouring landowners who they claimed were abusing the 'rights of passage' within the Priory's jurisdiction. In order to strengthen their position, they petitioned King Edward III and secured a Royal Charter dated 30th April 1330 granting the Prior and his successors for ever 'the right of passage' over the arm of the sea for men, goods, horses with leave to charge reasonable tolls. Within two weeks of the granting of the Charter, the Prior was accused by William Lascelles and other Seacombe men of removing an anchor and rope valued at £5 from a place called 'Mulne How'. The Prior stated that, in the sight of his Church, he was the Lord of Claughton and, as such, he exercised sole rights over the Mulne How anchorage. Lascelles and his friends argued that they were Lords of the Manor of Seacombe who had 'from time immemorial' held the right of passage for the conveyance at will of men, horses and victuals from any point on the coastline between Wallasey Pool and Raynylde's (Tranmere) Pool, both from their own lands and those administered by the Priory. The Prior refuted this claim and the dispute was referred to the Eyre Court in Chester which found in favour of the Prior and fined the plaintiffs thirteen shillings (65p). Outraged by this verdict, Lascelles obtained a Writ from the King's Chancellor which ensured that a record of their Plea was sent for consideration in London, an early form of the Appeal Court. The outcome of future quarrels suggests that the Eyre Court's decision was upheld.

The situation was further exacerbated when, between 1333 and 1339, the monks established a new 'right of passage' across the Wallasey Pool at a point known as the Hooks, so called because of irregular formations jutting out into the water. This was situated between the present day Duke Street bridge and the end of Limekiln Lane, Poulton under reclaimed land later occupied by Wallasey gas works. This passage was used by the monks to reach their lands in Wallasey. Strengthening their position further, as loyal subjects who took burgage in Liverpool (tenure of land in the town on weekly rent) were offered free use of the right of passage, the monks of St. James erected a granary or warehouse in Liverpool in 1346, thus entitling them to cross the river in either direction without paying tolls.

Further up river there was another example of royal patronage and monastic involvement. On 16th July 1357, the Black Prince granted the right of passage to the Poole family and at some date unknown it passed to the Abbey and Convent of St. Werburg at Chester. Abbot Thomas (either Thomas Highfield, (died 1527) or his successor, Thomas Marshall (translated 1529), put his signature to an undated Indenture leasing one ferry boat, a landing stage and a cottage in a wood to Thomas Deane, a Chester barber. The ferry passed from the Dean and Chapter of Chester after the Dissolution to Sir Richard Cotton who eventually sold it. By the early nineteenth century it was vested in the Stanley family of Hooton Hall.

The Lascelles family was prominent in an Inquiry convened in 1396-7 to examine evidence that they had suffered various deprivations at the hands of the Priory, having lost the right to load and unload boats on any of the Priory lands. The Inquiry was told that Lascelles and other Seacombe men held

shares in a ferry with boats from the 'high street' which ran through the County of Wirral to Tokesford, a name implying a ford at low water and a ferry at high tide. Tokesford is believed to have been at the site of the present day Poulton bridge, the westernmost crossing of the Wallasey Pool and was approached from a turning off Black Street, the main track connecting Woodside with Bidston and Moreton. Tokesford was used, not only for crossing the upper reaches of the Pool, but also as a starting place for sailings to Liverpool. It is arguable that the original Seacombe 'right of passage' may also have included Tokesford and the whole of the north shore of the Pool. Lascelles' grievance was that 'the religious of Birkenhead had established a rival ferry under the wood of Birkenhead to the injury of their (the men of Seacombe) rights'. However, Lascelles and his supporters had failed, through ignorance or default, to register their ancient rights at the special courts set up to verify such claims and the Inquiry ruled that they had forfeited their rights. The Tokesford passage was put under the control of the Earl of Chester who, in due course, either sold or transferred it to the Stanleys of Eastham and finally the Vyners of Bidston who, in 1814, were responsible for building the first embankment

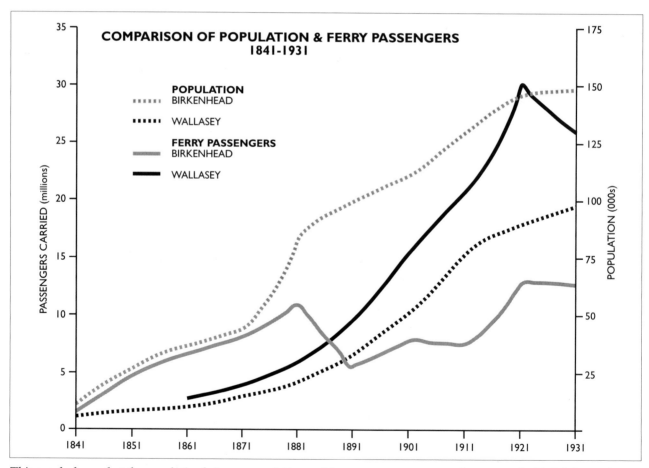

This graph shows that the correlation between population and ferry passengers was much more marked in Wallasey than in Birkenhead where the existence of considerable industry in the town resulted in fewer people having to cross the river in search of work. Until mid-century, it was easier to travel to Liverpool from Wallasey than to Birkenhead.

across the upper reaches of the Pool.

It is not clear if the Lascelles also lost the right to use the Seacombe passage; it depends on whether Tokesford and Seacombe were one and the same. Possibly Seacombe was quite independent or was created as the result of the Inquiry. However, there is no doubt that Seacombe continued to prosper albeit in a secondary role to Woodside which became the main ferry crossing. In 1516, Robert and Margery Dod (widow) sold certain lands to John Porte (Peart) including 'a fourth part of the passage of Secum', indicating that the passage was still jointly owned. But it is not clear if there was a well-defined landing place in the vicinity of the present Seacombe stage or whether it applied to any of the many inlets along the shores of the Pool as far inland as Poulton. These inlets would have afforded greater protection from the weather, been closer to the farms of Liscard and Poulton, involved shorter land journeys and avoided the exposed confluence of the Pool with the Mersey.

Following the dissolution of the monasteries, the Woodside passage (including the Hooks) passed to the Crown and from 17th May 1544, it was sold into private hands as described in Volume One. By 1541, Seacombe had also passed to the Crown and, in that year, it was leased at an annual rent of 9s. 8d. (49.1p) to William Bromley. In 1543 Bromley transferred the lease to John Minshull, the Lord of Tranmere who had ulterior motives in wishing to acquire it.

About 1552 he and his ferry man, John Bromborough, were accused by Ralph Worsley, owner of the Woodside passage, of violating his rights as successor to the Priory estates. Minshull had set up a rival ferry and a busy fish yard within the confines of Birket (Tranmere) Pool and claimed that as he owned 'the ferry of Secum', he had ancient rights to the passage of Tranmere; Bromborough stated that he was the only ferryman entitled to operate from Tranmere. Minshull produced documents which purported to show that as Birket's Pool was from time immemorial known as Raynolde's (or Raynylde's) Pool, he had an indisputable right to fish therein through his title of Lord of the Manor of Tranmere. Worsley maintained that the former Priory rights covered the whole coast from a creek known as Wallasey Pool in the west to a certain water 'Gonell's Pool' in the east. He reminded Minshull that only the Woodside boats had conveyed passengers and goods from these shores and the Seacombe boats had been limited to carrying goods only from the west bank of Wallasey Pool. Worsley lost the argument and the Tranmere crossing was permanently established as a rival to Woodside, continuing in operation with a few interruptions until 1904.

The association of the Tranmere and Seacombe passages has not been explained. By 1586, Seacombe had apparently fallen into disuse as, when John Poole, an important landowner in Wallasey and elsewhere in Wirral, addressed a Plea to the Queen's Exchequer seeking to obtain the lease of the Tranmere passage, he wrote that the Seacombe passage was decayed but that another passage (Tranmere) had been established two miles up river. 'The suitor humbly prayeth he may have lease of Her Majesty's interest in the said boat or passage at Tranmere and in consideration thereof he will revive the said rent of 9s. 8d for the said passage of Seacombe and yield the same rent yearly with twelve [old] pence increase for the said passage of Tranmere for which hitherto there hath been no rent paid to my knowledge'. The Exchequer agreed.

The statement that Seacombe was decayed is intriguing as he further wrote 'I am credibly informed the ground where the same [Seacombe] passage and ferry boat hath been used is grown into nature of an island so as people cannot have recourse to it as in times past they have been accostomed'. This suggests, perhaps, coastal erosion and the location of the landing is again unclear. A site further up the Pool would have had greater advantages, as previously mentioned. When Mother Redcap's Inn was built in 1595 it was described as the only building on the coast between the Rock Point herring house and the Seacombe boat house. One can speculate that the latter just might have been the building depicted in the Vyner estate map of 1665 at the foot of Limekiln Lane but it suggests that the ferry was again in existence before the turn of the century.

Further confusion arises from a record of a land transaction in Poulton in 1565 which included the ferry. Perhaps this referred to the Tokesford crossing but it could have been a part of the Seacombe rights. Alternatively there might have been a quite separate Poulton right of passage of which records have disappeared. Poulton was a relatively thriving port; according to the *Liverpool Year Book* for 1765 there were three fishing boats of 8, 14 and 20 tons, compared with Liverpool's twelve. It prospered and by 1839 there were regular sailing packets to Ireland. It declined swiftly following the damming of the Pool in 1844 prior to its conversion into docks.

Liverpool's Ferry Rights

Since 1537, the Liverpool right of passage had been held by the Molyneux family under lease from the Crown. The Liverpool ferrymen had two major grievances the first being resolved in 1577 when they were ordered to continue the traditional custom of providing free transport for all Liverpool burghers and their families; it was agreed that a toll of $^1/_2$d. should be levied if a burgher was accompanied by his horse. The second concerned the Cheshire ferrymen whom it was alleged were stealing the Liverpool trade. In 1584, Liverpool Town Council ordered that no Cheshire boat was to take or receive any goods originating on the Lancashire coast but this was widely ignored and in 1626 the Council reacted to demands for action by convening a Public Inquiry. The Liverpool men reasoned that one of their boats should always be the first to load on their side of the river and there should be fixed tolls applying to all Mersey ferrymen, thus preventing queue jumping, overcharging and undercutting. If approved, the agreement would apply only to Liverpool and not to Bootle, Kirkdale and Toxteth who, to some extent, supported the Cheshire men.

In the course of evidence by individual sailors, John Jumpe of Liverpool testified that the farmers of Eastham, Tranmore, Wallasey and Birkett boats usually paid to the farmers of the King's Ferry (Woodside) for such fraught (sic) and passengers as they carried from Liverpool. Before 1609, Jumpe stated that the owners of the Birkett boat paid half their receipts for goods taken at Wallasey to the owners of the Wallasey passage but he believed that due to a dispute the Birkett boat no longer loaded in Wallasey. Contradicting him, Peter Smith of the Birkett boat, said he still loaded at Wallasey and paid tolls. From this contradictory evidence it would seem that the Tranmere and Seacombe passages were still linked but Jumpe refers to the owners of the Wallasey passage. Perhaps they embraced both Poulton and Seacombe and it would be interesting to know the distinction between the Birkett and Tranmere ferries. Two witnesses cited examples of summoning the Liverpool Sergeant to arrest certain Cheshire ferrymen for non-payment of tolls.

The Inquiry advised that Cheshire boats loading in Liverpool should keep accurate accounts and proffer half their monies to the Liverpool ferrymen and the reverse procedure should apply on the Cheshire shore. Twenty years later, Liverpool made a further attempt to stamp out abuses, ordering that all cross-river ferry traffic should be divided equally by allowing the home boat priority loading from its own base; tolls were again regulated. During the Civil War, the boats were requisitioned by both sides for conveying troops.

Liverpool Loses Ferry Rights

In 1777 Liverpool Town Council acquired the right of passage from the Molyneux family, the annual revenue being £20. Having failed to control the numbers of Cheshire boats using their quays and wharves, the Council decided to make them available to all comers. In so doing they effectively surrendered their rights and opted out of the ferry scene. At an Inquiry held in 1856, they were accused of squandering their traditional 'right of passage' over the Mersey with the result that only the Cheshire ferry owners would benefit from the enormous increase in cross river traffic. Birkenhead and Wallasey ultimately secured the right to levy tolls for journeys both to and from Liverpool providing that no monies were taken on the Lancashire side.

Sail boats jockey for position on the Liverpool waterfront. Some of those depicted in this early 19th century view were almost certainly ferry boats. M. Jenkins collection

2 THE PRIVATE OWNERS 1761-1861

HORSE racing was an important generator of traffic for Seacombe ferry. Between 1637 and 1785, racing took place over a five-mile irregularly shaped course running from the present junction of Wallasey Village and Green Lane to Leasowe Castle and back. During race weeks the course attracted considerable numbers of wealthy racegoers many of whom sought accommodation on the Wirral. Several inns were opened and Seacombe Boat House was extended to provide rooms and dining facilities. Wagonettes and coaches were provided to convey visitors to the course over an indifferent road which skirted the north bank of Wallasey Pool, crossing the various inlets by wooden bridges. The Woodside boats were often called upon for assistance at the busiest times. When the races were transferred first to Lydiate and then to Aintree, probably because of flooding of the low-lying land by the sea, less salubrious sports were promoted – '...a main of cocks to be fought at the sign of the Ferry, being the Boat House at Seacombe in Cheshire opposite Liverpool'.

In 1761, John Wilson sold the Seacombe boats and other equipment to John Owen who, ten years later, disposed of them, together with $7^1/2$ acres of land, to Rear Admiral Richard Smith. The 'right of passage' was held by a number of joint owners one of whom was Smith's father-in-law, James Gordon of Poulton-cum-Seacombe who died in 1778. Smith inherited this share and, with the decline in patronage which followed the demise of the races, the other joint owners gradually waived their rights leaving Smith in sole possession. Upon his death in 1811, his son, also Richard Smith of Urswick in the Furness district of Lancashire, inherited and, as an absentee landlord, Trustees were appointed to act on his behalf, apparently in his capacity as Lord of the Manor of Poulton-cum-Seacombe. In order to place the ferry on a sound commercial footing, it was decided to resite the terminal and improve the landing facilities.

About 1815, Richard Smith completed a new earth and stone slipway about 100 yards north-east of the old Boat House where, at low tide, the water receded the least distance from the shore. The slip enabled the sailing gigs to approach at most states of the tide thereby easing the problems of embarkation and disembarkation. Having financed the new slipway, the Trustees were anxious to lease the site on an annual basis and the first lessee is believed to have been Stanley Garner, the proprietor of a newly-built Stanley Hotel which was situated on the main track leading from the ferry towards Liscard and Poulton – later Victoria

Road and now Borough Road. Other hotels were springing up all along the Wirral coast as enterprising investors catered for wealthier Liverpudlians who wished to escape from the squalor of the city. The Seacombe Hotel, owned by Thomas Parry, was built directly overlooking the new ferry slip and opened in 1819. This impressive two-storey building gained a reputation for good cuisine and luxurious appointments. There were gardens, a bowling green, a summer house and even an American-style bowling alley. Wagonettes were available to convey guests to such attractions as Leasowe Castle. There were miles of unspoilt beaches and pleasant walks along leafy lanes. The Parry family who ran the hotel until 1853, lived in a fine mansion, Brougham House (Frog Hall) which stood on the corner of Brougham Road and Brighton Street. Once the ferry trade began to improve, several of the previous joint owners of the right of passage challenged Smith's supremacy but seven separate court actions all failed.

The Changeover to Steam

Although opposed by the Guild of Watermen, the Merseyside shipbuilders swiftly adapted to the technology of steam propulsion. Their yards were huddled together on a strip of the river bank which was eventually used for the excavation of Albert Dock. The largest and best known yards were those of Humble and Hurry and Mottershead and Hayes. On 25th July 1816, the latter launched *Princess Charlotte*, the first Mersey-built paddle steamer which was ordered for the Eastham passage. She was quickly followed by Runcorn-built *Prince Regent* and *Duke of Wellington*.

The early paddlers were of a similar basic design and construction which evolved as vessels increased in capacity and tonnage. Traditional features of sailing ships such as bowsprits and flat sterns were retained. All machinery was located amidships below deck next to a cramped cabin with room for up to 100 passengers reached by a steep companionway protected from the elements by a small deck house. Coal was stored below deck forward. Part of the deck was flush to allow the carriage of carts and livestock. The tall, gaunt chimney stack, some 35ft high, lay abaft the paddle-boxes and attached to it was a mast and rigging for use in emergencies though later this feature was moved forward. There was usually no bridge, the wheel being positioned astern to minimise linkages with the rudder; later the helm was moved amidships but remained at deck level.

Machinery consisted of flue-type boilers and side lever engines, single or in pairs, with a cylinder, piston and side rods on one side and a cross-tail and connecting rods on the other. As the side lever was pivoted, the piston which raised one end lowered the connecting rod on the other. Accidents and explosions were quite common and in 1817 legislation required all future boilers to be made of iron or copper, fitted with two safety valves and capable of withstanding, under test, three times their working pressure, usually 3-5 lb. psi. Under no circumstances were they to exceed one sixth of their calculated maximum pressure. Coal consumption often exceeded 10 lb. per horse power per hour due to scaling in the boilers caused by the use of sea water. Speeds rarely exceeded 10 knots.

For the next 25 years, during which steam was adopted by all the Mersey ferries, steamers followed this basic primitive design, being underpowered and frequently unreliable and it was only after unification of the three northern ferries under the Wallasey Local Board in 1861 that larger, more robust vessels were gradually placed on the passages, designs closely resembling those adopted at Woodside.

Steam Comes to Seacombe

Parry acquired the ferry lease in 1819 and, two years later, to meet competition from other hotels on the waterfront, he ordered a steam paddle boat, appropriately named *Seacombe*, which made her first crossing in June 1822. With little regular passenger traffic, she at first ran on a demand basis, filling in time by towing sailing ships. However, by 1823, there was sufficient traffic to justify an hourly service with sail being used if Seacombe was not available. However, sail was eliminated the following year when he acquired *Alice*, named after his wife, and *Alexander*. He proudly advertised 'an hourly service worked entirely by steam at a single fare of 3d.', a fare which would have kept his clientele select.

To facilitate the maintenance of his fleet, Parry requested the Trustees to improve facilities. In 1826 a small dry dock with derrick and other lifting equipment was built with, to the north, a short stone wharf for use at high tide, all protected by a retaining wall. There was space for stockpiling coal which eased the problems inherent in coaling from river flats moored alongside. A flight of steps led directly to the hotel terrace and a clock on the hotel front regulated the ferry sailings, a warning bell at the top of the steps being rung two minutes before each departure.

All coaling was done manually, one of a number of arduous tasks undertaken by the ships' crews,

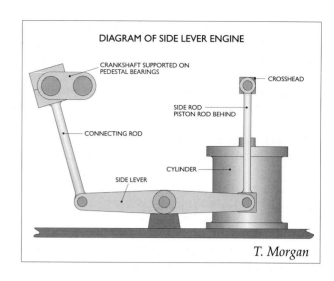

DIAGRAM OF SIDE LEVER ENGINE

CRANKSHAFT SUPPORTED ON PEDESTAL BEARINGS

CROSSHEAD

CONNECTING ROD

SIDE ROD
PISTON ROD BEHIND

SIDE LEVER

CYLINDER

T. Morgan

who were responsible for operating, maintaining and repairing their vessel. Normally they were on duty 12 hours a day, seven days a week and, even in the worst weather, a token crew was left on board. Routine maintenance was done after hours and on market days the decks had to be thoroughly swilled of all muck and filth. For the engineer and stokers the day began two hours before the first sailing; they cleaned out the ash cans, loaded the coal, lit the fires and raised a good head of steam. Once under way, they spent their time in the tiny hot engine room trying to coax the unpredictable machinery to keep going. On deck, the master and helmsman were exposed to the elements as they guided their frail craft through the ranks of vessels blocking the ferry route. Rough water, ice and fog were accepted hazards and it was undoubtedly due to the skill and devotion of these early ferrymen that public confidence in the 'kettles' increased. Fire was an ever-present menace; in 1825 *Alice* caught fire whilst riding at anchor and, being under-insured, she was scuttled. She was later raised, repaired and returned to service.

It was essential to improve embarkation facilities and the foundation stone of a new slipway was laid on 5th June 1835. With an incline of 1 in 20, the slip was 15ft wide with an extension running on two rails. A stationary winding engine was installed in a hut at the shore end of the extension so that the engine moved with it. The extension bucked and swayed in the slightest swell and the flimsy planking afforded little protection against the water which splashed through the cracks, drenching the ladies' wide-hooped crinolines and the gentlemen's frock coats. The rebuilt terminal was opened in the spring of 1836, the 1815 slipway passing into public use especially for handling domestic coal supplies. The ferry service was advertised as half-hourly, still at a fare of 3d. *Gore's Directory* listed four vessels on the passage in 1835, *Seacombe* (probably the second of the name or an extensive rebuild), *Alice*, *Liverpool* and *Admiral*, (sometimes quoted as *Admiral Lord Nelson*).

John and Richard Parry inherited the ferry on the death of their mother early in 1847 though official correspondence between the Birkenhead Dock Trustees and the Commissioners of Works refers to **Miss** Parry as the lessee. The hotel side of the business had declined and they branched out into other activities including haulage and hackney carriages for which they were granted four licences in February 1847. The decline may have been caused to some extent by the build-up of sand on and adjacent to the landing slip, alleged to have been caused by the building of the river wall between the dock entrance and the ferry in the 1840s. Between 1847 and 1852 the Parrys acquired three second-hand paddle steamers including the former Eastham ferry vessel *Sir Thomas Stanley*, enabling *Alice* to be broken up. Both the Parrys and the Coulborns, owners of New Brighton ferry, had been appointed Town Commissioners in 1845 and, as such, they were well aware that there were municipalisation proposals for the ferries. They were therefore reluctant to invest in new steamers and infrastructure.

It was an important day when, in June 1848, Liverpool Corporation, the owners of the Birkenhead ferry, reduced the passenger fare for the river crossing from 2d to 1d. This was no altruistic move but an attempt to stem the losses on this ferry, which lay between Woodside and Tranmere, and tempt passengers away from these competitors. In that respect it failed as the other ferries reduced their fares to the same level and it seems likely that Seacombe soon found that it had to do the same. The establishment of the 1d fare was a great step forward in creating mobility of labour on Merseyside and in stimulating the movement of people to reside on the Wirral side of the river. It meant that fares were one shilling a week instead of two shillings and in those days one shilling would buy quite a lot of food for a working class family. The Seacombe fare had certainly become 1d by 1853 and fares soon stabilised at Seacombe 1d, Egremont 2d and New Brighton 3d.

The Parrys decided to cut their losses and sold the hotel to Eliza Stokes. They informed the Smith Trustees that they would not be renewing the ferry lease in February 1853 and offered their steamers for sale. *Sir Thomas Stanley* had already been sold and converted into a general purpose tender, registered in the name of Thomas Doyle and others in which guise she reappeared at Seacombe in 1857, the year before she was finally scrapped. *Liverpool* was described as a hulk and was presumably scrapped and no buyer could be found for *Seacombe* which probably suffered the same fate. *Britannia*, *Invincible* and *Thomas Wilson* were either purchased by Thomas Prestopino, the Bootle shipbroker, who secured the ferry lease for one year in March 1853, or by the Smith Trustees and then rented to Prestopino. Details are scanty but it seems that during Prestopino's brief tenure conditions at the ferry sank to an all time low. A contemporary joke suggested that anyone foolish enough to use the ferry should first say goodbye to his friends, secondly take leave of his wife and family and thirdly make his will before setting off. Supplementing the ex-Parry steamers were *Egremont* which Prestopino had acquired in June 1849 and *Ramsgate Packet* which had been launched at Harwich in 1834. Neither was in good condition. An illustration of the state of affairs is given by these extracts from the Seacombe Ferry Log Book, now unfortunately lost.

1853 3rd Feb. *Invincible* to be second boat at 7.30am did not come until 9.45am. At 10.0am captain of *Egremont* came and said he could not come back from Liverpool as the boat was short of coal.

9th Feb. *Egremont* 45 minutes late for first trip. Then went to coal at 8.0am; did not return until 12.30pm. Great complaints about this boat.

11th Feb. *Invincible* should have been 7.30am boat did not come until 9.0am, 1$^1/_2$ hr behind time. Mr Littledale three calves to Liverpool – 9d.

13th Feb. *Egremont* broke machinery at 11.0am, did not run any more that day.

15th Feb. *Egremont* came on ferry at 6.30am. Took *Invincible*'s trip she being short of coal. *Egremont* 10.30am short of coal. *Invincible* took her trip. *Egremont* came on ferry again at 3.0pm. *Invincible* left at 7.0pm to get coal, did not come again.

23rd Feb. *Egremont* went to anchor at 6.30pm having at Liverpool side done some damage to her sponson on account of bad weather. Great complaint about irregularity of the boats. Many is going by Egremont ferry in consequence of the above named boat being by the passengers not deemed seaworthy.

1st Mar. *Egremont* first boat 6.15 am instead of 5.30am. All early passengers gone by Woodside. Great complaints.

4th Mar. All right with boats this day excepting *Egremont* which left Liverpool at 10.0am. She left quarter before 11 am when she got to Liverpool she could not return, consequence was all passengers went to Woodside. Great complaints,

Mr Ewart amongst them (a relative of Gladstone the great Prime Minister).

26th Apr.   *Britannia* did nothing till 11am in consequence of her having no coal. Great complaints from customs officers.

21st Jun.   *Ramsgate Packet* first boat at 5.30am. Came to stage, some-thing the matter with injection pump. Could not start until after 6.0am. Passengers on both sides detained. All labouring people lost quarter day's work. Great complaints by Wallasey people going with potatoes to market saying in future they would go by Woodside.

3rd Jul.   Steamer *Egremont* came on ferry early in forenoon. Engineer said he could not keep her going. At 1.0pm he said he could not go again. Told he must go and sent note to captain of *Ramsgate Packet* telling him to come immediately. He came with his boat to the stage and told me she could not run the ferry. By this time the *Egremont* had come again with great difficulty from Liverpool with passengers. Both boats lay together at the stage and neither of them could go. At last *Egremont* made a start and got half way down Prince's Wall. A tug boat went alongside and wanted to take the passengers from her. Lost a valuable trip, all or so going by the Egremont boat. Could not make her time good. Stopped in river and Woodside boat went alongside and wanted to take her passengers.

4th Jul.   *Egremont* should have come on ferry at 7.30am. Captain came at 8.0am and said she was done with altogether. BOILERS GIVEN WAY.

Under Common Management

The long-suffering passengers looked to the Local Board to take steps to effect an improvement and, in 1853, at the invitation of the Board, Lister and Mills presented estimates for redesigning the Seacombe running-out stage but because of legal problems, these had not been accepted. However, in the winter of 1854-55, the stage was badly buckled by tightly packed ice blocks and the stationary engine capsized; the Smith Trustees were compelled to rebuild the stage, employing Lister and Mills as contractors. The stone slipway was extended to a length of 540 ft and the extension, or 'telescopic' as the locals called it, to 180 ft. As added protection it was moved along three rails and divided by a central railing to separate embarking and disembarking passengers. Toll booths with turnstiles were installed and lifebelts attached to the railings. A large warning bell was suspended from a stanchion above the north side toll booth. The winding engine was repositioned in a separate housing on the quayside. This work took nearly two years, the facilities being opened to the public early in 1857.

During the reconstruction, the vessels departed at high tide from the south quay wall, passengers boarding by a narrow plank balanced precariously on top of a paddle box. Writing in the *Wallasey and Wirral Chronicle* in 1890, a Miss Dodo recalled that 'the plank would be pointing at the polar star one second and harpooning on an imaginary whale the next'.

Meanwhile, in March 1854, Edward Warburton Coulborn and William Rushton Coulborn, members of a wealthy merchant family with interests in shipbuilding and ferry management elsewhere in England and Scotland, took on the Seacombe lease from the Smith Trustees on a year-to-year basis and proceeded to revitalise the Seacombe passage just as they had done for Egremont a year or two earlier (see below). On 20th March 1857, they negotiated a new 14-year lease at an annual rent of £955. 15s. 0d. (£955.75) comprising £550 for the ferry, £30 for the forge and stable and £375 calculated as 5% per annum on the recently completed improvements. The rateable value of the site was reassessed at £348 per annum.

A simple fare structure was adopted – Seacombe 1d, Egremont 2d and New Brighton 3d. It is possible that the 1d Seacombe fare had been in operation since 1847. There were weekly, monthly and annual contract tickets and special rates for families and servants. Tolls were fixed for carrying farm produce, animals, carts and a comprehensive range of articles. To cut costs, for a time all evening sailings to and from New Brighton called at both Seacombe and Egremont. As there was no direct road linking all three districts, most people walked along the shore; for those who could afford it, the boats provided a local as well as a cross-river service.

New Brighton Ferry

In 1768, as a result of public protest, Liverpool Town Council discontinued the practice of allowing loaded gunpowder wagons to pass through the city streets en route from the port to their magazines in Clarence Street. They purchased a plot of land near to the safe anchorage lying between Mother Redcap's Inn and Rock Point and

New Brighton ferry owed its origins to a Liverpool businessman James Atherton, a retired Everton builder and his son-in-law, William Rowson, a Prescot solicitor, who advocated the establishment of a ferry service from Liverpool as part of a plan to encourage prospective residents. The first wooden pier was completed in 1834 and at high water, boats could moor at the 40ft structure pointing to the south but at low water, passengers had to wade to and from the steamers until 1835 when they were carried in a flat-bottomed landing craft hauled up and down by a horse powered windlass. The pier lasted until 1865.
M. Jenkins collection

built the Liscard Magazines. Every vessel entering the river had to off-load her powder for storage in the magazines until departure and during the unloading, some of the crew would be rowed across to Liverpool. As shipping using the port increased so the patronage of the Magazines grew and by 1820 a thriving passage had developed, much of it unconnected with the storage of gunpowder. Pleasure seeking Liverpudlians came to sample the unspoilt beaches and a hotel was built together with a number of exclusive residences. The hotel eventually became a school numbering among its fee-paying pupils Menotti and Riciotti Garibaldi, the sons of the Italian patriot. Anyone wanting to conduct business in the vicinity would agree to meet at the ferry. *Gore's Directory* for 1822 advertised a regular service of sailing packets and in 1826 a newly opened Liverpool-Hoylake service, worked by the paddle steamers *Hero* and *Paul Pry*, called at the Magazines en route. This service survived until 1832. The absence of a pier at the Magazines ensured that as the other ferries at Egremont and New Brighton were established, the regular service ceased though there were intermittent sailings until the magazines closed in 1851. All traces of the old stone slipway disappeared during the construction of the promenade between Holland Road and New Brighton in the 1890s

New Brighton ferry owed its origins to a Liverpool businessman James Atherton, a retired Everton builder and his son-in-law, William Rowson, a Prescot solicitor, who advocated the establishment of a ferry service from Liverpool as part of a plan to encourage prospective residents. Situated at the exposed mouth of the Mersey, New Brighton was hardly an ideal location from which to operate an all-year, all tides ferry for it could suffer from high winds and mountainous seas

and at low tide the water receded some 650ft from the shore. Undeterred, scores of prosperous Liverpudlians migrated across the water to build comfortable villas with unrivalled views of the Mersey approaches.

In 1833, part of the foreshore was leased from the Commissioners of Woods and Forests and the first wooden pier, which was completed in March 1834, was a curiously-shaped structure extending some 500ft from the shore. Built of heavy timbers embedded in the rock and supported by diagonal braces and cross beams, it was 9ft wide and 30ft long at its outer extremity. The first 135ft of the pier was angled due north-west; at the river end there was a further 40ft-long structure running due south at which boats could load at high water.

At extreme low water, passengers were forced to wade to and from the steamers but, in 1835, they were carried in a flat-bottomed landing craft which was hauled up and down by a horse-powered windlass. Access to the pier was through a toll house at the shore end or by two flights of steps leading direct from the beach. No formal lease from the Commissioners of Woods and Forests to work a ferry service was obtained until April 1851. This extended for 75 years at a rent of one guinea (£1.05) per annum and a grant of 100 yd. on each side of the ferry was made on 4th October 1859 for a further guinea per year.

Despite having only one vessel, Atherton advertised an hourly service using a second-hand Scottish-built paddle steamer, *Sir John Moore*. The journey time for the 2.75 mile crossing was 25 minutes which left little time for turnround or inclement weather. To provide additional revenue and to supplement the summer schedule, other vessels were permitted to disembark passengers at the pier on payment of a small toll. This practice continued for some

70 years.

In 1838, ownership was transferred to Atherton's two sons who placed the Tranmere-built paddle steamer *Elizabeth* on the station in 1840. In 1845, they disposed of their interest for £2,000 to the Liverpool firm of Lodge, Pritchard & Co. of which two of the directors were the Coulborn brothers.

Atherton's vision of New Brighton as a suburban Utopia failed to materialise though a few of his fine houses survive 160 years later. Although the ferry had been intended as a residents' link with their workplaces, the facilities tempted droves of working class people to cross at weekends to enjoy a relatively inexpensive day by the sea. Recognising that New Brighton catered for two different types of clientele, the Coulborns purchased a former gentleman's yacht *Queen of Beauty* to provide a superior residents' only service in summer as well as offering elegance and luxury during the winter. She was followed in 1846 by the Liverpool-built *James Atherton* which, with a capacity of 529, catered for the fluctuations in loading in the summer. Over the next five years, the Coulborns spent over £3,000 on improved facilities. Various extensions to the pier brought passengers to within 80ft of the low water mark and the old flat-bottomed boat was replaced by a crude version of the running-out stage which comprised a wooden platform running on rails attached by spikes to the rock surface. This clumsy contraption could be raised and lowered over a distance of 200ft. Sometime in 1848 part of the shore end of the pier was damaged during a gale. During the rebuilding, a shack selling anything from tea to wine was erected near the toll house and rented out at £35 per year. Local residents were outraged by this open invitation to imbibe strong liquor and were increasingly concerned by the unchecked growth of the

Queen of Beauty, a former yacht, was placed on the New Brighton service by the Coulborns to provide a luxury service for their regular commuters to save them from having to mix with day trippers. She worked from about 1845 to at least 1856. From a painting

'Devil's Nest', a row of huts and stalls hugging the high water mark which sold alcoholic drink.

Special constables were sworn in to control the rowdy elements among the day trippers and for over a century many residents resented their influx, feeling that they lowered the tone of an otherwise select neighbourhood.

Following the acquisition of the Egremont ferry lease by the Coulborns in May 1848, they established their administrative headquarters at Egremont and suspended the New Brighton sailings from 1st October 1849 until Easter 1850 to the disgust of regular users. New Brighton residents were advised to walk along the shore to Egremont. The combination of the two passages resulted in considerable savings in staff and coal and, in winter, doubled the prospective clientele. The Coulborns received a new lease of the ferry from the Commissioners for Woods and Forests for 75 years from April 1851 at a rental of £21 per annum and a grant of 100yd. on each side of the ferry on payment of 21 shillings per annum on 4th October 1859.

Egremont Ferry

The Liverpool Harbour Master, John Askew, built a fine villa about one mile north of Seacombe and named it Egremont after his birth place in Cumberland. The name was gradually applied to the whole district. Askew was 'pulled across daily in his galley' to reach his work in Liverpool and by 1823 he was allowing friends and others (on payment of a fee) to use the landing place at the bottom of his garden. Concerned at these developments, the Smith Trustees accused Askew of infringing the Seacombe rights of passage and started court proceedings aimed at preventing Askew using his private landing for public purposes. The judgement went against the Trustees, the court ruling that 'the owners of the Seacombe passage exercised no rights over the strand to the north'.

With his position apparently secure, Askew purchased the ferry rights from the Commissioners for Woods and Forests for £3,000 and leased the shore line. He planned to build an iron pier, purchase a paddle steamer and start a regular ferry service with a view to opening up the district for industrial and residential purposes, financing the erection of a two-storey hotel with gardens reaching down to the water's edge. The site was hardly ideal for a ferry as the river bed was very flat, falling only 3ft 10in in every 100ft so to provide the depth of water for a paddle steamer to approach at low tide, a pier needed to be at least 750ft long. Such a structure was unlikely to be approved by the River Conservancy so Askew decided to build a shorter structure to be used by steamers only when it was absolutely safe to do so. It was 200ft long and built entirely of wood, stakes being driven deep into the rocks. It ran out from a stone concourse protected by a high quay on which stood a ferry house and several small workshops. To warn shipping, three tall masts, each carrying an enormous storm lamp, were mounted on the end of the pier. Construction was hampered by foul weather and the official opening was delayed until the summer of 1830.

Askew purchased a second-hand paddler, *Loch Eck* in August 1830 and a service commenced. It was evidently sufficiently successful for Askew to order a similar but larger new paddler *John Rigby* which entered service in 1831; a third vessel, the second-hand *Hero* was added to the fleet in 1832. In that year, *Gore's Directory* listed an hourly service from North Pier, George's Dock Basin either by steam or sail. The latter would have been used at low tide when the pier was inaccessible to steamers or when they had been withdrawn for towing becalmed sailing ships, generally a more lucrative proposition. In 1834, shelters were provided on the pier and a mercury clock mounted on the hotel front to regulate the sailings.

The service was frequently suspended without warning when towing work was on offer; this was one of the charges which Askew faced during a Public Inquiry into his involvement with the Wallasey Pool conversion scheme. As an employee of Liverpool Corporation, he was ordered to disclose details of all his business activities as his employers were angry that he had given moral and financial support to a scheme which was likely to damage their interests; this was in direct contravention of an undertaking made to the Corporation as part of his conditions of service. Ferry users criticised the poor management of Egremont ferry and questioned the morality of the Harbour Master despatching his privately-owned vessels to rescue becalmed ships. Askew retained his job until 1841 but was required to relinquish control of Egremont ferry. He sold his assets to the Egremont Steam Ferry Company, formed in October 1835 with a capital of £15,000. Askew retained ownership of the land on which the ferry buildings stood and on 22nd February 1836 renewed his lease of the shore line, agreeing to pay the Commissioners of Woods and Forests £50 per annum for 31 years. As a placatory gesture, Askew undertook to finance a 50ft extension of the existing wooden pier.

Seacombe ferry, probably in the 1850s, with the running out stage extended. The vessel is thought to be Thomas Wilson.
M. Jenkins collection

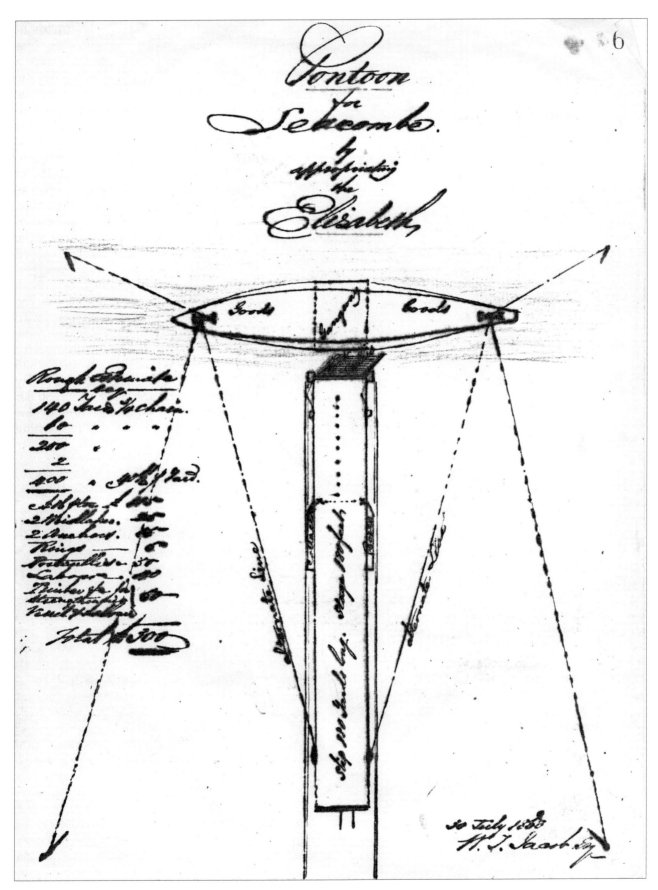

Elizabeth was built in 1840 as a goods boat at New Brighton for the Athertons and passed to the Coulborns with the ferry; she became a passenger boat with a certificate for 401 persons. She was at first refused by the Local Board but they were obliged to buy her. She again became a goods boat and, as a hulk, was used as a landing boat at both New Brighton and Seacombe; the sketch shows the mooring arrangements at Seacombe. T. B. Maund collection

The original Egremont ferry looking north with the running out stage retracted. The boatyard was on the extreme left of the picture. The vessels cannot be positively identified.
M. Jenkins collection

Egremont Steam Ferry Company

With a view to improving the service, the company constructed the extended landing stage and bought an iron paddler, *Ennishowen* which was delivered in July 1836. She was an early example of iron construction and attracted considerable attention but was severely underpowered. In October 1837 a second iron paddler, *Egremont* was placed in service and, with more than twice the power, completed the crossing in 12 minutes. *Thomas Royden*, named after her designer and builder, was built of wood and joined the Egremont fleet in 1837. Despite these innovations, the Egremont Steam Ferry Company was not financially successful and was dissolved in 1838; it was replaced by the Egremont Steam Packet Company which met with no more success. Even with the extension stage and four steamers, the ferry continued to be worked by a mixture of steam and sail; suspensions continued and public confidence was further eroded.

The Steam Packet Company was wound up in 1845, the assets being bought by Mary Sharples who was managing the hotel. She quickly disposed of the ferry business to John Owen Sothern who had been a friend and partner of John Askew. As part of the transaction, Sothern purchased land south of the ferry on which, in 1847, he established a small shipbuilding yard known as South Bank with facilities by which boats could be launched during the Spring tides. By 1846 Egremont was already quite a thriving area with brickworks either side of the ferry using clay from the neighbouring cliffs. They worked day and night and their products were mainly distributed throughout Merseyside by vessels which used the ferry pier.

Ennishowen had been laid up in 1843 and scrapped in 1845 and *Egremont* had been relegated to a last resort stand-by leaving only *John Rigby* and *Thomas Royden* in regular use. Sothern had an iron paddler *Duke* which he used while he built in his yard to his own design a new steamer *Wallasey*. She was made of wood but included some modern features and could carry 650 passengers. She cost £2,500 and was launched in October 1847, probably the first launch from the yard; several men engaged in her construction, Messrs. Anson, Cartwright, Evans and Pye were later to find employment as masters and engineers.

However, before *Wallasey* was launched, Sothern sold the ferry for £18,000 or £19,000 (reports differ) to John Fletcher of Toxteth who assumed control on 28th July 1847 having first negotiated a new 75-year lease at £50 per annum for the considerably reduced area of land occupied by the ferry. The Agreement covered 'the terrace, stone and wooden pier, coal yard and long strip of land running into the river'. In less than a year Fletcher sold the lease to the New Brighton ferry owners, the Coulborn brothers, provided they entered into a strict covenant 'to ply with steam boats at regular intervals'. The brothers secured 'the public ferry with tolls for 20 years' and on 1st September 1849 purchased from Fletcher all the ferry land and property for the same price as he had paid for it.

However, from 1st October 1849 they closed New Brighton ferry for the winter, obliging their passengers to use Egremont which was, of course, less affected by the weather. This saved working expenses and enabled them to lay up two vessels, employing their crews on maintenance and repair work. When they reopened at New Brighton the following Easter, the New Brighton and Egremont services were combined, establishing a pattern which was to survive with minor variations for 90 years. They established their headquarters at Egremont and in 1850-56 spent £5,500 on several capital projects. The upper pier was extended to 238ft and the slipway carrying the extension stage to 798ft. A larger stationary engine and boiler were installed to move the heavier stage, the old equipment being held in reserve. Offices were improved, new stores for oil and tallow were built and an open yard for 6,000 tons of coal laid out. Plans to extend the running-out stage a further 20ft were shelved as the estimated cost was £1,800. Edward Coulborn pioneered the use of gas lighting in the town when, in 1850, he laid supply pipes under Tobin Street and erected gas lamps throughout the terminal area.

At the time of their purchase of Egremont ferry, the Coulborns' total investment, excluding vessels, was quoted in a report by Braithwaite Poole (see Chapter 3 and Appendix 1) as follows:-

Cost of Egremont ferry which to Mr Fletcher was £18,000 but to Mr Coulborn only	£14,500
Additional outlay	5,500
Cost of New Brighton ferry	2,000
Additional outlay	3,000
Stores and other extra works	6,000
Stationary engines, gas works, smiths' and fitters' tools and utensils valued at	1,607
Residual of leases; 60yr for Egremont (to July 1922) and New Brighton (to April 1921) & goodwill of ferries	27,393
TOTAL	£60,000

All three ferries passed from the Coulborns to the Wallasey Local Board on 1st August 1861 as described in Chapter 3.

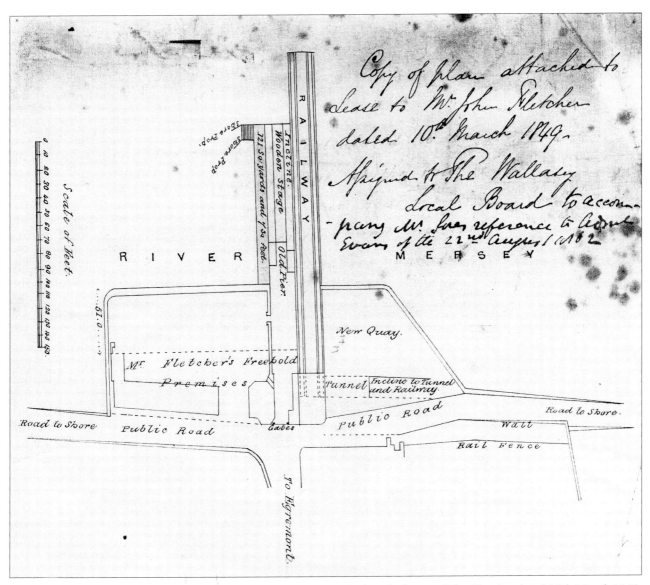

A plan of Egremont ferry inscribed to the effect that it was attached to the lease to John Fletcher dated 10th March 1849. However, there is no evidence that the tunnel and the railway in the form shown were ever constructed. The plan was used in 1862 in a submission by the Wallasey Local Board to the Conservator, Admiral Evans, as discussed in Chapter 3.

Wirral Archive Service

The approach to Seacombe pier, probably in the 1860s or early 1870s. The building with the tall chimney was the power house for the running out stage. Note the pay box on the left with the sign 'Fare 1d' and, on the other side of the approach, the brake lever for the stage.
Wallasey Tramway Preservation Group

3 THE EARLY MUNICIPAL YEARS

TOWN Commissioners for Wallasey (including Seacombe-cum-Poulton and Liscard) were appointed in 1845 under the Wallasey Improvement Act; they met for the first time in a room above the stables of the Queen's Arms Hotel, Liscard on 12th June 1845. Their powers included paving, lighting, cleansing, generally improving the Parish and providing a police force and market. They were empowered to lease or purchase the ferries at Seacombe and Egremont, the wharves, landing places and conveniences connected therewith and to provide and purchase steam boats and other things for the efficient working of the ferries. Their prime concern was to eliminate the health hazards arising from the stagnant waters blocked in the upper reaches of the Wallasey Pool but bringing the ferries under municipal control soon became a prime objective. As the concept of local government was in its infancy, many of the Commissioners, all local business men, must have experienced difficulty in balancing their public duty with their private interests. For example, the Parrys of Seacombe were forced to resign for hiring their own carts to the Parish although they were subsequently reappointed.

The Commissioners' first action in connection with ferries was to write to Liverpool Corporation in August 1845 complaining about the landing facilities at Liverpool. In fact Seacombe fared better than the other ferry operators but Liverpool, under pressure from all the ferry proprietors the previous year, had already decided to build a floating stage which opened in 1847. A ferry sub-committee was appointed in July 1846 to examine the implications of public ownership. The only immediate action was the adoption of the Seacombe slip in 1847.

The Sea Bank Ferry

In November 1847, the Town Commissioners considered the viability of a rival ferry to Egremont which was designed to serve the Sea Bank estate of luxury villas and a luxury hotel to be built in an area bounded by Maddock Road and Manor Lane and stretching inland to Liscard. However, the Commissioners for Woods and Forests refused to sanction a pier at the foot of Manor Lane. Three hundred ratepayers petitioned the Town Commissioners to appoint a committee to examine immediate methods of improving Egremont ferry and ultimately taking it into public ownership. However, the acquisition of

the lease by the Coulborns in May 1848 and their undertaking to provide a regular service silenced the critics and the Sea Bank ferry was quickly forgotten.

In 1851 much housing in Wallasey was described as abominable and the infant mortality rate was worse than that of Liverpool. Hundreds of workers who had poured into the tiny community seeking work on the new docks were housed in cramped hovels without running water or sanitation. The poorest dwellings were in Mersey Street, behind the Seacombe Ferry Hotel. When the dock scheme collapsed amid allegations of corruption, the workers were immediately dismissed. Health hazards stemmed from the water bottled up behind 'the Stank', a causeway across the Pool on roughly the line of the later Four Bridges. Despite the partial opening of the Great Float on 10th April 1851, sanitary conditions in Seacombe were so bad that a petition, signed by some of the Wallasey Commissioners was sent to the General Board of Health demanding a Public Inquiry. The Inspector expressed the opinion that the Commissioners had failed in their responsibilities and should be replaced by an elected Local Board.

His recommendations were not carried out for two years during which the Commissioners made a serious attempt to acquire the Seacombe ferry lease from the Smith Trustees. However, when, on 7th April 1853, they announced that they had reached agreement, they were opposed by an influential group of landowners who threatened to take legal action if the Agreement was ratified. Nevertheless, the Commissioners decided to proceed but, at that juncture, they were replaced by the newly-elected Local Board who met for the first time on 7th July 1853 under the chairmanship of Isaac Penny.

After health matters, acquisition of Seacombe ferry was high on the agenda but members opposed to the latter questioned the legality of spending monies raised on the security of the rates for the purchase of new ferry boats. Negotiations with the Smith Trustees were suspended in November and on 2nd January 1854 the Attorney General ruled that funds borrowed in terms of the Public Health Act 1848 were not to be used for the acquisition of steamboats or ferries. It seemed that the 'anti's' had won the day.

Despite the improvements made by the Coulborns since taking over the Seacombe ferry lease in March 1854, there was local agitation for an even better service and a Special Committee of the Local Board presented five recommendations on 7th January 1856:

1. There should be better boats, better manned and kept in better order and cleanliness.
2. The Seacombe crossing should take 7 minutes and the Egremont crossing 12 minutes.
3. The boats should run as follows (except Sundays): Seacombe to Liverpool 5.30am to 8.0pm half-hourly; 8.0pm to midnight hourly. Egremont to Liverpool 6.0am to 8.0pm half-hourly; 8.0pm to midnight hourly. The boats running after 8.0pm to serve Seacombe, Egremont and New Brighton (suggesting that this practice had been discontinued).
4. Day trippers should be carried to New Brighton on separate boats at concessionary fares.
5. A luggage boat should be provided from Seacombe.

In September 1856 the Local Board announced that they proposed to obtain Parliamentary powers to acquire all three ferries but, if unsuccessful, they would establish a rival ferry at Seacombe financed by monies not collected from the rates; only Edward Coulborn voted against this resolution.

With the threat of municipal expropriation, the Coulborn brothers, reluctant to relinquish control of New Brighton, transferred the lease to their nephew Richard in 1855. Despite low winter receipts and a further suspension during the winter of 1854-55, the ferry was a summer gold mine. According to figures quoted later by Braithwaite Poole in his pamphlet supporting the Local Board, New Brighton was the most profitable passage. During 1859, receipts were £9,042 compared with £6,134 at Seacombe and £5,390 at Egremont. On one single day takings were £290 – equal to 23,000 single journeys at 3d. To cater for sudden excess demand, extra boats were drafted into use to supplement the two vessels maintaining the basic service. In 1859, a half-hourly service was maintained for most of the day between 8.15am and 9.30pm from New Brighton and from 8.0am to 8.15pm from Liverpool.

At a formal Ratepayers' Meeting on 19th November 1857, the Local Board put forward their proposals:-

'Certain, regular safe and frequent communication with Liverpool is indispensably necessary to every inhabitant of the Parish. No individual can supply this and make a profit until the Parish becomes more populous; the Board therefore seeks powers to pursue, improve and work the ferries so as to secure the desired ends and to devote all this and all other objects required by the public good...'

The vote was 454 in favour and 254 against and the necessary powers were included in the Wallasey Improvement Act, 1858 which, to some extent, superseded the powers granted by the 1845 Act.

Independent arbitrators had been appointed in November 1856 to assess the value of the assets of the three ferries and the Board formed a Ferries Committee on 27th April 1858 initially chaired by Henry Pooley. Opponents of municipalisation published pamphlets and carried on a newspaper campaign aimed at persuading their fellows that the purchase of the ferries was little short of financial suicide. The Board's case was helped by the sinking of two of the Coulborns' vessels. In January 1857, *Wallasey* sat on her anchor at Seacombe and one the the flukes pierced her wooden hull and in March 1858, *Thomas Wilson* sank after colliding with the Woodside steamer *Prince*. Both were raised and returned to service.

The Coulborns' terms for disposing of their business which was rising in value under their competent management, were as follows:-

Egremont would be leased at £1,000 per annum plus 5% interest on an estimated capital outlay of £2,000. Seacombe would be sub-let on exactly the same terms as it was held from the Smith Trustees and New Brighton, if required, would be rented at a figure based on the average of receipts since 1852. These terms were subject to the Board purchasing all their steamers and operating equipment. These terms were rejected and a new sub-committee was chosen to deal specifically with Seacombe.

In November 1858, the Local Board accepted the terms relating to Seacombe but rejected the others. Instead, they offered to pay £30,000 for the outright purchase of both Egremont and New Brighton, including all the rights and privileges, land, buildings, slipways, piers, machinery and all improvements made by the Coulborns. The latter refused the offer and engaged C. H. Beloe, an eminent Liverpool engineer, to represent them and a Mr Bancroft to act as their arbitrator. The Board engaged a Mr Harrison to recommend minimum and maximum prices; there was then disagreement as to who should arbitrate between the arbitrators!

Final agreement was reached after three months of negotiations in London which commenced on 28th January 1860. Coulborns were to receive £60,000 for Egremont and New Brighton and a nominal £2 for Seacombe. The Board paid the legal costs of £3,000 and the Law Clerk was instructed to put the recommendations into effect as swiftly as possible. On 30th November 1860, Isaac Penny, the former chairman of the Local Board and by then legal representative of the Smith Trustees, rejected the Board's offer of £3,000 for the Seacombe right of passage. Another 18 months elapsed before agreement was reached in the sum of £30,000, payable in mortgages over five years with interest at 4%. The sale included all manorial rights south of Brougham Road.

Even at this late stage rival factions were still arguing about the merits of municipalisation. One

Liscard supporter in a letter dated 7th March 1861 wrote:-

'...the fact is notorious the boats are too slow, the cabin accommodation very repulsive, the landing at Egremont most uncertain and the state of the slip wet and disagreeable and to those permanent evils may be added the not unfrequent withdrawal of the boats from Egremont and occasionally from Seacombe also. How are things to be altered for the better – how are we to be relieved from the discomforts at which everyone is constantly grumbling – how to give our Parish a fair chance of material improvement and progress and how to gain our Parish a full share of the prospective advantages of the Birkenhead Great Float, one side of which skirts our Parish? – public control of our ferries.'

But the opposition, led by Mr D. C. Buchanan, said that such a move would simply place a costly millstone around the neck of the entire Parish. Rival figures were produced. The Board estimated an annual profit of £4,000 – Mr Buchanan a loss of £12,000. The Board claimed the capital outlay bearing interest in the third year of working would be £92,000 incurring annual interest of £3,833; Buchanan said it would be £165,000 with interest of £8,250. The Board's calculations were based on six vessels each costing £1,200 to work while the opposition thought seven vessels would be needed with expenses of £1,500. They also allowed for a Sinking Fund of 5% which was not contemplated by the Board and depreciation of $7^1/_2$%, equal to a new boat every two years; the Board allowed for 5%.

One of the pamphlets in support of the Local Board was written by Braithwaite Poole, a former Goods Manager of the London and North Western Railway, which is summarised in Appendix 1. It was circulated to all Board members on 5th December 1860. Poole claimed expertise gained in the study of the various steamer services operated by the railway companies. Furthermore he had been based in Liverpool and had an intimate knowledge of the river and its traffic. He resided in Marine Terrace, Magazines and observed the movements of the various ferry vessels through a telescope. He prefaced his pamphlet with the following remarks:-

'In reviewing this subject, I do not intend disrespect to Messrs. Coulborn; on the contrary, I much respect their economical management and can well imagine that any private gentlemen, similarly situated, would hesitate to incur the risk of building new and expensive vessels for a private speculation, howsoever advisable it may be considered to do so as a public enterprise'.

When the position of Ferries Manager was advertised, Poole was offered the job after a close run contest with a Captain Reid. It was agreed that the Local Board would assume control of the ferries on 1st August 1861 and Poole took up his position a month earlier. The Board, being without vessels, had agreed in June to purchase four of the Coulborn steamers, *Fairy* (which had just been reboilered), *Thomas Wilson*, *James Atherton* and *Tiger*. *Elizabeth* was rejected as too old and *Liscard* and *Wallasey* were to be sold by the Coulborns. The valuation of these presented some problems as indicated in Appendix 1. The Wallasey Improvement Act, 1861 authorised the Local Board to take out mortgages on security of the Ferries account, the assets or the general rate fund, expenditure of £50,000 being sanctioned for the purchase of the reversionary rights in Seacombe and other ferries.

The colourful era of private ownership had come to an end.

Under Public Ownership

Operation of all three ferries passed from the Coulborns to the Wallasey Local Board on 1st August 1861 and, to ensure continuity, all employees were retained. The ceremonial occasion was linked with the opening of the municipal waterworks and 300 distinguished guests were taken on a cruise from Egremont to New Ferry then to the Crosby lightship and back to Egremont in the Rock Ferry steamer *Wasp*. In the evening a banquet, hosted by the Local Board chairman, was held in the water tower.

A house flag with the initials 'W F' in white on a red background was adopted and the Admiralty-approved method of river signals was observed. One employee at each terminal was sworn in as a special constable, bye-laws being introduced to control passenger conduct. One which banned singing and the playing of musical instruments was relaxed to allow 'music boxes' to be played on the northern boats between 11.0am and 3.30pm. Hawkers and pedlars were barred from ferry premises, causing some protests from the public about the exclusion of an old woman who had sold oranges and gingerbread at Seacombe. W. H. Smith was allowed to open a newsstand at Seacombe and advertising billboards were erected at all three terminals.

Daily half-hourly services were provided on all three passages except that there was no service to New Brighton on Sundays. First boats left Seacombe at 5.30am, Egremont at 5.45am and New Brighton at 8.15am and last boats from Liverpool were at 12.0 midnight, 10.30pm and 8.30pm respectively. The Seacombe service was augmented at peak hours. From 23rd August all contract holders were allowed to travel on all three ferries without extra charge and books of 12 'pass tickets' were sold at slightly reduced rates. The practice of issuing reduced contracts to members of the families and servants of holders was continued. To aid public confidence through good timekeeping, a large clock was placed on the frontage of the Ferry Hotel at New Brighton, the proprietor being paid a rent of one shilling (5p) per annum. A Mr Cunliffe was appointed to maintain and regulate all ferry clocks for a fee of 30 shillings (£1.50) annually.

Poole soon set about making savings on the northern services. From 1st November 1861, the New Brighton service was reduced to hourly with last departures from Liverpool at 6.0pm and New Brighton at 6.30; however, direct boats, not calling at Egremont, were introduced at peak hours. To reduce costs, all three passages were soon being worked by a maximum of four boats and coal contracts were renegotiated and tenders invited for several coal barges to be towed behind steamers to eliminate costly refuelling stops during revenue earning hours. In the event of bad weather causing suspension of the Egremont and New Brighton sailings, flags were hoisted at the ferry terminals, the top of Tobin Street and at the junction of Victoria Road and Rowson Street. In fog no boat could leave Seacombe until the other vessel had been sighted and her paddles stopped.

James Hall was engaged to handle luggage and other goods to and from Seacombe at a fixed scale of charges and in October he started an omnibus service between New Brighton and Seacombe. Following the introduction of a 'street railway' in Birkenhead and flanged-wheel omnibuses along the docks at Liverpool, the Local Board was asked to approve a tramway but this was rejected in October 1861.

A Change of Manager

Poole complained bitterly about conditions at New Brighton. Despite £200 having been spent on dredging, the public were still regularly required to transfer to a landing boat and occasionally the service was stopped. The old running-out stage was unreliable and unstable, frequently becoming dislodged during heavy seas. Poole recommended that the moving stage should run on rails fixed to the surface of a smooth incline some 150ft long. Although his scheme was rejected, the Local Board accepted that the terminal needed completely redesigning.

But the ebullient Braithwaite Poole was frustrated by the Board's failure to adopt a policy for modernising the whole ferry operation due to lack of funds. At a Town's Meeting in September 1862 there were strong protests about a ferry rate

of 8d in the £. Impressive as Poole's achievements were, they were insignificant compared with the improvements at Woodside. On 8th June 1863 he wrote to the Chairman as follows:-

'My duties have become onerous and the assistance offered me so inadequate. I feel much disposed to retire'.

He was invited by the newly-formed Hoylake Railway Company to become their Secretary and chief adviser and he left the ferry service on 30th September 1863. One of his last acts was to write to W. & M. Scott of the Tranmere Foundry from whom balanced gangways had been ordered for Liverpool landing stage. A special boat sent to fetch them on 1st December was sent back empty and the gangways were still in a half finished condition on 9th.

He was succeeded by William Carson, a 27-year old engineer and designer, who had been employed by the Cork Steamship Co. He took over on 1st October at a salary of £300 and during the 15 years he spent with the Ferries Department he was to transform the undertaking. An Assistant Manager, William Drummond, was appointed on 1st January 1864 at £90 per annum.

The 'Flower' Boats

Having refused to purchase *Elizabeth* in June, the Board paid £500 for her on 22nd July 1861 followed on 15th August by *Wallasey* which was purchased with the aid of a £1,000 bond. To supplement the fleet, two iron paddlers were hired from the Hetheringtons, lessees of Rock Ferry. *Ant* for three months and *Nymph* for one month. The contract to build a new steamer designed by E. W. Coulborn was awarded to H. M. Lawrence & Co. of Liverpool who were also to design and install her boiler and engines. They recommended that the vessel should be redesigned to include two funnels and two boilers and increased in length. The Board agreed only to the latter and appointed a Mr Furlong to superintend construction on their behalf.

Because of the age profile of the fleet, the Ferry Committee decided to order a second new vessel, the successful tenderer being Jones, Quiggin & Co. of Liverpool with whom an order was placed on 1st May 1862 for an iron hulled paddler with engine and boiler to be supplied by Forrester & Co. Meanwhile *Elizabeth* was declared unfit for passenger service and £247 was spent to convert her into a dedicated luggage boat. Furlong was now engaged as the Board's Consultant and Superintending engineer at £80 per annum. His first inspection resulted in the withdrawal of *Fairy* on which some of the panels had worn to a thickness of one sixteenth of an inch. *Tiger* was little better and Furlong advised that she be cemented on the inside to render her seaworthy. With three vessels out of service, the Board asked the Coulborns if they could hire *Gem* (the former *Liscard*) but it was not available and to cover the Easter traffic, *Hercules* was hired, complete with crew and coal, from Crouse and Downham at £14 per day. On 24th April *Invincible* returned to her old haunts having been chartered for £9 per day while *James Atherton* was undergoing emergency repairs. She was released on 22nd May when W. R. Coulborn agreed to hire *Gem* for three months at £7 per day.

The Board now placed an order with G. Forrester & Co., in conjunction with Jones, Quiggin, for an iron hull suitable to accommodate the engines and boiler taken from *Fairy*. The saloons were to be entirely below deck in order to leave a flush deck except above the engine space. The position was so desperate that, following the launch of the first new boat, *Mayflower* or *May Flower* on 14th May 1862, she was pressed into service over Whitsuntide incomplete and unpainted. Faults emerged, the Local Board claiming £1,621. 15. 4d (£1,621.76) before finally accepting delivery on 1st August. The second 'flower boat', *Waterlily* or *Water Lily*, was launched on 14th June 1862 and after successful trials, entered service during August. Both vessels were broadly similar with two raised deck saloons, the aft one flush with the stern and

the fore cabin forward of the stack and paddle boxes. They were light and airy with large sliding windows. The roofs of the cabins were railed off and provided with seats. There were nine watertight compartments and Bremme's steam steering and anchor raising gear was fitted. Technically they were in advance of and occupied less space than the earlier side lever engines having 70hp diagonal oscillating engines in which the cylinder was mounted on trunnions to allow it to follow the movement of the crank. *Waterlily* differed from *Mayflower* in having a narrower, smaller stack and a more confined bridge but, at 140ft long, she was the longest ferry vessel yet seen on the river and anticipated the more or less standard 150ft length which was to evolve commencing with Woodside's *Cheshire* six months later.

The third 'flower boat' was the hull designed to take the innards of *Fairy* and was named *Wild Rose*. On a test run she sailed from New Brighton to Eastham, 9 miles in 48 minutes, and was handed over on 16th October 1862 but was soon rejected as being totally unsuitable. She consumed coal at the rate of over five tons per day and had an alarming tendency to 'crank' or 'tender' when fully loaded. It was found that her moulded depth had been exceeded by nine inches, requiring ballast. Her builders argued, with some justification, that it had been difficult to

Heatherbell *was launched in 1865 at Thomas Vernon's yard on the Mersey. She was licensed for 807 (later 837) passengers and gave good service until withdrawn in 1891. The wooden structure on the foredeck housed the companionway to the below deck saloon.*   M. Jenkins collection

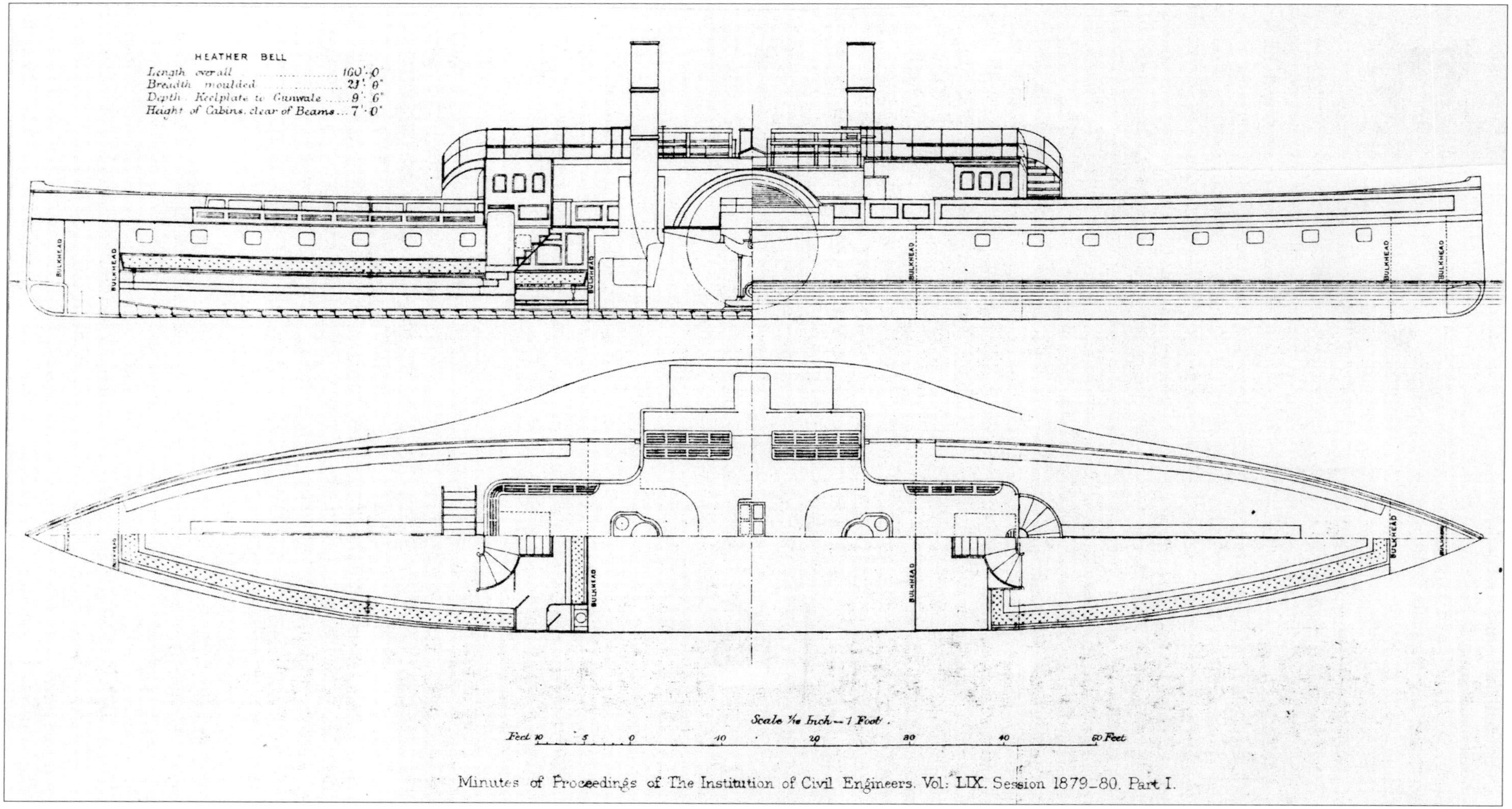

HEATHER BELL

Length overall ... ... 160'. 0"
Breadth moulded ... ... 21'. 6"
Depth Keelplate to Gunwale ... 9'. 6"
Height of Cabins clear of Beams ... 7'. 0"

BULKHEAD
BULKHEAD
BULKHEAD
BULKHEAD
BULKHEAD
BULKHEAD
BULKHEAD
BULKHEAD
BULKHEAD
BULKHEAD

Scale ¼ Inch = 1 Foot

Feet 10   5   0   10   20   30   40   50 Feet

Minutes of Proceedings of The Institution of Civil Engineers. Vol: LIX. Session 1879–80. Part I.

Proceedings of Institution of Civil Engineers

General arrangement drawing of Heatherbell, launched in 1865.

Heatherbell *was sold to a Dublin towing company and renamed* Erins King *but evidently became a pleasure boat as the words 'To Refreshment Saloon' can be discerned on the original print. Here she is seen in this role and fitted with taller funnels. She was broken up at Garston in 1900.* G. H. Peers

design a hull to accommodate old engines and equipment and estimated that for another £1,500 they could rectify all her faults. They advised lengthening her by 20ft and lowering her cabins and bulwarks. Jones, Quiggin recommended relocating her coal bunkers and enlarging her rudders so that she would steer correctly. The Board adopted a simpler and less expensive remedy; they fitted a new £50 rudder outside her sternpost which effectively made her single-ended. Throughout her life on the Mersey, *Wild Rose* remained cranky and unsteady, shipping gallons of water on the turn. She stood high out of the water and the new rudder protruded above the water line. Carson once said that he always expected her to capsize but she always came up smiling. The derelict hull of *Fairy* was sold for £80 and during the winter of 1862-3, the steering gear of *Tiger, Mayflower* and *James Atherton* was relocated amidships in the interests of safety in foggy conditions.

One of Carson's first projects was to design a new vessel which was eventually ordered from Thomas Vernon & Sons in January 1865. She was a double-ended flush-decked paddle steamer with 7ft high cabins below deck and a 70ft long cabin amidships on deck with promenade deck above. She was named *Heatherbell* and had an official capacity for 807 passengers. The hull was divided into seven watertight compartments, a feature of all Carson's designs. There were two funnels and provision for two gangways each side, one on each side of the paddle-boxes. Heavy timber sponsons and rubbing pieces extended all round her. She was launched in May 1865 but, because of engine defects, did not enter service until September. She had a speed of 10 knots and remained pride of the fleet for 14 years, being used mainly on the New Brighton service.

An Ageing Fleet

The optimistic forecasts of 1861 were not attained and there was no money to renew the ageing fleet. In January 1864 *James Atherton* was withdrawn to undergo alterations to the hull, receive a new boiler and engine repairs. In May 1864 *Wallasey* was declared unfit to carry passengers and was relegated to the goods service while two months later *Tiger* was withdrawn and sold, having been previously fitted with a second-hand boiler. *Waterlily* had to undergo repairs and the undertaking was left very short of boats so was obliged to hire extensively during the summer and continuing into early 1865. These vessels included *Hercules, Columbus, Helen, Dispatch* and *Bridgewater*, the New Ferry boats *Sylph* and *Sprite* which were new and had not yet entered service and the Rock Ferry boat *Star*. A luggage boat *Favorite* was also hired for a time. *Gem* was purchased from Coulborns in September 1864, an unusual example of a vessel being rejected and then later purchased to do the work for which she had been designed.

On 1st December 1867 *Wallasey* sank during a violent gale; she was raised on 23rd January but, being beyond repair, was broken up. *Gem* received a new boiler during a refit in 1869 and was given a 50-seat deck cabin. *Wild Rose* was reboiled in 1870 but other modifications were not proceeded with until 1873 when deck shelters were provided. On 12th August 1869 both *Gem* and *Heatherbell* were chartered to act as tenders to the s.s. *Great Britain*, a useful source of extra revenue. The oldest vessel in the fleet, *Thomas Wilson*, fitted in 1863 with engines built by Fawcett, Preston for the former Woodside steamer *Ann*, suffered frequent mid-river breakdowns and *Mayflower* was in need of a major refit. During the summer of 1871, the Board was obliged to hire boats to maintain the service at Bank Holidays and during July and August. These included *Hercules, Bee* from Rock Ferry and the former Birkenhead Ferry steamer *Cato* from E. G. Willoughby of Tranmere.

New Brighton

The Local Board was in the difficult position of having taken over an undertaking which, while essential to the future growth of the town, was in need of considerable capital investment on both vessels and landing facilities. In order to maximise revenue there was a need to retain sufficient vessels and staff to cope with the peak summer demand but also to maintain a winter service for a small voluble band of annual contract-holders with minimum staff. The need to dredge the approaches to New Brighton ferry pier and protect the landing facilities from the ravages of sea and wind were costly items in the accounts. The population in 1861 was only 10,700 so the revenue base was low but an influx of new residents would be encouraged only by the provision of safe, all-weather facilities. In this respect, the way ahead had been demonstrated by the installation of a new floating landing stage at Woodside in February 1862 and the Local Board grasped the nettle and decided that floating stages should be provided at

all three ferry terminals as soon as they could be afforded. New Brighton, the most profitable passage, was chosen for attention first and powers were incorporated in the Wallasey Improvement Act, 1864 which also authorised further mortgages of £45,000 of which £15,000 was earmarked for the New Brighton pier and stage. The Act required the plans to be submitted to the Admiralty for approval.

The new terminal was based upon James Brunlees' plans used for New Ferry and comprised an iron pier, a floating landing stage and a connecting passenger bridge. The contract, valued at £9,300, was awarded to Peto, Brassey and Potts of Birkenhead on 1st October 1864. Within a month of signing, the contractors realised that the completion date of 1st July 1865 was unduly optimistic; furthermore the Local Board had failed to appoint James Brunlees as engineer-in-charge, preferring instead their own engineer. On 5th January 1865, the partially built pier was transferred to contractors Rothwell & Co. of Bolton who undertook completion by 1st May at a cost of £9,250. They, too, proved incompetent and progress was further hindered when the connecting bridge collapsed while being placed in position, toppling on to the four linked pontoons which served as a temporary stage during the reconstruction works. This broke up, depositing some 200 people in the water, fortunately without loss of life.

The temporary pontoon stage was repositioned but it was condemned in October as unsafe, being replaced by the hulk of *Elizabeth* which had been used in a similar capacity at Seacombe. The new works were then entrusted to the distinguished engineer, Henry Hooper but, when the Local Board finally took possession on 1st March 1866, they still declared themselves thoroughly dissatisfied. The final work was completed by Bowdler, Chaffer and Co., the Seacombe shipbuilders, the cost having escalated to £23,906, exceeding the original estimate by £14,000. When asked to comment on the discrepancy, Brunlees said 'the pier at New Ferry had been built for one proprietor and in that case I was permitted to appoint my own resident engineer and was fortunate in having a good contractor whereas the New Brighton pier was under the superintendence of a Board who appointed their own resident engineer and was unfortunate in its contractor'.

The opening ceremony took place on 20th May 1866 when *Heatherbell* was brought alongside the new floating stage. On 3rd October 1867 the stage and bridge suffered major structural damage when the Lamport and Holt steamer *Galileo* ran out of control in a strong south-east wind and smashed into the southern end of the stage as her pilot, in an effort to avoid running aground, fought to bring

The Wallasey Local Board took over all three ferries from 1st August 1861 and, realising the traffic potential of New Brighton ferry, decided to provide a new ferry pier connected to a floating landing stage by a hinged bridge. This view, taken from the end of the Promenade Pier, shows the ill-fated paddle-steamer Gem *approaching the new landing stage with a good load of passengers. The landing stage opened on 20th May 1866 after a series of calamities attributed to incompetent contractors. The pier was based on plans drawn by the celebrated engineer, James Brunlees, for New Ferry pier. The stage and bridge were severely damaged on 3rd October 1867 by the Lamport and Holt steamer* Galileo *and did not reopen until 28th May 1868. The structure continued to be plagued by problems and also by insufficient depth of water for many years.*

G. H. Peers collection

her alongside in heavy seas. There was an ebb tide running and the impact broke the mooring chains, the stage then swinging round. Watching from the shore, a Mr Haughton observed 'The vessel blew across the head of the stage and, after a time, the pressure became so great that the moorings yielded, the bridge curled up in the air like a sapling and fell in three fragments into the water. The landward edge of the bridge was torn from its connection but the riverward end retained its attachment to the arch by means of the chains until someone on the landing stage cut it loose with a chisel and let it go by the board'. The landing stage drifted out to sea and was rescued by the combined efforts of *Wallasey* and *Waterlily* under the personal command of William Carson.

At the subsequent enquiry, Brunlees was completely exonerated. However, during the subsequent reconstruction, the offshore end of the bridge rested upon rollers embedded in the stage thus making the movement of the whole structure more flexible. However, Brunlees' recommendation that protective dolphins be positioned either side of the stage was rejected by Admiral Evans, the river conservancy officer. Whilst the new bridge was being installed, passengers reached the boats from the pier by means of a temporary wooden stairway and four flats anchored abreast of each other and connected by gangplanks. The landing stage was reopened on 28th May 1868, the repairs having cost £4,850 although it was rumoured that the Board received £10,000 in compensation. But there were recurring problems with the stage and it was removed for examination on 11th November 1869, passengers using an iron landing boat bought for £45. After an abortive reopening on 15th December, the service was suspended while further work was done to anchor the stage more securely. During the closure, the ferry staff were employed in constructing larger toll booths at the pier entrance. The bridge was finally repositioned on 24th December but the problem of insufficient depth of water was not solved and for several years there were times when boats had to be hired to act as an extension to the stage.

Most Victorian seaside resorts boasted a pleasure pier and New Brighton was no exception. Constructed adjacent to and north of the ferry pier, the 560ft long 75ft wide structure was opened on 9th September 1867 at a cost of £27,000 and became a popular attraction for visitors. Access was gained from the ferry pier for which a rental was paid by the pier's owners but later a separate entrance was added leading directly from the horse shoe-shaped promenade protrusion at the foot of Victoria Road.

Forward Planning

Meanwhile, on 6th January 1866 the Local Board formed a Special Committee to formulate plans for improvements to Seacombe and Egremont ferry terminals. Carson prepared detailed plans based on his own ideas which were presented to the Committee in February 1867 but the Board also announced a competition for the best schemes. The offer of two prizes of £100 and two of £50 attracted engineers of some status. The winners of the Seacombe prize were Messrs. Benjamin Haughton, C. E. and G. J. Crosbie Dawson of the London & North Western Railway while the Egremont prize was won by Mr Charles Cubitt, nephew of the late Sir William Cubitt. Awards were made to the winners on 9th January 1868 by which time the

Local Board had decided what it was going to do.

Carson persuaded the Board to adopt his plans but tactfully submitted three variations for Seacombe which was by far the major scheme. The plan was a bold one, involving the reclamation of a considerable area of land and it was necessary to obtain the approval of the River Conservancy and the Mersey Docks and Harbour Board. This process took some time and it was late in 1871 before the Local Board was able to seek Parliamentary approval. Both the Seacombe and Egremont schemes were authorised by the Wallasey Improvement Act, 1872.

During the summer of 1867, the three passages were worked by only three boats with the New Brighton/Egremont service ceasing to call at Seacombe after 7.30pm. For the winter of 1867-68, the New Brighton sailings were hourly on weekdays with only five crossings on Sundays. The next winter the Egremont and New Brighton services worked hourly, the boats also calling at Seacombe at off-peak times. Forced by mounting winter losses, the Board considered replacing the northern boats by a horse tramway linking Seacombe to Trafalgar Road, Egremont at a cost of £4,446 but this was rejected as the Board would have needed Parliamentary powers. A similar plan to use horse buses was likewise dismissed in September 1868. A 1d fare between Egremont and New Brighton had been introduced on 1st April 1866.

From 1st August to 10th September 1871, and again in 1872, the midnight Liverpool-Seacombe sailing was extended to New Brighton experimentally at a special high fare of 6d. A short-lived daily luggage boat return sailing was introduced from New Brighton to Liverpool on 13th June 1872.

Second-hand Vessels

Ten years after municipalisation, three of the Coulborns' boats were still in service and, in the absence of funds for new boats, the only alternative was to buy second-hand. Bowdler, the Seacombe shipbuilder, was Chairman of the Ferries Committee and he inspected a yacht *Swallow* lying at Scarborough. Although rather light for service on the Mersey, she was purchased in May 1872 for £1,300 although damage caused whilst in transit needed expenditure of another £1,000. She was very fast, making the Seacombe crossing in under five minutes on one occasion and in June 1873 inaugurated an express peak hour service to and from New Brighton which does not seem to have lasted very long. *Cato* was considered for purchase but she had been built in 1849 and was in poor condition so an offer was made for another Willoughby steamer, *Seymour*, an iron paddler built at Bowdler Chaffer's yard in 1869. After some

bargaining, £4,000 was paid for a vessel of somewhat old fashioned lines but nevertheless economical in service. Both acquisitions were initially used on the New Brighton service which was increased to half-hourly during peak periods.

In December 1873, *Gem* was sent to Allsup's at Preston for a complete rehabilitation including lengthening by 11ft 4in to enable gangways to be placed either side of the paddle boxes and was given new engines. She was also divided into seven watertight compartments, *Waterlily* being similarly treated in November 1875. A wooden steam-powered coal barge *Maggie*, built at Northwich in 1867, was acquired in March 1874. A $2^1/2$-ton steam crane was fitted and she was used to coal the larger steamers, eliminating the slow, costly and dirty process of coaling by hand.

Swallow was laid up for the winter of 1875-76 but in July 1876 was employed on a direct Egremont-Liverpool service. At the end of that season both *Mayflower* and *Waterlily* were fitted with new boilers by Fawcett, Preston & Co. *Mayflower* was also thoroughly refitted by Gilchrist and Smith. This involved lengthening by 20ft, providing additional water-tight compartments and re-newing and extending her poop deck. Her new length was 155ft and passenger capacity had risen from 793 to 863. Like *Heatherbell* she was too long for the berthage at Liverpool stage but the Dock Board decided to take no action. *Waterlily* was equipped with Partridge's Gas Apparatus which comprised a large holder below deck supplied from the mains by equipment mounted on Egremont stage. *Gem* was similarly equipped. The warm yellow glow of the gas lamps was no doubt attractive but a spark in the wrong place could have blown the vessel up. Both vessels returned to service by Easter 1877.

Thomas Wilson and *James Atherton* were both nearing the end of their usefulness. The latter went on hire to Tranmere ferry for two months at the end of 1876 and replaced *Thomas Wilson* as luggage boat in July 1877, the former having lost her passenger certificate in March. During the major works at Seacombe she served as a temporary workshop. *Seymour* worked the railway ferry between Liverpool and Monks Ferry in November 1876 at £12 per day.

During the winter of 1877-8 there were many dense fogs and, despite strong representations from the Local Board, the Dock Board Pilotage Committee refused to take action to prevent ships being moored in the river on the Seacombe passage. It was decided to equip all deck seats with detachable tops and fit cork to the bottoms to sustain buoyancy in case of an accident. Extra watertight compartments were to be created in *Gem* and *Waterlily*, the latter being chosen for immediate attention.

The Gem Disaster

One of the worst fogs in living memory blanketed the Mersey on Tuesday 26th November 1878. As was the custom in foggy conditions, the manager personally conducted operations and authorised every departure. There were strict rules for masters notably never to exceed half speed and strict observance of the code of fog signals in use on the river. On this occasion *Seymour* arrived from Liverpool and, after her passengers had disembarked, *Gem* was ordered alongside and proceeded to embark about 250-300 waiting passengers, leaving half an hour late at 9.30am commanded by Captain Cartwright, an experienced master, with 27 years ferry service. A Brocklebank sailing ship, *Bowfell* was anchored a little west of mid-river between the temporary Seacombe stage and Alfred Dock and *Gem* crashed sideways into her, just forward of her starboard sponson. As *Gem* swung on, she fell across the clipper bow of *Bowfell*, the bowsprit of which swept the decks causing considerable damage including knocking her funnel down. Panic ensued and several passengers jumped overboard though, in fact, there was no danger of *Gem* sinking as she had not been holed below the water line. Estimates of fatalities varied between eight and 20 as many bodies were never recovered. *Gem* finally made a landing at Woodside cattle stage.

At the subsequent inquest, the jury were to recommend that '...the time had arrived for the Dock Board to be unanimous in putting a stop to ships anchoring in the ferry track between Seacombe and George's Landing Stage, especially during winter months. Our inevitable conclusion is that it borders on criminality to anchor ships in the ferry track during foggy weather'. But these sentiments were not shared by the Wreck Commissioner who presided over an official Inquiry which opened on 10th December 1878. Cartwright was criticised for exceeding half speed as he had apparently ordered full speed to try to clear the bowsprit thus increasing the force of the impact. The Inquiry concluded that 'the blame, therefore, if blame there is, rests more with the ratepayers and the Wallasey Local Board who are the owners of the ferry steamer *Gem* in giving no discretionary power either to their manager or their captains to stop the Seacombe Ferry boats when it is dangerous to run'. As soon as the Inquiry was over, *Gem* was repaired, an iron bulkhead replacing the staircase to the aft cabin. Early in 1879 both *Mayflower* and *Heatherbell* were fitted with extra watertight compartments, the latter having had a near miss in fog with an anchored vessel which was not displaying regulation lights or sounding a warning bell.

The collision between the ferry steamer Gem *and* Bowfell *in November 1878 had a serious effect on the public's confidence in the safety of the ferries. The funnel of* Gem, *felled in the collision is seen on the deck after the vessel had been docked.*
M. Jenkins collection

Reconstruction at Egremont

Elaborate plans of proposed new embarkation arrangements at Egremont were drawn up in 1862 on behalf of the Local Board by Furness and Kilpin of Lawton Street, Liverpool. An ambitious scheme envisaged a railway 517ft long being laid on the river bed with a steam-operated locomotive carriage on stilts, capable of carrying 215 passengers and some freight, which would have connected the land with a movable stage, also using the same railway. This structure included jacks and a screw device to keep it in position but, as it had no motive power, it is not clear whether it would have been moved along the track by the locomotive carriage or by the boat. The railway terminated in a short tunnel under the quay and there were lock gates creating a dry dock behind which the carriage and stage could be parked at high tide when the boats would have tied up at the quay. The carriage measured 36ft x 16ft and power was supplied by two 7 hp engines mounted on each side of the vehicle. Two 7ft wide doors, one each side, would have enabled loading and unloading to take place simultaneously at the landward end, passengers transferring to the movable stage by an end gangway. The height of the deck above rail level was about 15ft and above water level about 5ft. An endorsement on one plan notes that it was provided to accompany an application to Admiral Evans, Conservator of the River Mersey on 22nd August 1862. The railed contraptions would have been totally unstable in bad weather conditions and might well have been overturned by a fast-running tide and it is not surprising that nothing more was heard of this scheme.

A survey in 1871 showed that the Egremont pier, slip and walls were in need of urgent attention and the Local Board decided that the provision of a complete new infrastructure would give the best value for money in the long term. The problems were formidable as the landing stage needed to be 750ft from the shore to provide sufficient depth of water at low tide but the river conservancy would sanction a structure no longer than 360ft.

Carson and the ferries engineer, James Lea, were entrusted with superintendence with Charles H. Beloe as engineer-in-charge. Beloe was to be involved with tramway development in both Liverpool and Wallasey and with several railway and shipping projects.

The ferry was closed after operation on 12th January 1874, contract holders being free to use either New Brighton or Seacombe. The old movable stage and its machinery was sold for £300 and most of the works buildings were demolished. Carson's plan was for a pier 275ft long to be built 35ft above low water level. 85ft beyond the pier's outer end, a dolphin consisting of two groups of wrought iron columns, filled with concrete up to high water level were arranged as a tripod. This dolphin was connected with the pier by a bow string wrought iron bridge, hinged to the pier and supported at its outer end by two hydraulic rams by means of which the height of the bridge could be adjusted according to the water level. A gangway, worked by a small hydraulic ram, was placed at the end of the bridge and between the half-tides and high water passengers were embarked by lowering this gangway directly on to the deck of the steamer.

A movable carriage 370ft 6in long and weighing 80 tons traversed the slipway under the pier, with heavy cast iron wheels running on three rails. It was moved by means of winding gear driven by the same Brotherwood 3-cylinder hydraulic engine which powered the hydraulic rams. It was run in or out between the half tides and low water to form a pier extension to which the vessels tied up.

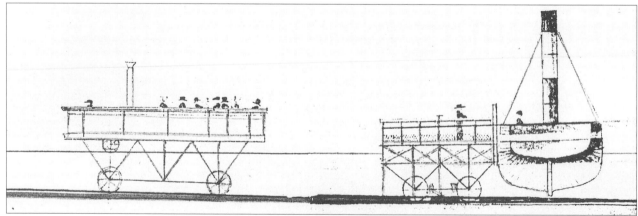

Plans have been found of an elaborate scheme in 1862 to run passengers out to the boats at Egremont in a high-built railcar powered by steam. Strangely there is no reference to this in the Local Board's proceedings. Most of the plans are too large and fragile to copy but the general view of the steam car, the movable landing stage and the boat have been adapted from the original. The means of transmission on the car are unclear and it seems doubtful that the car and landing stage would have been able to withstand a swift moving tide.

Wirral Archive Service

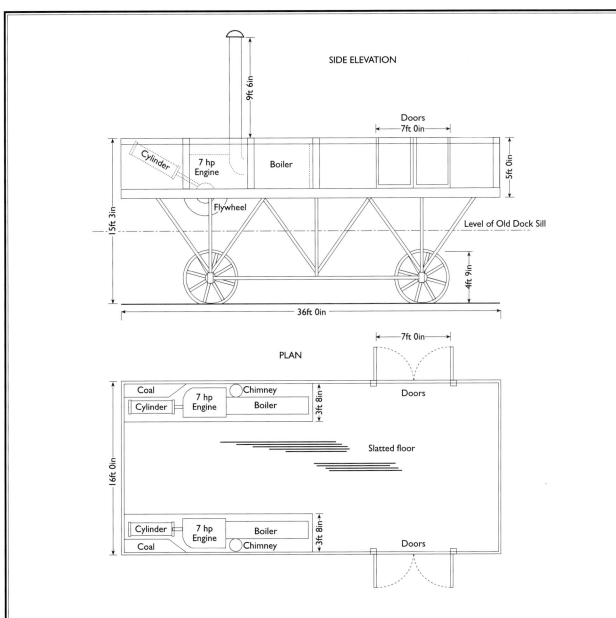

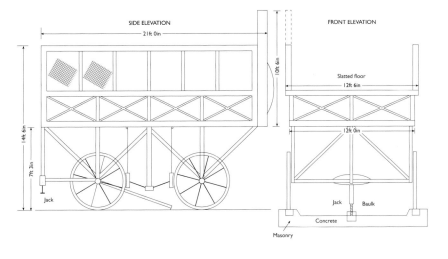

SIDE ELEVATION

9ft 6in

Doors
7ft 0in

Cylinder

7 hp
Engine

Boiler

5ft 0in

15ft 3in

Flywheel

Level of Old Dock Sill

4ft 9in

36ft 0in

PLAN

7ft 0in

Coal

Cylinder

7 hp
Engine

Chimney

Boiler

3ft 8in

Doors

16ft 0in

Slatted floor

Cylinder

7 hp
Engine

Boiler

3ft 8in

Coal

Chimney

Doors

Details of the carriage linking the shore with the landing stage at Egremont in the abortive 1862 scheme.

SIDE ELEVATION

21ft 0in

FRONT ELEVATION

10ft 6in

Slatted floor
12ft 6in

14ft 6in

7ft 3in

12ft 0in

Jack

Jack   Baulk

Concrete

Masonry

The proposed movable landing stage.

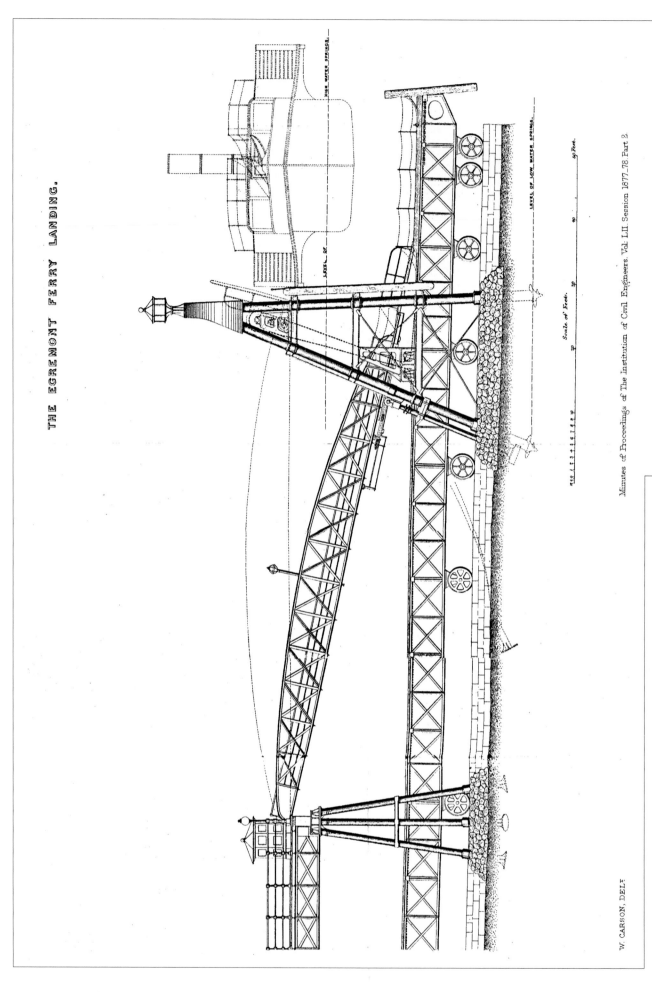

THE EGREMONT FERRY LANDING.

Scale of Feet.

W. CARSON, DEL.ᵀ

Minutes of Proceedings of The Institution of Civil Engineers. Vol. LII. Session 1877-78. Part 2.

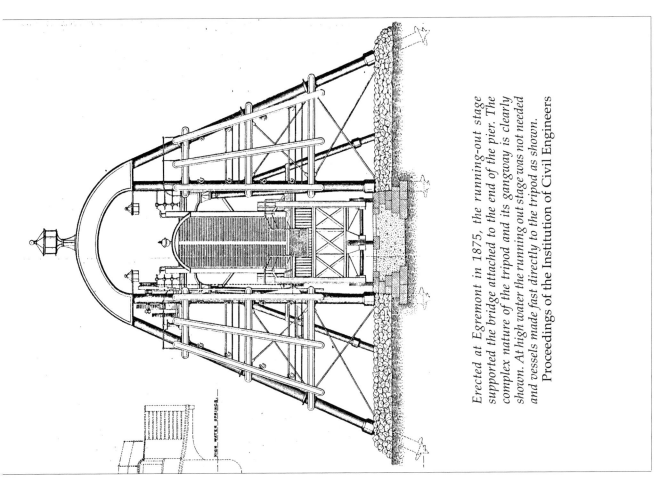

Erected at Egremont in 1875, the running-out stage supported the bridge attached to the end of the pier. The complex nature of the tripod and its gangway is clearly shown. At high water the running out stage was not needed and vessels made fast directly to the tripod as shown.
Proceedings of the Institution of Civil Engineers

During the construction period there were several spells of bad weather as a result of which work was delayed and the new terminal was not reopened until 12.0noon on 25th March 1875, with much civic ceremony. New offices, workshops and a booking hall were built at the shore end and Egremont was established as the headquarters of the Ferries Department. The works cost £14,000.

On 29th September 1875 the boiler in the hydraulic engine house exploded and the building collapsed, rendering the movable stage immobile. The stage was out and was caught by the swiftly rising tide. Two vessels moored themselves to it hoping that their added buoyancy would help to move it up the ramp but they failed and the extension was derailed. From 1st October the ferry operated only for $6^1/2$ hours during high tide and this situation continued for some time until the boiler was repaired. A duplicate engine and boiler were installed to avoid a future problem of this kind and in a belt-and-braces exercise, a powerful crab winch with a steel wire rope, worked by a capstan and handspikes was also installed. A dozen men could thus move the extension by hand. The whole structure was coated with a preparation of crude brown glycerin and water at a ratio of 1:4 and, following some accidents, a gong was sounded before the stage was moved. Ferry staff had their work cut out to catch fare dodgers who raced across the beach and climbed on to the extension to reach the boats.

Unfortunately some of the work turned out to have been shoddy and extensive repairs were made to the slipway in July 1878. A demand by passengers for a waiting room at the end of the pier was rejected but it was eventually built in 1888. An ambitious scheme in 1878 for installing a hydraulic lift capable of raising a 250-ton ship above the high water mark was finally rejected as impracticable and a plan to build a £4,500 graving dock south of the pier in 1880 was also abandoned. The objective was to eliminate the use of the Great Float for major repairs to the Board's vessels as heavy dues were payable to the Dock Board. Minor repairs continued to be done on the gridiron at Egremont or by beaching at low water.

The problems at Egremont were not entirely solved by the new pier and landing difficulties continued. In February 1879, a strongly worded letter was sent to the Dock Board complaining of the practice of dumping mud dredged from the docks along the coast between Egremont and the Magazines and it was decided to seek authority for a 35ft extension of the slipway but the Board of Trade, successor to the Commissioners for Woods and Forests, would not agree on the grounds of interference with navigation. Although Egremont was the headquarters of the Ferries Department,the accommodation was cramped and inefficient and it was said that a move to Seacombe would save £200 per year in wages and cartage charges.

A windy walk along the exposed pier. Everyone wears a hat and some have umbrellas for protection against the sun. Egremont pier was completely renewed in 1874-75. Because the conservator of the Mersey would not allow a pier sufficiently long to ensure deep water at all states of the tide, this ingenious structure was devised with a 370ft 6in. long extension mounted on wheels which ran on rails laid on a slipway beneath the pier. A bowstring bridge connected the end of the pier with a tripod dolphin which guided the extension. The extension was moved by winding gear driven by a 3-cylinder Brotherwood water engine. In this picture of the pier in 1890, the rails can be seen near the edges of the slip. The notice reads 'Persons are warned against being on the slipway when the stage is in motion'. Priestley & Co.

CAUTION
PERSONS ARE WARNED AGAINST
BEING ON THE SLIPWAY WHEN THE
STAGE IS IN MOTION.
By ORDER.

Despite the department's financial problems, a plan to modernise the existing workshop at Egremont for £500 was rejected in favour of building a new workshop at Seacombe to cost an estimated £1,557. Two months after the contract was awarded it was rescinded as the Local Government Board would not approve the full loan requested for the various capital projects then in prospect.

Reconstruction at Seacombe

The land reclamation plan at Seacombe, where the ferry slip was in a small bay, was virtually a northward extension of the Birkenhead dock scheme which had been taking shape over the previous 25 years and was undertaken jointly with the Dock Board with whom the 3.4 acres reclaimed by straightening the river bank was to be shared. The Local Board had to take into account that it was politically impracticable to burden the ratepayers too heavily.

Carson originally put forward three plans but one (Plan B) was discarded at an early date. Both remaining plans envisaged a floating landing stage 310ft long and a passenger bridge fixed at the shore end. Plan C, on which the Parliamentary plans were based, proposed a floating roadway with only one intermediate pontoon for use by vehicles while Plan A included a goods bridge fixed at the shore end in the same way as the passenger bridge. The existing slip had a permanent incline of 1 in 20 and

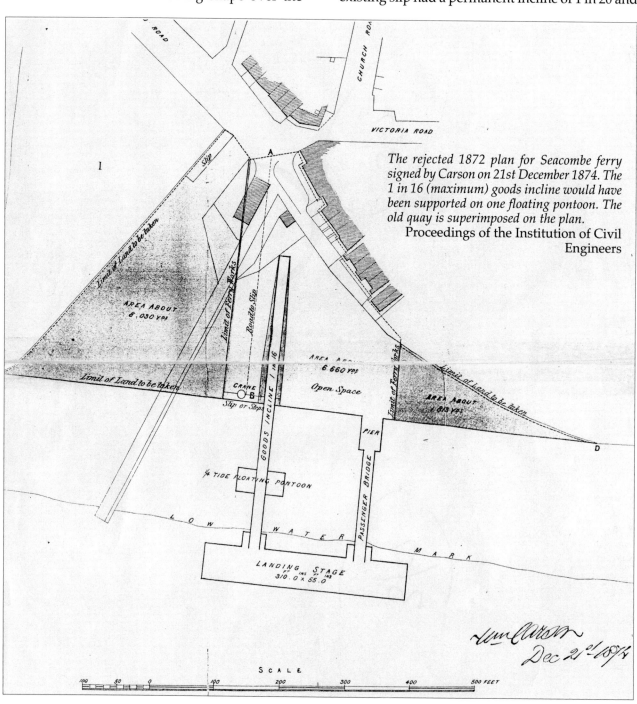

The rejected 1872 plan for Seacombe ferry signed by Carson on 21st December 1874. The 1 in 16 (maximum) goods incline would have been supported on one floating pontoon. The old quay is superimposed on the plan.
Proceedings of the Institution of Civil Engineers

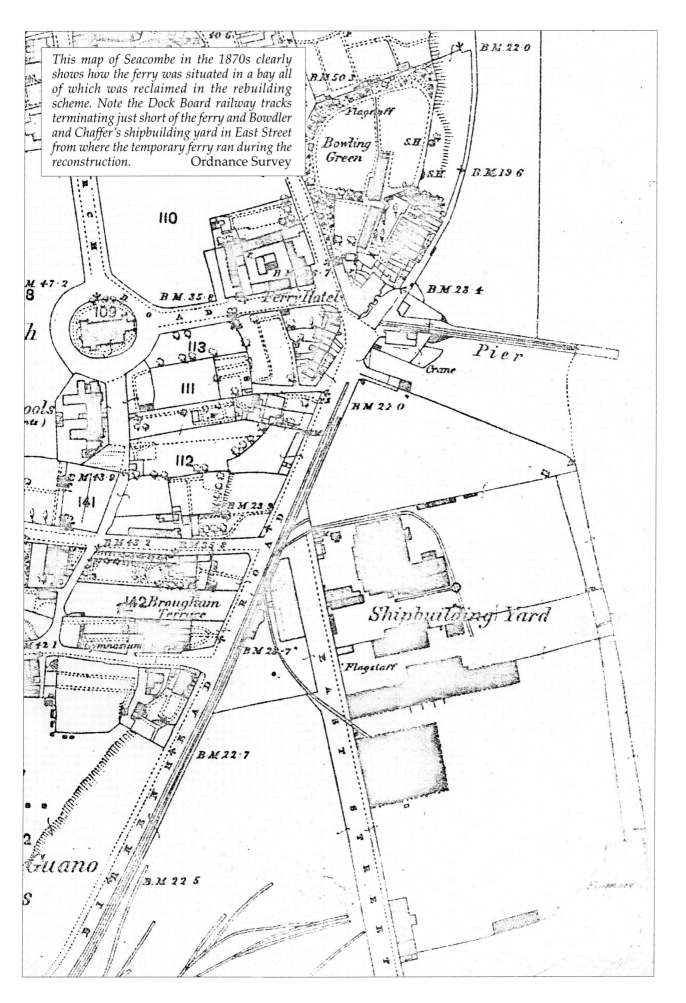

This map of Seacombe in the 1870s clearly shows how the ferry was situated in a bay all of which was reclaimed in the rebuilding scheme. Note the Dock Board railway tracks terminating just short of the ferry and Bowdler and Chaffer's shipbuilding yard in East Street from where the temporary ferry ran during the reconstruction. Ordnance Survey

A picture of Seacombe taken just before the bay was filled in in 1876. In the foreground is Swallow, *bought second-hand in 1872 and behind it is* Thomas Wilson, *built in 1845. By this time passenger and goods traffic had been separated and the luggage boats loaded from the gangway to the left of the picture. This was a public quay. Stokes (formerly Parry's) Hotel is in the background.*

G. H. Peers collection

varied in length from 370ft to 25ft according to the tide. A 160ft bridge would have had an unacceptable gradient of 1 in 5.3ft at a low water spring tide of 21ft whereas a floating structure would have lifted over its entire length with a 1 in 16 gradient at extreme low water and a level plane at high water. Plan C was adopted by the Local Board in 1867.

However, during the years of planning, the floating roadway at Woodside had been opened and the practical problems associated with its use and the cost of its maintenance had become apparent. The Woodside and Liverpool roadways, opened in 1868 and 1874 respectively had several pontoons thus providing a very flexible structure. It became apparent that a floating roadway would provide inadequate mooring for the stage and an expensive mooring boom would have been needed to maintain rigidity. The 1867 plan was amended in 1872 and a revised Plan A was adopted the following year incorporating, in addition to passenger and goods bridges, a high level pier with two hydraulic lifts connecting it to the stage for use at low water. The stage was redesigned from a width of 55ft to 70ft with an end-loading embayment at the south (goods) end. The pier and lift were to have railway tracks connected to the dock railways.

The Board of Trade approved the change in plans without the need to seek new Parliamentary powers and active planning for the continuation of the ferry service during the estimated three-year construction period begun in late 1875. William Carson was appointed Engineer at a fee of £1,000 with Wilfrid S. Boult and John J. Potts as resident engineers. The Conservator refused to allow a temporary pier to be erected but fortuitously Bowdler and Chaffer's shipyard to the south of the ferry slip which had been damaged by fire in 1872, had become vacant and the Local Board rented part of the site with a 450ft frontage to the river and access from East Street. An asphalt surface was laid, existing buildings being adapted as passenger facilities and to accommodate carriages, cabs and omnibuses. A floating stage and 150ft connecting bridge, redundant from a failed service between New Ferry and Toxteth, were purchased from Mr R. A. MacFie and floated across the river on 2nd February 1876. The stage which, for some reason, had been registered as a ship, *South End*, by its previous owner, measured 120ft x 30ft x 7ft 9in with a projection under the bridge of 20ft by 10ft and was moored with $1^3/4$ in. chains. As the shipyard sloped down to the river wall, a 16ft wide timber pier was built to within 35ft of the wall, the inshore end of the bridge being hinged to a cross-head with a similar connection to the stage.

The first contract, for the 1,000ft river wall, was let in May 1876 and from 11.0am on 26th July 1876 all Seacombe sailings were transferred to the temporary landing; this functioned reasonably well except at low water when a steamer was beached at the stage to give extra depth and landing craft were brought into use. During an exceptionally low Spring tide on 30th March 1877, two Tranmere boats were hired and beached alongside but these failed to reach low water mark and passengers had to be transferred to 'a small armada of little craft'.

Demolition of the Seacombe Hotel and other properties which flanked the bay began immediately, the old slip being retained for a time for the removal of waste. The foundation of the river wall was very hard boulder clay; it was built of random soft-stone masonry, two thirds being in blocks of not less than 20 cu.ft. The wall rose to a height of 27ft above Old Dock Sill behind the piers and 24ft elsewhere. For infilling behind the wall, rock rubbish was dumped for a width of 24ft behind which was clay most of which was obtained by levelling ground behind the old Seacombe hotel and adjoining properties, including a bowling green. The whole structure was massive, being designed not only to withstand the weather but also to resist, as far as possible, damage which might be caused by a drifting steamer. The work, which was undertaken by Thomas Monk of Bootle,

had to be fitted in with the tides, the founding of the wall alone occupying 471 tides.

As Seacombe is situated at the narrowest part of the Mersey, the tide sometimes flows at $6^1/_4$ knots with a range of 32ft 6in, so the Conservator would not allow a protrusion into the river greater than about 300ft. Two piers extending 80ft from the river wall were supported by six cast-iron columns 5ft in diameter above water level and 6ft 6in for 14ft below. The two 160ft bridges rested on these which were extended over the land for 29ft and a brick terminal building was constructed over the whole structure, the builders being Holme and Nicol of Liverpool who had built the Woodside terminal building. The high level bridge giving access to the lifts lay between the two bridges. The landing stage as built was 310ft 6in long by 80ft wide at the passenger end, the overall distance from the river wall to the outer face of the stage being 308ft.

The piers, landing stage and bridges were built by Thomas Brassey & Company's Canada Works on the West Float at Birkenhead. Work began on erecting the piers on 4th April 1877 but the project became bogged down because the contractor did not hire suitable dredgers. Eventually, a large centre ladder dredger was hired from the Clyde

Above: Swallow, *a former Loch Lomond steamer named* Queen Victoria *was built in 1852 and purchased second-hand in 1872 for £1,300. She was fitted with feathering floats and was sold ten years later being broken up in 1883.* From a painting

Right: *The feathering paddle wheel fitted to many ferry steamers adjusted the angle of the paddles so as to give maximum thrust.* T. Morgan

FEATHERING PADDLE WHEEL

AFT FOR'D

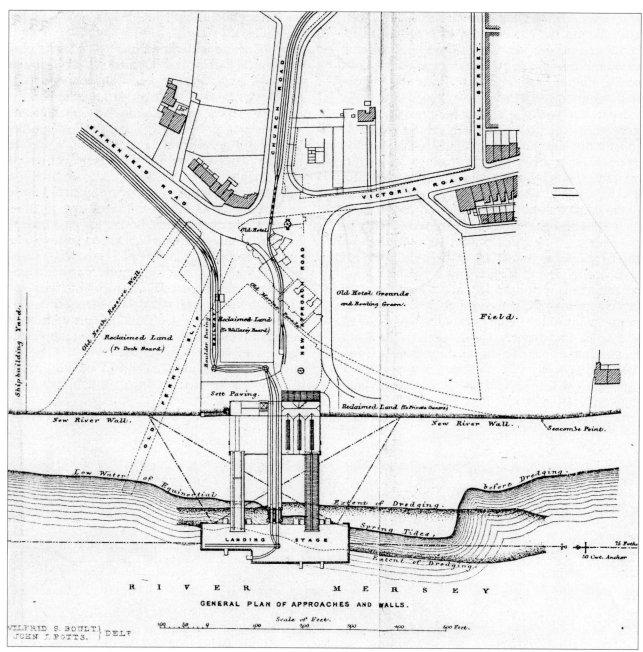

GENERAL PLAN OF APPROACHES AND WALLS.

Scale of Feet.

WILFRID S. BOULT
JOHN J. POTTS. } DEL.ᵗ

Plan of the new works at Seacombe completed in 1879-80 with the old coastline shown by a broken line. Note the embayment at the south end of the landing stage and the railway tracks connected to the tracks in the ferry yard and the Dock Board lines in Birkenhead Road by turntables. The tracks on to the High Level bridge and landing stage were not, in fact, laid following the refusal of the Dock Board to provide matching facilities on the Liverpool side of the river.

Proceedings of the Institution of Civil Engineers

Trustees for six months during which she was able to work for only 30 days because of Spring tides and periods of rough weather. Finally, the Local Board hired a powerful dredger from the London & North Western Railway. The stage was then floated into position with two paddle tugs forward and another two aft on 20th November 1879. The two main mooring chains had already been positioned and buoyed and these were hauled in followed by the fore and aft anchors. The bridges were floated down on Dock Board camels on 21st and 22nd November and dropped into place as the tide fell. The cross-bridle mooring chains were then

picked up, the lengths of the moorings adjusted and the stage fixed in its proper position. A glazed roof over the passenger bridge was constructed *in situ.*

The machinery building comprised an engine- and boiler-house and a 70ft accumulator tower incorporating a clock tower with four 6ft diameter faces and an ornamental finial. The cast iron accumulator cylinder and ram, 18in in diameter by 20ft stroke had a weight case 9ft 9in in diameter by 21ft deep attached to the ram head by a wrought iron crosshead to give a pressure equal to 600lb per sq in of the ram. Pumping power was derived from two direct-acting horizontal high pressure engines, the steam cylinders being of 15in diameter and 24in stroke. The engines were automatically controlled by the accumulator, the pumps being supplied from the return water-tank with a head of 18ft. Two Cornish boilers supplied the engines with steam at 80lb per sq.in.

Hydraulic power was used in three ways. The goods lifts were mounted on hydraulic rams 40ft long with a maximum stroke of 32ft 9in, the cylinders being attached together so that advantage could be taken of a descending load. The length of stroke, which varied with the state of the tide, was controlled from a hut on the stage. Two passenger and two goods gangways were also powered as were three of Brotherwood's patent three-cylinder capstans. One of these was mounted on the stage for moving railway wagons on the stage and on and off the lifts; another on the high-level pier for working wagons along it and a third at the head of the goods bridge for helping carts when the gradient was steep. All the machinery was supplied by the Hydraulic Engineering Co. of Chester.

The Grand Opening

The new Seacombe terminal opened on 5th January 1880 but, at that time, the approach roadways and railway had not been started. The ferry buildings and the whole fleet were dressed overall and the first boat left the new stage as the clock on the accumulator tower tolled noon. On board were civic dignitaries from Liverpool, Birkenhead, Wallasey and surrounding districts, representatives of all the firms involved in the construction and as many ordinary passengers as could squeeze on. The luggage service was conducted by *James Atherton* from the temporary stage until 31st March when *Sunflower* took over from the new stage. The temporary stage and bridge were removed on 23rd July 1880 and the site handed over to the Dock Board on 17th August. The cost of the project was £143,000 which was a little over half the total capital investment of £275,000 made in terminals and vessels by the Local Board since the takeover in August 1861.

One feature of the terminal which was never

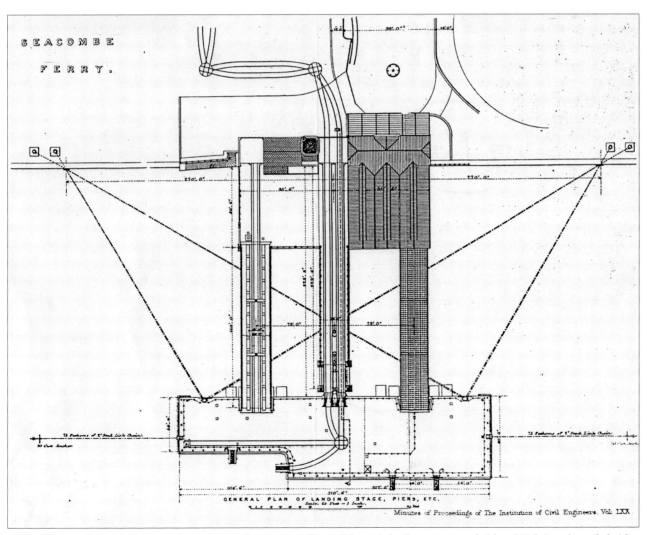

General plan of the 1879-80 works at Seacombe showing from right to left, the passenger bridge, High Level goods bridge with lifts and goods bridge. Note both end and side gangways in the luggage embayment.

Proceedings of the Institution of Civil Engineers

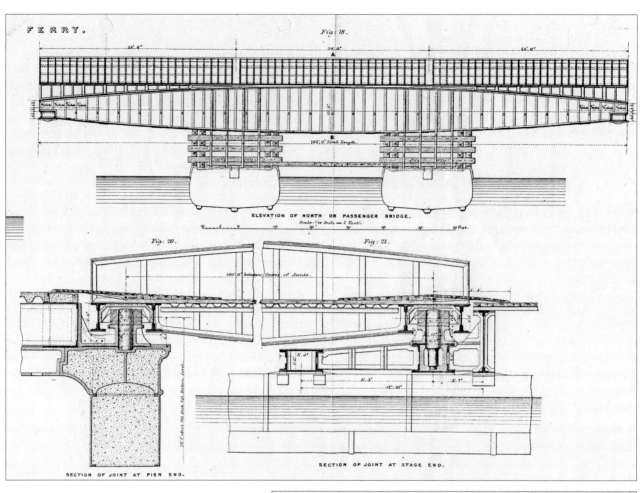

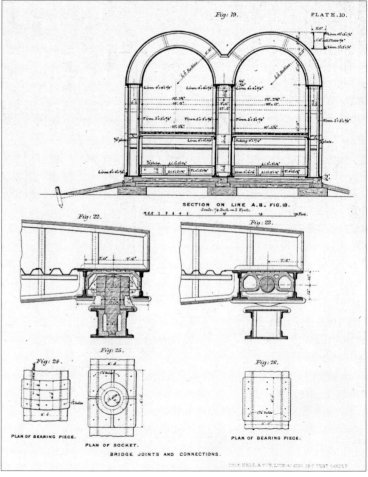

Detail drawings showing mechanical and design features of the north (passenger) bridge installed at Seacombe in 1879.
Proceedings of the Institution of Civil Engineers

Pier Entrance, Seacombe   Valentine's Series

The Seacombe ferry approach soon after opening in 1880 with a line of cabs waiting for custom.   Valentine's postcard

utilised was the facility to carry railway wagons across the river and it is extraordinary that the Local Board allowed Carson to have his head and spend so much money on a project which was seriously flawed. The facility would no doubt have been very useful and lucrative as the rail distance to Liverpool was about 40 miles but the Dock Board had no plans to provide matching facilities on the Liverpool side and showed no sympathy for the scheme.

Following the completion of all the maritime facilities, the 122ft-wide approach road was laid out. This was not part of the public highway and when the street tramway which had opened on 30th June 1879 was extended down to the ferry terminal, the company paid £1 per annum to the Ferries Committee for the privilege. A cab rank with shelter was eventually provided in the centre of the 92ft carriageway.

The *Gem* tragedy of November 1878 had many repercussions. Ferry traffic slumped, house prices fell and the building trade went into recession. Whether as a direct result or not, Carson resigned from 30th June 1879 and Capt. Cartwright was

dismissed for drunkenness on 30th December. Carson moved to the Whitecross Iron Co. of Warrington but continued as Engineer for the Seacombe ferry reconstruction until completion. The Board of Trade refused to be drawn into the dispute about anchoring vessels in the ferry track, declaring that the matter was at the discretion of the Dock Board. However, after the new Seacombe terminal was opened in 1880, the importance of the crossing was recognised and the same pilotage rules were applied to both Woodside and Seacombe though there were many breaches over the years.

The opening of the new terminal was marked by the inauguration of a 24-hour service between Seacombe and Liverpool with hourly sailings throughout the night at a fare of 6d.

In the course of 19 years of municipal ownership, the three ferry terminals of the Wallasey Local Board had been transformed and a fleet of roomy, modern steamers placed in service. This investment laid the foundations of the growth of Wallasey and its hinterland and the remarkable increase in population over the next half century.

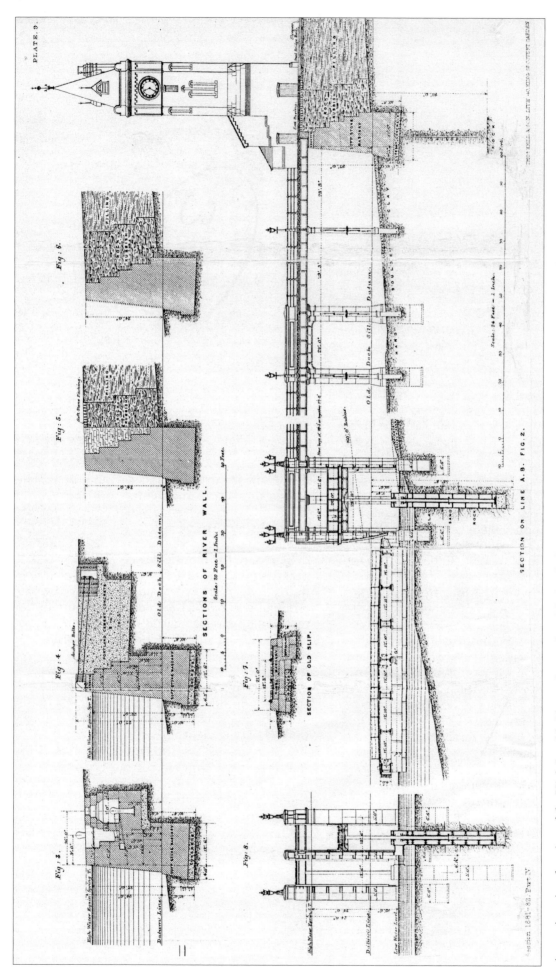

An engineering drawing of the High Level bridge at Seacombe with the clock tower, which housed the hydraulic equipment at one end and the double goods lift at the other.
Proceedings of the Institution of Civil Engineers

The iron paddle steamer Waterlily, *built locally in 1862 is seen in its last years in the 1880s or early 1890s after the forward saloon had been removed to enable it to carry carts as well as passengers. Square windows in the forward part of the hull slid open to provide ventilation to the below-deck cabin, a feature peculiar to this vessel. She was scrapped at Garston in 1892.*

Commercial postcard

A group of ferry steamers just off Liverpool landing stage include Seymour *(left) and* Waterlily *with its square portholes (centre). The Woodside boats in the picture are probably* Cheshire, Lancashire *or* Woodside, *all vessels of the 1860s.*

M. Jenkins collection

A view through the pierhead dolphin at Egremont with the extension stage fully extended as passengers come ashore from Primrose destined for New Brighton. A Cunarder passes in the background.
Priestley & Co.

4   1880-1914

WILLIAM Carson's successor as manager of the ferries was George Harries, a Birkenhead engineer who had been selected from a short-list of nine, including J. G. Bowdler, the former Chairman of the Ferries Committee whose shipyard had been destroyed by fire. Harries' salary was £400 per year. Another applicant, a retired naval architect, Frederick Ash, was appointed assistant manager. Harries' immediate task was to consolidate Carson's work and maximise the use of the new facilities which acted as a catalyst to Wallasey's spectacular growth leading to a situation where 40% of employed adult residents worked in Liverpool.

The contractor who laid out the ferry approach also laid out the goods yard, providing double track, a 12ft wagon turntable and a weighbridge serving both road and rail traffic. A rail connection with the Dock Board line in Birkenhead Road was completed on 28th October 1880 enabling coal for the steamers to be brought by rail to the ferry yard instead of having to be carted from Mortar Mill Quay on the East Float at one shilling a load. But the stillbirth of the cross-river wagon service had now been accepted and there was no rail connection to the High Level Bridge. The yard was opened to the public in September 1881 as compensation for loss of the parish slip and cattle and sheep pens and an abattoir were erected. It became a very busy place with small steam locomotives bringing coal and cattle wagons and taking the empties away.

The slump in revenue following the *Gem* disaster was arrested by 1881-82 and the following figures show how traffic was stimulated by the new Seacombe terminal.

	1878-79	1881-82
Daily receipts	£6,403. 9. 9	£9,436. 3. 2
Pass Tickets	520. 5. 3	359.13. 0
Contracts	319.17. 6	1,525.12. 6
Freight	757. 2. 8	2,450.11. $1^1/2$
Rents	30.19. 8	84. 1. 9
Rents, Goods Yard		49. 0. 6
TOTAL	8,031.14.10	13,955. 2. $0^1/2$
INCREASE		5,924.12.$9^1/2$
		(73.76%)

However, the wage bill had risen from £8,000 to £10,000 and the coal bill from £4,397 to £5,297, consumption in 1881-82 being 12,668 tons.

New Vessels

Carson had prepared drawings for a new passenger steamer in 1871 but it was not until July 1878 that he was instructed by the Committee to finalise plans for two passenger vessels and one luggage boat, the latter to be end-loading and capable of transporting railway wagons. This was despite the Dock Board having now firmly indicated that it would not allow railway wagons on the Liverpool stage. The tender of T. B. Seath of Rutherglen of £9,100 for each passenger vessel and £7,800 for the luggage boat, was accepted from ten submitted. J. G. Bowdler, was paid a retainer of £25 as technical adviser.

The design of the 150ft long passenger vessels was influenced by the Woodside steamers of recent years and established the general design principles adopted by Wallasey ferries for the next 70 years. They were double-ended paddle steamers with two funnels powered by two diagonal oscillating engines with 36in cylinders and a stroke of 5ft 6in, supplied by David Rowan & Co. of Glasgow. The hull was divided into 16 watertight compartments of which four were for coal. The paddle shaft was amidships so that they could travel equally fast in either direction. The 93ft long saloon had large picture windows, a great improvement on the portholes of earlier designs. The tradition of flower names was continued, the passenger vessels being named *Daisy* and *Primrose* and the luggage boat *Sunflower*.

The trials of both passenger vessels began in September 1879 but defects in the steam-powered steering gear delayed their entry into service until 3rd October in the case of *Primrose* and even later for *Daisy* which had the steering gear replaced. *Wild Rose*, *Gem* and *James Atherton* were offered for sale. *Sunflower* was launched on 13th August 1879 and steamed into the Mersey on 15th October. She had two funnels and resembled the two passenger ships in some respects. As described in Chapter 6, she proved unsuitable for the traffic so, in December 1880 Allsup's tender of £11,300 for a new double twin-screw iron luggage boat to be named *Wallasey* was accepted. She was to be the Wallasey ferries first screw driven vessel. The tender price included a second boiler, bilge keels and some rearrangement of bulkheads from the original specification. She was designed for end-loading but later converted to side loading. Launched on 10th September 1881, she had her trial trip on 2nd December, but all was not well and she did not enter service until February 1882. She improved the performance of the luggage service and had an uneventful career apart from sustaining severe damage in a collision with s.s. *Winnipeg* on 11th March 1898, drifting towards Tranmere, horses and carts being taken off by *Snowdrop*.

Following the success of *Wallasey*, in March 1882, *Sunflower* was converted into a passenger ship by Gilchrist & Smith but she retained her basic shape and the tendency to dip and slop about in the water. Her two on-deck cabins differed from those of *Daisy* and *Primrose* in having round glazed ends but her promenade deck extended to the edges of her paddle boxes, giving a little more covered accommodation beneath, her certificate being for 951 passengers. Each paddle box was ornately decorated with the ship's name prominently displayed in the centre. She could always be recognised at a distance as the black band on her funnel was much deeper than those of her contemporaries.

Wild Rose was taken off the market in February 1880; she was made ready for Easter and continued in the fleet as a stand-by for a further three years. *James Atherton* was finally sold for scrap in January 1881 after 35 years on the river. *Gem* was now the last of the Coulborn fleet to survive and in March 1881 it was decided to give her a new boiler. However, possibly as a result of public memories of her accident, she was never popular and had been involved in four further minor collisions; renovation work was suddenly stopped and she was sold to Allsups for £250 in May 1881. Ill luck still dogged her for, following sale to West African owners, she was wrecked off the Scilly Isles on her delivery voyage.

The cabin accommodation started to take the form which became familiar up to the mid-20th century. The underused ladies' saloons were gradually abolished and separate accommodation was designated for smokers and non-smokers. Upholstery gave way to shaped mahogany laths mounted on the existing seat frames. *Daisy* and *Primrose* were among the first vessels to be converted. The public were now becoming more discerning and wanted modern steamers to match the terminal facilities. *Swallow* had been laid up since the end of the 1881 season and was sold by auction for £130 in July 1882, the Board said that *Heatherbell* would also be auctioned but sent her to Forresters for a refit and reboilering instead, the condition of the contract being that she must be ready for 1st July 1883, otherwise a penalty of £5 per day would be incurred. Forresters also reboilered the coal barge *Maggie* at the same time. When *Heatherbell* returned, *Wild Rose* was sold; it was said that boys could cause her to rock by simply running from one side of her deck to the other. Her contemporary *Mayflower* remained in service, awaiting a buyer and *Seymour* spent most of 1883 on hire to Tranmere ferry, whence she had

Sunflower, launched in 1879, echoed the style of the steamers of the previous decade. She was built as a luggage boat but was unsuccessful being too narrow, and was converted for passengers in 1882, with a passenger certificate for 951. The picture dates from January 1899; the 'soup-plate', as she was called, was broken up by the ferry staff in 1904. E. R. Dibden

The ill-fated Gem *is shown wrecked on the Scilly Isles on 26th November 1881 when en route to Sierra Leone after sale by the ferries.*   R. T. McMahon collection

originally come. The Board continued to hire various steamers at busy times.

At the end of 1882, the Board decided to order a new steamer and considered commissioning a twin-screw vessel to carry both goods and passengers. However, the order to Allsups was eventually for an iron paddler for passengers only at £10,900. A teak deck was later specified for another £350 and patent feathering floats were added for £250. Three names, *Blue Bell*, *Moss Rose* and *Violet* were considered, the latter being chosen. She was to be the last iron steamer to be built for Wallasey.

New vessels were the subject of much debate as new marine designs and technology were being closely watched. Steel was taking over from iron but there was some fear that the extra weight of the steamers would cause damage when berthing and the proposed 7ft draught would reduce manoeuvrability. Screw propulsion was also taking over from paddles and Flannery, the ferry engineer, dismissed the earlier objections and pointed to the lower coal consumption of screw vessels. Tenders were put out for two twin-screw steamers and, despite the fact that Allsups were weeks behind with *Violet*, they were again successful in winning the order worth £25,000 less £1,700 for *Mayflower* which was to be traded in when the first vessel was delivered.

Being short of boats, the Local Board was forced to hire the incomplete *Violet* from Allsups at £10 per day for the Easter and Whit holidays in 1884. During her first stay it was realised that her specified draught had been exceeded and the Board refused to accept her. In retaliation Allsups suspended work on the two new boats and then suggested that they should build one new twin-screw boat according to specification and one paddler similar to *Daisy* and *Primrose*. This was rejected and the matter was resolved by Allsups agreeing to deduct £1,150 from the cost of *Violet* and build the new boats according to specification.

Violet failed to reach her stipulated speed of 12 knots at her first two trials on 30th May and 23rd June 1884 but she finally made it on 3rd July. Allsups then objected to the Board deducting £2,500 for late delivery. She had a tendency to ship water due to her excessive weight and roundness in the bilges and would plough through the waves instead of rising to meet them, subjecting all on deck to a soaking. Outwardly, she resembled *Daisy* and *Primrose* with two funnels, on-deck saloons and promenade deck extending over the full width of the paddle boxes. Her service with the ferries was short as she was disposed of in 1900 after only 16 years.

The steel double twin-screw *Crocus* and *Snowdrop* were launched in August and November 1884 respectively and, after successful trials entered service on 26th January and 27th February 1885.

Violet, *launched in 1883, was the last iron steamer to be placed in service new by Wallasey ferries. Her general lines were based on the steamers of the 1860s. As a paddle steamer, she became obsolescent and was withdrawn and scrapped at Garston in 1900.*   Commercial postcard

They were shorter and wider than *Violet*, at 130ft 9in long and just over 35ft wide. They had certificates for 1,303 passengers, the extra capacity being in a below-deck smoking saloon. The saloons were wide and airy and the promenade deck was approached by stairways positioned behind the port and starboard lookouts which were mounted on narrow platforms above the exposed main deck. There were two funnels, a central wheelhouse and four gangways; propulsion was by two compound engines. *Crocus* was experimentally lit by electricity, the fittings being supplied by Manchester Edison Light Co. for £185 and six further vessels were converted during 1886. It is not known if the gas-lit *Waterlily* was among the conversions.

Seymour was sold back to Samuel Davies of Tranmere ferry in 1886. She had been on hire to him for most of the time since 1883; she was hired by the Wallasey Local Board on several subsequent occasions, acting as a grounding boat at Egremont at Easter 1886 and was last mentioned at Easter 1888 when she was hired as a landing boat at New Brighton.

In June 1885, the Board of Trade agreed that the weight of on-deck saloons should be excluded from the tonnage measurement on which survey fees and dock dues were based.

Throughout 1883-84, three urgent capital projects were under consideration by the ferries management – enlarging the landing facilities at New Brighton, designing and commissioning two new passenger steamers and building new workshops at Seacombe. Since 1861, £355,602 had been spent on capital account and the interest and capital repayments were a serious burden on the undertaking and on the long-suffering ratepayers. The Local Government Board showed sympathy with the ratepayers to the extent that, other than £30,000 for two new steamers, it refused to sanction further loans.

Through Bookings

As New Brighton grew in popularity as a resort, the railways regarded it as a potential source of traffic but the lack of a branch line limited their options. In August 1878 the Local Board endorsed an agreement with the Cheshire Lines Committee for the issue of through tickets between stations in the Manchester area and New Brighton throughout the year, passengers making their own way between Liverpool Central station and the landing stage. A similar arrangement was made with the London and North Western Railway in July 1879 and with the Great Western for the month of July 1880 only, no further arrangements being made with that company for many years. Some bookings involved two ferry trips, from Woodside to Liverpool then to New Brighton. In 1899, by which time there were more amenities at New Brighton, the management were pressing the railways and agreements were made with other companies, including the Liverpool Overhead Railway with whom through tickets were offered in both directions as the round trip on the 'Overhead' giving unrivalled views of ships in the docks was a popular pastime with Wallasey people. These were the first through fares to be reinstated in 1922 after wartime suspension. The success of these through bookings depended on their promotion by the railway companies in the inland towns and the Local Board in some cases agreed to contribute towards these costs. The ferries' share of through tickets was usually four old pence. Revenue from through railway passengers 'up to 31st December 1906' was given as £1,278.50 which represents 76,710 return journeys but unfortunately it is not clear what period this covered. Through tram tickets from St. Helens, involving two trams each way, were introduced in 1905 and continued until 1939.

Special summer only tickets between the three Wallasey ferries and Eastham were offered from 1st July 1900 at 6d, 7d and 8d; 1,184 were sold in the first month but patronage gradually declined and the agreement lapsed in 1913. Through tickets were issued including admission to various attractions at New Brighton such as the Tower Ballroom, the Palace and the Promenade Pier.

Competition for New Brighton ferry

Although there had been plans to build railways to both Seacombe and New Brighton in the 1850s and 1860s, these had lapsed and it was not until 1881 that the Seacombe, Hoylake and Deeside Railway obtained parliamentary powers to construct a line from Bidston to Seacombe, following this in 1882 and 1886 with other schemes for Wallasey and New Brighton. These lines were not a threat to the ferries until three interconnecting lines were brought into use on 2nd January 1888. These were the Mersey Railway's branch from Hamilton Square to Birkenhead Park, the Wirral Railway's Birkenhead Park-Docks line and the Seacombe, Hoylake & Deeside line thence to Wallasey which was extended to a station at Atherton Street, New Brighton on 30th March 1888.

Shallow water at low tide was a problem at both New Brighton and Egremont for many years and old vessels were frequently used as landing boats, their function being to extend the length of the pier. Thistle of 1891 is tied up to Shamrock at New Brighton. The latter was two years younger but had been bought second-hand from Birkenhead that same year with a view to its use as a luggage boat. It proved unsatisfactory and was used as a landing boat until sold in 1902. The low level of the water is emphasised by the steep angle of the bridges.

M. Jenkins collection

Connecting trains with some through carriages brought New Brighton to within 25 minutes of the centre of Liverpool. The original plan to bring the trains down to Rowson Street was never carried out, because of the gradient and shortage of funds, so the station was inconveniently situated for many residents.

Since its opening in February 1886, the Mersey Railway had already deprived Woodside and Tranmere ferries of many thousands of passengers but, although it was unaffected by the weather and took passengers further into Liverpool, it had certain disadvantages, mainly the sulphurous fumes from the locomotives in the tunnel which gradually worsened over the years despite all kinds of expensive ventilation measures taken by the company. Furthermore, not all trains had through carriages and connections at Birkenhead Park (which was dubbed Pneumonia Junction by sufferers) were not always maintained. After the Wirral and the Mersey Railways fell out for a time in the 1890s, the through carriages ceased altogether.

Even before the railway opened, the ferries had been experiencing a slump in revenue, takings in 1885-86 being £2,000 below the previous year's. In both 1887-88 and 1888-89 revenue at about £44,000 was £5,000 down on 1884-85. New Brighton, being dependent on good weather, fell from £27,000 in 1886-87 to £20,500 in 1888-89, 24% down, much of it due to railway competition. Various economy measures were taken including a reduction in manning levels in June 1886 and halving of the bonuses paid to masters and engineers. Holidays were reduced from two weeks to one week and the manager's salary was cut from £425 to £350 per annum.

In anticipation of railway competition, direct 'express' boats were run to and from New Brighton from February 1887 between 7.15 and 9.50am and 5.0 and 7.0pm. In January 1888 a monthly contract was offered at 7s 6d (37$\frac{1}{2}$p) and other fare concessions were made. However, the cost of these measures exceeded the benefits and the direct boats had all been withdrawn by August 1888. The experiment was repeated from 1st October 1893 to 28th February 1894 with no more success and again from 1st May 1899 when a half-hourly all day direct service was started and lasted until the end of summer 1900. They were never revived. Over 1.5 million passengers deserted the ferries for the trains and it was 11 years before revenue fully recovered. However, the worst of the financial crisis had been overcome by February 1890 when holiday, salary and bonus cuts were restored in full. Some passengers came back from the railway to the ferry but they had a difficult choice. In the winter they could either freeze at 'Pneumonia Junction' and suffocate in the tunnel or face the full fury of the river at its most malignant.

More Terminal Problems at New Brighton

By 1879 the growth of seasonal traffic at New Brighton swamped the facilities and at Whitsuntide 1879 the crush was so great that some boats had to be sent straight back to Liverpool without unloading. On this occasion four boats were hired, two tugs, the Woodside steamer *Liverpool* and a Tranmere vessel for beaching as a stage extension at Egremont. In October 1879 they accepted plans by the well-known engineer, Dowson, for a new stage measuring 240ft by 55ft and a second passenger bridge for £6,500. But there was a backlash from ratepayers and the Board was obliged to drop all plans for the time being, spending a small amount on repairs to maintain the status quo.

In 1881, the Local Board succeeded in raising a

An unusual early aerial view of the new longer landing stage installed at New Brighton in 1885 clearly shows how the two bridges were placed at an angle of 15 degrees. Note the end of the promenade pier.
G. Parry collection

The suction dredger Tulip *was built on the Severn at Sudbrook being launched in September 1897. She did good work deepening the river at New Brighton and Egremont and went on hire to other authorities. Latterly she was underused and was sold to Grayson, Rollo & Clover Docks in 1934, being finally broken up in 1964.* M. Jenkins collection

loan of £8,500 and Dowson prepared a modified scheme for a stage 220ft long but it was February 1884 before the contract for the work was awarded to Head, Wrightson & Co. for £7,327. This embraced an additional bridge, enlarged landing stage, strengthening and alterations to the main pier and a pay gate recess. The pier head was strengthened to take the strain of the new bridge which was placed at an angle of 15 degrees to the north-east of the existing bridge and attached to the enlarged floating stage by well-lubricated sliding plates. There were four balanced gangways and two vessels could load or unload simultaneously. These improvements and the increase in the number of reversible turnstiles greatly reduced overcrowding.

The Board wanted the work finished by Good Friday 1885 and accused Dowson of spending too little time on the project. The deadline was not met, the two bridges being put in position on 23rd April and the whole job was not completed until 30th July. The estimate was exceeded by £3,440 though this included £1,196 for new shelters on the stage and turnstiles which were not in the original budget. But all was still not well. Soon after the official reopening, the stage was strengthened to avoid serious damage by heavier steamers and by 1888 was said to be in poor condition. By 1896, a report by consulting engineer J. J. Webster revealed serious weaknesses in the whole structure which was in urgent need of major repairs.

In 1900 Allsup's of Preston were awarded a £6,000 contract to replace the northern bridge, which was the original one built in 1866, and to widen the pier alongside the toll booths so that more of them could be provided. The work was done during the winter, the new steel passenger bridge being lifted into position on 27th December 1900. A new southern bridge, built by Heenan and Froude of Manchester was installed on 29th August 1907 and the northern bridge and the stage twice needed repairs following the March 1907 gales and others in November 1908.

Throughout the 1890s, the New Brighton service was plagued by insufficient depth of water at low tide and much time was spent in trying to find a solution. Contacts with the Dock Board brought forth no assistance. In March 1895 the manager tried to hire a dredger from the Ribble Navigation but this fell through. Formal permission to dredge the river was given by the Mersey Conservancy Board and enquiries about dredging were made as far afield as Irvine and Whitby. An offer by the Manchester Ship Canal Co. for the hire of a dredger for £1,000 per month was considered too expensive. The manager calculated revenue losses caused by suspension of the service and, on the strength of this, in June 1896 it was decided to seek a loan of £10,000 to purchase a suction dredger. An order was eventually placed with T. Walker of Sudbrook, Mon. and the vessel, named *Tulip*, having been launched on 28th September 1897, was delayed by a strike and problems with her equipment, which included a Gwynne's Pump. She was a substantial vessel of 432 gross tons measuring 160ft long by 27ft 1in and she started work at New Brighton on 13th May 1898. Initially there were doubts about her ability to tackle the marl and clay deposits at Egremont, another dredger, *Sicily* being hired. A dispute with her builders finally went to arbitration. As much as 23,000 cu.yd. of sand was removed by dredging in February 1901, resulting in 40 passenger crossings being cancelled. A further 29,000 cu.yd. were removed in August 1904.

The Conservator turned down a plan to lengthen the pier, advising the Council to 'pursue a policy of much more active dredging'. However, at Easter 1905, the traffic was very heavy, revenue being 22.5% higher than the previous year; doubtless the weather played a part. But on the Monday, an exceptionally low tide resulted in the suspension of the service at New Brighton for much of the afternoon and evening, resulting in Seacombe having a record day, 106,119 adult fare-paying passengers passing through the turnstiles. The tram services between Seacombe and New Brighton were filled to capacity. In November 1906 the Council decided to borrow £10,000 to finance dredging and employed a consulting engineer, A. F. Fowler, who recommended scraping the river bed with a bucket dredger. In February 1907 a contract was given to the Tilbury Contracting and Dredging Co. to keep the approaches clear throughout the year. The bucket dredger *Beaufort* lifted 43,000 cu.yd. of hard material including mussel shale in the early months of 1907. While the work was in progress, a violent storm on 16th March tore the stage from its moorings and drove it out to sea. The south end bridge and several pontoons were badly damaged. The stage was salvaged the following day and towed into dry dock for repair. Temporary landing arrangements obliged the ferry to close two hours before each low tide, seriously affecting traffic on Good Friday and Easter Saturday. However, more or less normal services were restored on the Monday and thousands of pleasure seekers were carried from Liverpool, the two luggage boats being pressed into service in addition to the ordinary passenger steamers.

Dredging operations were completed on 10th June 1907 and, by the end of May, 42,784 cu.yd. of material had been removed giving an average depth of water of 11-12ft. *Tulip* had assisted *Beaufort* for which the contractors reimbursed the ferries, and she was fitted with a new suction pump in January 1908 so that she could maintain the new depth of water. Sand eroders were placed underwater in 1911-12 by which time boats could approach at almost all states of the tide. She was very successful in keeping Egremont and New Brighton landing stages free of silt and on occasions she was hired to Birkenhead Corporation who had similar difficulties at Rock Ferry. In 1903 she was hired to Wexford Harbour Board for £400 per month, being insured for £10,000 for the voyage.

Later in 1903 she worked at Heysham and in 1906 at Port Talbot. *Tulip* removed 63,000 cu.yd. of sand and shale in 1911 and the effectiveness of her value to the undertaking was demonstrated when she had to cease work during the coal strike of 1912 and *Snowdrop* had to be grounded alongside the stage.

The 1890s

In 1891 there was a reversion to paddle steamers when *Thistle* was built by J. Scott of Kinghorn. She had a steel hull 150ft long and a passenger certificate for 1,200 passengers. She resembled *Daisy*, *Primrose* and *Violet* but was easily distinguished by her single rather squat funnel placed forward of the paddle boxes. Her powerful diagonal engines gave her great speed but she remained in the fleet only until 1910 by which time paddlers were considered obsolescent. *Heatherbell* was withdrawn, sold and renamed *Erin's King* to work pleasure cruises between Dublin and Kingstown.

As a standby for the luggage service, the Woodside steamer *Woodside*, an iron paddler built in 1865, was purchased from Birkenhead Corporation in 1891 for £750. A greater sum was spent on clearing the decks and making other improvements and this vessel, now renamed *Shamrock*, had a dual role as a relief for *Wallasey* and a landing boat. She was not satisfactory on the luggage service and was sold in March 1902.

In July 1893 *Daisy* certificate was renewed for only six months. Her boilers needed to be lifted and thoroughly repaired or steam pressure would have had to be reduced to 10lb which was completely impractical. The work, which included replating, was done by D. Rollo & Co. and she re-entered service in April 1894. A proposal to increase accommodation by lengthening the cabins was shelved but revived in September 1897 when work started by direct labour to extend the forward cabin by six feet, with a rounded end and lengthen the upper deck by 15ft with two additional staircases.

In 1895 further orders were placed with J. Scott of Kinghorn for three vessels after 17 tenders had been received. The first was a steel-hulled coal barge, *Emily*, slightly larger than the wooden flat *Maggie* which was described as 'in a very defective condition' but was taken in part-exchange to the value of £260. *Emily* was launched on 18th December 1895, cost £2,041 and remained in the ferry service for 39 years. The others were virtually identical steel paddle steamers which were rather long for ferry service at 160ft. They were named *Pansy* and *John Herron*, the latter in honour of the Ferry Committee chairman, and were authorised to carry 1,240

The steel hulled coal barge Emily *was used to collect coal from the various coal berths on the Mersey Docks or from Garston and deliver it to Seacombe where it was unloaded by the grab crane shown. She was launched in 1895 and served the Wallasey ferries for 39 years.* G. Parry collection

passengers. Whilst technically similar to *Thistle,* they were of different appearance having a single raked funnel and a foremast. The specification was changed during build, the cabins being lengthened by 10ft and made continuous. It was agreed that their trials should be on the River Forth so that the makers could quickly remedy any faults but *Pansy* failed to achieve her contract price of 12.75 knots. A 6-hour continuous reliability trial was satisfactorily completed on the Mersey in December 1896 but the Council still demanded the full penalty of £200 from the builders for lack of speed.

At 11.0am on 24th March 1898, in thick fog, s.s. *Lake Winnipeg* was in violent collision with *Wallasey* and *Thistle* whilst moored at Seacombe stage, causing considerable damage to all three vessels. The stem and bows of *Lake Winnipeg* were so firmly embedded in the starboard side of *Wallasey* that as the former drifted up-river, *Wallasey* was torn from her moorings and eventually beached on Tranmere shore. Water was pumped out and she was placed on the gridiron at Egremont. The incident caused serious damage to Seacombe stage, one of the hydraulic gangways being broken and both goods lifts put out of action, one being restored only by cutting away part of the stage. It was several weeks before operations returned to normal.

Increased Traffic

Although New Brighton was developing rapidly as a bathing resort it mainly attracted day trippers and, on fine weekends, the ferries were hard pressed to cope with the traffic. The last section of the riverside promenade, from Holland Road to New Brighton, was completed in 1891 and this enabled people with tight budgets to cross by Seacombe ferry and walk at any state of the tide along the promenade to New Brighton, enjoying the panorama of passing shipping as they went. If they tired they could settle for the beach at Egremont. The Local Board agreed to the operators of pleasure cruises calling at New Brighton pier, $1^1/_2$d per passenger landing fee being charged. Agreements on these lines were made in 1890 with the Southport, Preston & Blackpool Steam Packet Co. and the Birkdale, Southport and Preston Steamship Co. Vessels sailing between Liverpool and North Wales also called at the pier occasionally on the same conditions. Between 1898 and 1900, the impressive amusement grounds, dominated by the 600ft high Tower (almost 100ft higher than Blackpool's), were laid out and greatly enhanced New Brighton's attractions. There were now several hotels of quality and considerable optimism about the resort's future. However, the year 1895 was best remembered for the exceptional weather in February, when the River Mersey froze and the steamers had to fend off ice floes.

Charter and cruise work had been undertaken from the earliest days of municipal ownership as it is on record that on Whit Monday 1875 a Wallasey steamer was sent to Runcorn to carry a group of pre-booked excursionists to New Brighton at an inclusive price of £21. On 11th June a similar trip was organised from Garston at £16. *Seymour* was hired to the Rock Ferry Co. for three days from 1st May 1875 at £2 per hour, with a minimum of six hours. In November 1876 the same vessel was chartered by the L.N.W. and G.W. Joint Railway companies at £12 per day to run the railway ferry between Monks Ferry and Liverpool.

The opening of the Manchester Ship Canal created a demand for vessels to cruise the new waterway and in June 1893 the Ship Canal Passenger Steamer Syndicate Ltd, formed specially to meet this demand, enquired about hiring a steamer for three months though this apparently proved over-optimistic. Nevertheless *Crocus* and *Snowdrop* spent several days on the canal at rates of between £10 and £12 per day. Not all these trips were in the summer as *Crocus* was hired by the Manchester Ship Canal Co. on 7-8th December and both vessels on 1st January 1894 when the canal officially opened. The following day *Waterlily* managed to collide with the Birkenhead steamer *Claughton* on the canal. Later that month the Co-operative Wholesale Society wanted to hire both ships for the ceremonial opening on 25th May but the Committee told them to enquire again nearer the time. In June 1894 the Syndicate offered £20 per day but the Committee, sensing that demand exceeded supply, demanded £30. During Whit Week 1894 steamers were hired for private trips between Runcorn and New Brighton and from Manchester to New Brighton and back. These occasional charters continued as a useful source of extra revenue and, following the loss of a hire because of delay awaiting a committee meeting,

the chairman and manager were allowed to quote.

Another source of charters was R. A. MacFie, owner of New Ferry, which was just about holding its own with one old steamer, *Firefly* which broke down frequently. *Violet* and *Daisy* and perhaps some other Wallasey vessels spent many days working the New Ferry service in 1893-94. In August 1897, a vessel was hired to the Eastham Ferry Co. each Saturday, Sunday and Monday at the rate of £40 per half day.

The New Century's Steamers

Two twin-screw steamers, named *Rose* and *Lily* were built on the Mersey by John Jones & Son in 1900. At 42ft 1in they were wider in the beam than any previous passenger steamer and had certificates for 1,831 passengers. As built the three lookouts were at deck level and the single funnels were rather squat. There were five portholes between the gangway doors, *Lily* having the sheeting painted white whilst *Rose* had buff. *Rose* was equipped with a flying bridge of skeletal form, apparently in 1901 but no pictures of *Lily* have been found with this addition.

Seacombe was the name given to a new steel double twin-screw luggage boat built by

Crocus which entered service in 1885 is seen loading at Liverpool for Seacombe with Lancashire behind. She and her sister ship Snowdrop *were the first screw passenger vessels in service with the Wallasey ferries; she was sold in 1908, seeing a brief period sailing between Rhyl and Llandudno until she sank off Rhyl in the same year. She was licensed for over 1,300 passengers despite the restricted deck space compared with the later steamers. Note that the master occupied either the starboard or port lookout when berthing. The speaking tube by which he communicated with the engine room is discernible. Also visible is the fog bell tower between the Seacombe and Woodside berths.* G. Parry collection

Rose, *built in 1900, was licensed to carry 1,831 passengers. As built she had a short funnel and a navigation bridge at promenade deck level. She was the first ferry boat to be fitted with a flying bridge and in 1906 received a taller funnel to improve the draught. She was distinguishable by having buff porthole surrounds amidships instead of the usual white.*

Commercial postcard

Lily was a sister ship to Rose and identical in most respects but she did not receive a flying bridge. She is shown in original condition with short funnel and later with tall funnel. Both vessels were sold to Dublin in 1927 and had long after lives.
M. Jenkins collection/G. Parry collection

Cochran of Annan at a cost of £18,000. She was launched on 28th September 1901 and, at 50ft, her beam was five feet greater than the successful *Wallasey* which had been in service for 20 years. Her arrival enabled the second-hand *Shamrock* to be disposed of. Her deck was completely clear and, apart from a brief spell as an oil-burner in the early 1920s, she had an uneventful career, being withdrawn in 1929 and broken up.

Further Reconstruction at Egremont

The crumbling slipway at Egremont was renovated early in 1884 and the engine house boiler renewed the following year. Following the accidental death of a boy who had been crushed by the running-out stage, a ferryman walked the slip carrying a red flag to give warning that the stage was about to move. Any suggestions of closing the unprofit-able service were met with strong protests from regular passengers of whom there were really insufficient numbers to justify operation. In March 1888 the ferry

was closed at periods of low water to avoid disruption of the New Brighton service, contracts being made valid for use at the other terminals.

In January 1896 a survey by J. J. Webster, revealed serious weaknesses in the tripod which vibrated at high tide when the impact of the boats gave greater leverage. The pier and bridge girders were adjudged satisfactory but the running-out stage was described as almost beyond repair. Its early replacement was advised. The landing stage was severely damaged by storms on 29th November 1897 and a comprehensive inspection showed that it clearly needed major rebuilding, the tripod having been eroded to the extent that it was only four or five feet in the ground. The bottom plates of vessels were being worn through by frequent grounding and vessels had to be hired as landing boats at £30 per day. There was clearly a case for closing the passage down. However, the Council continued to be swayed by the vociferous minority of regular users. The movable stage was patched up at some expense but in 1903 there was another serious attempt to close it down as the introduction

After two successful screw passenger boats had been added to the fleet in 1884, Wallasey surprisingly ordered a new paddle steamer in 1891. Thistle was built of steel by Scott of Kinghorn and had a certificate for 1,200 passengers though not all were protected from the weather. She was virtually obsolete when delivered and served only 19 years. Note the squat funnel mounted forward of the paddle boxes and the signpost type of destination indicator. She is moored at the foot of the Liverpool floating roadway; the New Brighton berth was moved south when the stage was lengthened in 1921. Priestley & Co.

of electric trams resulted in a drastic fall in the Egremont traffic and an increase at Seacombe. Again the opportunity was lost and matters drifted for another five years by which time the Egremont traffic had picked up again though not to the extent to make it profitable. However, in February 1908, the Council decided that the terminal should be redesigned and rebuilt and again appointed Webster as consulting engineer. His recommendations to extend the existing pier and affix a floating landing stage were accepted in May and the contract awarded to Alex. Findlay & Co. Ltd of Motherwell for £13,361. 18s. 9d. The Acting Conservator of the Mersey, Admiral Nares, ruled that approval for building the pier round the existing slipway would only be forthcoming provided the slipway could, at some future date, be broken up and to this the Council was forced to agree. An agreement was made with the Board of Trade to pay £5 per year for a lease of the land needed for pier piling and mooring the floating stage.

From 7th October 1908 the ferry was closed for about a month while a bucket dredger accompanied by two barges deepened the river bed where the pier extension was to be built. On 2nd February 1909 the ferry closed for over nine months and work started on dismantling the tripod, running-out stage and passenger bridge. Tragedy struck on 19th February when the partially knocked down tripod collapsed, killing a foreman and injuring three other workers. The Council's Works Department demolished the cluster of old buildings which had served as offices and workshops. The river walls were raised and the site adapted for recreational purposes with a shelter and a bandstand.

The gridiron on the south side of the ferry had been last used in 1908 and the rotting baulks of timber were gradually removed and carted away. All cleaning and repairs to the hulls were now done in the commercial graving docks.

The old high level pier had been 280ft long and the new one measured 342ft 6in being made up of six 52ft spans, one of 15ft 6in and one of 15ft. The structure was carried on cast iron piles of 12in diameter except for the cluster at the river end which supported the bridge which were 14in in diameter. The 153ft long bridge was 16ft wide and was connected to the pier by rollers and by swivels at the stage end. It was built on the West Float and placed in position by the Dock Board floating crane *Atlas* during September 1909. The floating stage was kept in position by dolphins consisting of greenheart piles braced together with creosoted pitch pine, the dolphins forming a groove between which the stage rose and fell with the tide. Thirty-

Passengers coming down the north bridge to board the Liverpool steamer at Seacombe early in the 20th century, before the stage was roofed over. Note the High Level bridge with a horse drawn lorry approaching the lift and the tip horse at the far left waiting to assist a cart to climb the south bridge.
Priestley & Co.

A strangely unfamiliar Liverpool waterfront before the erection of the three great buildings. The towers are (left to right) St. Nicholas Church, St. Peter's pro-Cathedral, Church Street and the Custom House, Canning Place. The Pier Head baths can be seen behind the ferry boat approaching the stage from Eastham. M. Jenkins collection

two of these 60ft long piles were driven to a depth of 12ft into the boulder clay of the river bed.

The ferry was officially reopened on 8th November 1909 by John Joyce, the Chairman of the Ferries Committee who used the occasion to criticise the Mersey Docks & Harbour Board for failing to dredge the river sufficiently and also for the inadequate passenger bridges at Liverpool, a matter which was put right in 1913 as described elsewhere. The first steamer, *Iris*, departed at 9.30am on what was a grey and windy morning. There had been some uninformed reservations about the safety of such a long pier and the consulting engineer, Webster, made a public statement to allay fears:

'It has been a most difficult piece of work to erect for, in addition to strong tides and rough water, the weather unfortunately has been very bad. I am afraid the sub-contractors under-estimated these difficulties and did not commence their work as soon as they otherwise would have done. The columns of the pier are of a very strong form having, in addition to the strength of the column's casting, a steel and concrete backbone so that, should a derelict boat unfortunately foul the columns, they will not snap off and drop the superstructure into the river.'

At first delays were caused as stragglers hastened along the pier to catch the boat and eventually a warning bell was sounded five minutes prior to departure and again immediately before the gates were closed three minutes before the scheduled departure time. It had been calculated that three minutes was sufficient time to allow even the elderly to reach the boat but many of the regulars

objected and there were several cases of irate passengers vaulting the barriers and racing along the pier.

From 12th January 1910, a 15-minute service was run between 8.0am and 7.0pm on weekdays to encourage use of the ferry.

During the closure of Egremont there was a crisis when, on 12th February 1909, s.s. *Octopus* – attempting to avoid colliding with other vessels – ran into Seacombe stage dislodging the north bridge which fell into the river. Emergency passenger facilities were provided at the south end of the landing stage. After recovery the north bridge was damaged by *Maggie*. During the repairs, hydraulic gangways were replaced by balanced gangways.

The Railway Reaches Seacombe

The Wirral Railway absorbed the Seacombe, Hoylake and Deeside in 1891 and work on a branch terminating at Seacombe ferry commenced in 1893. A formal Agreement was made between the railway company and the Local Board on 3rd August 1893 granting the railway authority to issue through tickets to and from Liverpool landing stage and granting a 33% rebate on the tolls. This was similar to the arrangement reached over a decade earlier at Woodside. Passengers' luggage was to be conveyed free of charge and the railway company's servants were to be given all necessary facilities for free travel on the ferry when engaged on the company's business.

In June 1894, the railway company, which was short of money, proposed to build a 'temporary station' on the corner of Church Road and Victoria

The ferry goods yard at Seacombe with the old ferry workshop. The arches of the goods bridge can just be discerned on the right and there is an electric tram on the left. The yard was used by coal merchants as well as holding coal for the steamers.

Wirral Archive Service

(later Borough) Road so that passengers would have to walk the full length of the ferry approach but assured the Local Board of its intention to extend to the ferry as soon as funds were available. The Wirral Railway Act 1895, to which the 1893 Agreement was attached as a Schedule, set out the scheme in detail. The station was to be built almost on the water's edge with a 18ft wide covered way between the entrance and the ferry terminal building. In addition, Church Road, part of Birkenhead Road and Victoria Road were to be diverted to permit a rail connection with the Dock Board lines in Birkenhead Road with a turntable connection with the lines in the ferry coal yard. Unfortunately, the company was never able to afford to proceed with this scheme and although powers for the extension were renewed twice, they finally lapsed in 1912.

The railway provided a service from West Kirby to Seacombe which was a viable alternative to the route via Birkenhead Park and the Mersey Railway. From 1st May 1898 the trains of the Dee and Birkenhead Railway (later renamed the North Wales & Liverpool Railway and in 1906 the Great Central) from Wrexham ran over the Wirral line from Bidston to Seacombe, again with through bookings and this created a considerable volume of traffic. Inclusive excursions to Caergwrle at one shilling (5p) attracted hundreds of passengers and, even at this low rate, were apparently good business for both ferry and railway.

The railway company continued to exert pressure on the Urban District Council (which replaced the Local Board from 1st January 1895) to gain further concessions on fares and, in May 1896, a 33¹/₃% discount on through contracts was agreed. Concessions were also made for excursion passengers.

In the summer of 1897 the Wirral Railway inaugurated a train service between Seacombe and New Brighton with through fares from Liverpool, a development which the ferries management had not foreseen but were powerless to prevent as no restriction had been put on the destination of through passengers. The service had mixed success and ran seasonally until 1911 when it was killed off by the extension of Wallasey's tramways.

Management Problems

George Harries retired as ferries manager in June 1897 being succeeded by his assistant Frederick Ash (at £350 p.a.) who was preferred over 250 applicants. However, Ash retired due to ill-health on 19th September 1899, H. E. Martin being appointed in his place. Thomas B. Hughes, Senior Toll Collector at New Brighton, was appointed Sub-manager at £150 p.a. and the status of an engineer,

Orme, was enhanced. Relations between Martin and Orme deteriorated, the latter maintaining that he should be directly responsible to the Ferries Committee rather than to Martin. Matters came to a head in May 1902 when Orme dismissed five boilermen without consulting Martin. The men were reinstated but the Committee took no decisive action to resolve the hostility between the two managers though they criticised inadequacy and incompetence in the workshops. Following criticism of the safety of Seacombe landing stage in 1904, the Committee asked Orme to resign and advertised for a foreman engineer at £200 per year. The manager's job was also advertised but this was later withdrawn and Martin remained in his post.

Tramway Connections

The Urban District Council had obtained powers to lay electric tramways in the town in 1900 and acquired the horse tramway company's route from 31st March 1901. Electric cars started running in March 1902 and by May cars were running on three routes all connecting Seacombe with New Brighton. These facilities were much more extensive than those previously provided by horse trams and buses as well as being faster and cheaper. Traffic built up rapidly at Seacombe but fell at Egremont as people preferred to ride straight through to the tram terminus rather than break the journey and walk down Tobin Street. The tramways also took their toll of railway traffic and this benefit was shared with the ferries.

Although separate committees controlled the ferries and tramways, it was recognised that close co-operation was essential and from 12th July 1902, cars on the Seabank Road and Rake Lane services connected with every boat. Once more, there were thoughts of closing Egremont down or selling off both northern ferries but after some public discussion, a half-hourly service from New Brighton, calling at Egremont, requiring two vessels, was provided from 1st December 1902. Requests for an all day 10-minute service from Seacombe and concessions on the trams for New Brighton contract holders were turned down. From 1899, notice of closure of the northern ferries was given by hoisting red balls on chains at both ends of Church Street, Egremont and at Victoria Road (Rowson Street), New Brighton. Flags were flown at the ferry stations. From November, the trams displayed flags on their trolley ropes when the northern sailings were suspended – a blue square flag for New Brighton and a red swallow tail flag for Egremont. This practice continued for the life of the tramways and special roller blinds for the purpose were later fitted to the buses which eventually replaced them.

The bow end of Sunflower *at Seacombe stage. The vessel's name is carried on the curve of the embossed paddle box. Note the open bridge, ornate gas lamps, gangway arch and the narrow hand-gangway. The fog bell tower is just visible to the right.*
Priestley & Co.

Sunflower *of 1879 gave good service during the last two decades of the 19th century and this bow on view shows her fully loaded and en route to New Brighton. Note that the bulwarks are built of wood.*
M. Jenkins collection

In 1902 the ferries made a loss of almost £3,500 and carried 55,000 fewer passengers than in 1901. Nevertheless, from 1st April 1903, a 20-minute service was restored to the northern ferries and from 5th June the Seacombe service was operated alternately every 7 and 8 minutes, using three boats, between 8.0am and 7.0pm. This continued throughout the summer but a 10-minute Seacombe and 30-minute New Brighton/Egremont service was operated from 5th October. The electrification of the Mersey Railway on 3rd May 1903 accelerated the rail service between New Brighton and Liverpool and eliminated some of the draughty waits at Birkenhead Park station as the electric trains ran much more frequently. However, an influx of new residents (which increased the passengers carried on the ferries from 15.5 million in 1901 to 22 million in 1911) and an increase in summer visitors in response to new facilities brought a prodigious increase in ferry passengers, the numbers carried rising from 17 million in 1903-04 to 24 million in 1913-14, an increase of 40%.

Improvements at Seacombe

To facilitate handling the increased traffic, new toll booths and turnstiles were installed in April 1902; wider balanced gangways replaced old hydraulic gangways at both Seacombe and Liverpool stages. To speed up passenger movements a second stairway was added to the upper-deck gangway on the Liverpool landing stage and walkways mounted on outriggers were built on both sides of the passenger bridge. Some alarm was caused in 1904 when an article in the influential *Journal of Commerce* alleged that the pontoons supporting the Seacombe landing stage were unsafe. Following a rebuttal from the Council, the Secretary of the Admiralty wrote seeking positive assurances. The pontoons had had little or no attention since 1880 but should have been removed for a detailed inspection during the filling-in of the embayment. This work had been proceeding very slowly and it became clear that there was some truth in the allegations. After an official inspection, the Board of Trade expressed extreme dissatisfaction and cautioned the Council to replace some defective pontoons and to clean, repair and paint others.

In 1905 roller shutters were approved for the front of the terminal building so that portions could be kept closed to alleviate draughts. Two more turnstiles, additional toll booths and a larger bicycle shed were provided. It was also agreed to move the manager's office from Egremont to Seacombe and to close the Egremont workshop and build a new one at Seacombe. The Council's engineer, W. H. Travers, prepared the specifications

and a building was erected south of the terminus adjoining the goods yard. Machinery was moved from Egremont in November 1907 and the workshop was officially opened on 2nd January 1909.

Birkenhead Corporation suggested in 1905 that each authority should provide a single vessel by rotation to run the loss-making night services between Liverpool, Woodside, Seacombe and Liverpool but after the legal position had been investigated it was decided that statutory powers would be necessary. Regrettably, neither authority made the necessary provisions in any subsequent Bill.

A New Generation of Boats

In September 1904 the manager was instructed to prepare specifications for two new ships with three-cylinder triple-expansion engines, each capable of carrying 1,700 passengers at a speed of $12^1/_2$ knots. The order was initially awarded to Scott of Kinghorn at £19,000 per vessel but the Council negotiated some sort of reduction. On the second of two occasions when the builder attempted to reopen negotiations on the price, the Council cancelled the order which was then given to Stephenson & Co. of Hebburn-on-Tyne. Names proposed were *Iris, Mayflower* and *Speedwell* but *Iris* and *Daffodil* were eventually chosen.

Several of the older boats were in need of expensive repairs and *Sunflower* of 1879 was offered for sale in October 1904. There were no takers and she was broken up by ferries staff. *Thistle* received an expensive overhaul, all her deck planks which had worn to less than half the stipulated $2^1/_2$in, being replaced. In April 1905 *Primrose* was given only a six-month passenger certificate and at the end of the season was sold to R. & D. Jones, a firm running short cruises. She was used by them for two seasons and broken up in 1908. *Crocus* went to the Merseyside Trading Co. who used her on a Rhyl-Llandudno service until the end of the 1907 season; the following year she sank off Rhyl. *Tulip* which had been offered for sale at the same time, was reprieved when a six-week charter for the Port Talbot Railway at £50 per week was secured. At the end of the 1908 season, she and *Daisy*, which had had no takers when offered for sale, were given minimal overhauls to enable them to work for one more summer season. However, *Crocus* was sold to Robert Smith & Sons of Chester in June 1909.

Iris was launched by Mrs. Martin, wife of the ferries manager, on 24th March 1906, followed by *Daffodil* on 20th April and both were towed to the Mersey via the English Channel to be finished at Rollo's yard. They had two sets of triple-expansion engines, supplied with steam from two boilers. They embodied improved features which became standard for the Wallasey ferries fleet for the next

Crocus *leaves Liverpool amid ice-floes with icicles hanging from her stern during the cold spell in January 1900. Her sister ship* Snowdrop *(lower) was virtually identical and is seen in company with a single-funnel vessel which could be* John Herron, Pansy *or* Thistle. Crocus *and* Snowdrop *were both launched late in 1884 and placed in service early in 1885. Built by Allsups at Preston, they were the largest steamers yet with a beam of 35ft, (10ft more than their immediate predecessors), passenger certificates for over 1,300, the first double twin screw passenger vessels and the first steel boats in the fleet. They were withdrawn in 1908-9.* E. R. Dibden courtesy G. E. Langmuir / M. Jenkins collection

30 years. The promenade decks, surmounted by a raked funnel and tall foremasts, extended to the full width of the vessels and flying bridges right across the upper deck gave their masters uninterrupted views from the two fully-enclosed lookouts. The main deck had three separate saloons. Despite their wrangle with Scott's over the £19,000 price, Stephenson's final account was for £20,850 each. The section between the gangway doors had square windows instead of portholes. *Iris* easily achieved her contractual speed of 12.5 knots at her trials on 28th May and entered service as a stand-by vessel on 2nd June with a single crew, coming into all-day use on 12th June. *Daffodil* was less successful, failing a trial with experimental propellers on 13th June. Soon after a propeller was damaged and had to be replaced. Then solicitors for the Myers Screw Propeller Syndicate claimed that the propellers fitted by Rollo's infringed their patent and the Council agreed to substitute Myers steel propellers of the same design for the cast iron ones. These had been patented in 1889 by Charles Myers of Manchester and the Woodside steamers *Mersey* and *Wirral* were the first vessels to have them fitted. All subsequent Birkenhead Corporation passenger steamers were so fitted. *Daffodil* achieved a speed of 12.51 knots on 18th July and entered all day service on the 30th. A central covered wheelhouse was added to the bridge in March 1911. As a result of experience with these vessels, both *Lily* and *Rose*, were given a longer funnel to create more draught and improve performance; they were equipped with the Scarab oil-burning system in 1921 and both were withdrawn in 1927 being sold to Irish owners.

As described in Chapter 5, in 1918, *Iris* and *Daffodil* were extensively altered for naval service

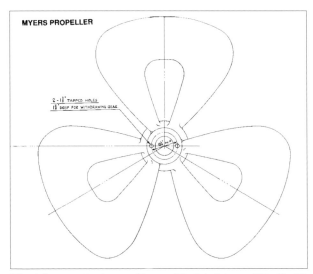

The Myers patent propeller as fitted to Iris *and* Daffodil *gave greater thrust at low revs and reduced vibration.*
T. Morgan

and subsequently given a 'Royal' prefix. They were returned to normal condition in 1919 and *Iris* was the cruise boat from 1923, being withdrawn and sold in 1931 to Cork Harbour Commissioners who renamed her *Blarney*. In this guise she survived until 1961. *Royal Daffodil* became the cruise boat in 1932-33 with grey hull but retained her white funnel. She was sold in 1934 to the New Medway Steam Packet Co. for £1,000 and broken up at Ghent in 1938. As cruise boats, both vessels had metal frames and canvas awnings over the after promenade deck. Unfortunately the ferries' management failed to protect the names and it was many years before they regained control of them.

In December 1908, the Council approved the purchase of two further vessels and the contract

A well-loaded Primrose *approaches Egremont pier about the turn of the 20th century. An iron paddler, she and her sister ship* Daisy *were built by Seath at Rutherglen on the Clyde in 1879 and had passenger certificates for 965. This broadside view clearly demonstrates their double-ended symmetry.*
Priestley & Co.

A circa 1900 picture of Egremont pier with the stage fully extended. The passengers' lot has been improved by putting windbreaks along the sides of the pier and a shelter has been built at the river end. In the foreground is the gridiron, last used in 1908, on which the steamers were beached for inspection of the hull and minor repairs. Priestley & Co.

Egremont pier at high water with the extension fully retracted on 14th February 1895 when the river was full of ice floes. Note the gangway on the end of the bridge for direct access to the boats. The vessel in the picture is the ferries' coal barge Maggie *built at Northwich in 1867 and acquired by Wallasey Local Board on 19th March 1874. She was fitted with a steam winch to lift $2\frac{1}{2}$ tons and was eventually taken in part-exchange for her replacement,* Emily, *on 18th December 1895.* Priestley & Co.

By 1908, the condition of Egremont ferry pier and its installations had deteriorated to the extent that rebuilding was essential in the interests of safety. The Conservator now agreed to a longer pier being built and the Council decided to install a floating landing stage. The dolphin collapsed during demolition, killing a workman and injuring others. The pier was lengthened and the deck strengthened and the ferry was reopened on 8th November 1909 by John Joyce, Chairman of the Ferries Committee. In this illustration, the old pier is discernible by the bracing on the pillars. Note New Brighton Tower (1897-1921) and pier in the distant background.   Priestley & Co.

A view from the waiting shed on Egremont landing-stage of the bowstring bridge connecting the pier with the stage.
Priestley & Co.

The ferry buildings, turnstiles and landward end of Egremont pier as rebuilt in 1908-9. Note the decorative roof tiles and railway style valance.

Priestley & Co.

The upper deck and starboard lookout of Thistle, *a steel single-funnelled paddle steamer, licensed for 1,200 passengers. She was built in 1891 and plied the Mersey until 1911.*

R. T. McMahon collection

was awarded to Cammell Laird & Co., Birkenhead in May 1909 at £38,890. The vessels were to be very similar to *Iris* and *Daffodil* but they had very rounded sterns and, surprisingly, they were two feet less in the beam, the innovation whereby the promenade deck extended for the full width of the vessel not being repeated, except for the section between the gangways. Their passenger certificates were thus for 1,563 passengers. Compared with their predecessors, they had very rounded stems. It was proposed to name them *Bluebell* and *Snowdrop* and both were launched under those names. However, the Board of Trade rejected the name *Bluebell* and subsequently also disapproved of *The Bluebell*. *Bluebell* started her trials on 16th August 1910 under her 'illegal' name and initially failed to reach her contractual speed, 12.107 being finally achieved on 1st September. She was renamed *John Joyce* after the chairman of the Ferries Committee. *Snowdrop* had no such problems completing her trials on the 5th and entering service on 10th October 1910. Both vessels had two sets of three-cylinder triple-expansion engines. They were placed on the New Brighton service where their speed was most useful.

Both *Daisy* and *Thistle* were offered for sale in March 1910. The former, the last of the two-funnellers with 31 years ferry service, was sold for scrap in May but, when it became clear that the new vessels would not be ready for the season, the much younger *Thistle* was retained for another summer being sold for scrap in January 1911.

Incorporation & Industrial Unrest

In July 1910, Wallasey received its Charter of Incorporation as a municipal borough, followed in 1913 by county borough status whereby the town took control of its own police, fire, ambulance and education services.

The years immediately preceding the 1914-18 War were marked by much industrial unrest though there was no disruption of the ferries, new working conditions for crews coming into effect on 25th April 1911. But strikes in the coal mines led to coal shortages. From 17th to 20th August 1911 the New Brighton service was reduced from a 15- to a 20-minute frequency to conserve stocks and, as stocks were down to 10 days' supply and 1,000 tons were stockpiled in the works yard at Seacombe. This was a short strike but there were further trials to come. A more serious coal strike

The lines of Thistle *(upper) and* John Herron *were similar though the latter was 160ft long (which was longer than the berths at Liverpool) and licensed for 1,240 passengers. This was the ultimate in paddle steamer design for Wallasey ferries.* John Herron *which entered service in 1896, was requisitioned during the 1914-18 war and finished her days as a tender at Cherbourg, being broken up in 1925.*

M. Jenkins collection

Snowdrop *well loaded is seen off New Brighton with a sailing ship in the background. The 'signpost' amidships would be* set to 'Egremont' and 'New Brighton'.
M. Jenkins collection

which started on 6th February 1912, coincided with heavy snowfalls which disrupted supplies by rail. The boats were coaled from flats alongside Seacombe stage but by 4th March reserves in the yard had fallen to 770 tons and an emergency timetable, mainly affecting the northern ferries, was put into effect. These boats ran at 8.0am and every 20 minutes to 10.0am then every hour to 4.0pm then every 30 minutes to 7.0pm and hourly to 10.0pm. Seacombe sailings were reduced to every 15 minutes after 8.0pm.

Three days later, the New Brighton service was suspended altogether, Egremont running every half-hour from 7.30am to 10.0am and 4.0pm to 7.0pm; Seacombe was reduced to 15-minutes at all non-peak times and on Sundays only the Seacombe boats ran with a 15-minute service from 2.15pm.

Some crewmen were laid off and others told to take their annual holidays, hardly an ideal time of the year! Contingency plans provided for the total withdrawal of the Egremont service and the hiring of a steam barge for coaling purposes. Gradually, however, the situation eased; New Brighton reopened on 1st April and operated throughout Easter though *Snowdrop* grounded 10ft from the landing stage as *Tulip* had suspended dredging to save coal. There were frequent last minute cancellations and on 9th April several trips were lost when engineers failed to raise reasonable heads of steam because of inferior coal. The table below shows the number of miles worked on each service, the number of hours actually in steam and the amount of coal consumed in the month of February 1912 (29 days).

Vessel	Seacombe miles	Egremont miles	New Brighton miles	Hours in steam	Coal Used tons
Wallasey	1,015			400	109.65
Emily					16.00
Pansy	42	48	1,826.5	389	179.50
John Herron	31	109	2,485	529	233.40
Tulip				504	72.00
Lily	554	77	866.5	334	256.05
Rose	2,015	119	466.5	606	383.75
Iris	1,745.5	119	466	529	408.95
John Joyce	600.5	167	1,607.5	525	327.80
Snowdrop	506	92	1,224	397	247.55
TOTAL	6,509	731	8,942	4,213	2,234.65

During the emergency, the paddlers, though in the minority, were preferred because of their lower coal consumption. The following figures for June 1912 show the relative performance of all types.

	miles	tons	miles per ton
Screw	11,307	1,590	7.11
Paddle	6,062	503.25	12.05
Luggage	1,050	189.20	5.55
Tulip	288	19	15.16

The effect of the coal shortage on the railways became so serious that, on 26th March, the Wirral Railway warned the Ferries department that it might be necessary to close the Seacombe branch temporarily; a request for a refund for passengers holding through rail and ferry contracts was refused by the department but, in the event, closure was avoided.

Improved Services

The increased traffic led the Corporation to change the services on the northern passages in order to encourage their use by regular passengers. Seacombe, with its 10-minute service throughout the day, tapering off to an hourly frequency throughout the night was able to absorb many additional passengers and, in fact, after a complaint of overcrowding was investigated, it was found that no boat was ever more than 60% full. For the winter of 1912 a 20-minute morning peak service from New Brighton via Egremont was followed by a 15-minute service to Egremont with every other boat going on to New Brighton until 8.0pm when a 30-minute service ran to the close. From 1st December a 20-minute service was run at Seacombe between 11.20pm and 1.0am when the hourly service commenced. For the exceptionally busy month of July 1913, during which there was a Royal visit to Liverpool for the opening of Gladstone Dock, a 15-minute service ran to and from New Brighton until 11.0pm on weekdays with a 20-minute Sunday service until 10.0pm.

For the winter of 1913-14, the all day 15-minute Egremont service was not repeated. A 15-minute service from New Brighton via Egremont was given between 8.0am and 10.0am followed by a joint 30-minute service, augmented to double the service to Egremont between 12.0noon and 2.0pm and between 5.0pm and 7.0pm, requiring three boats with a fourth in reserve.

Encouraged by a record summer in 1913, from 1st May 1914, the northern boats were run every 15-minutes throughout the day until 10.0pm. From 1st June two late boats up to 10.35pm from New Brighton were added and an ambitious morning peak service was started with a direct boat from Egremont every 15 minutes and a direct boat from

One of the last pair of paddle steamers built for Wallasey ferries in 1896, Pansy *had assumed the general appearance of the screw steamers which followed her in the early 20th century.*
M. Jenkins collection

Iris and Daffodil *(below), with their characteristic square portholes, in their 'intermediate' state with flying bridge but no central wheelhouse. The vessel seems to have given way to a London & North Western Railway lighter.*

Commercial postcard

The south bridge at New Brighton ferry on 16th March 1907 after the landing stage had been carried away by a storm. The north bridge was entirely submerged.   Wallasey Tramway Preservation Group

New Brighton every 20 minutes. This proved to be excessive and was replaced from 12th August by a combined 20-minute service between 6.30am and 11.0pm, using three boats. On Sundays a 15-minute service ran between 10.0am and 10.35pm.

These improvements were matched on 1st April 1914 by a reduction in the price of contracts to a new low level (see Appendix 5).

A New Manager and a Royal Visit

The Ferries manager, H. E. Martin, retired on 26th July 1913 after 17 years' service. He had led the team which designed the modern vessels introduced during his tenure of office and planned and oversaw the reconstruction of Egremont pier. There was keen competition for his job, 109 applying and a short list of 14 being drawn up from which the Council appointed a local man, Lt. Cdr. William Henry Fry, RNR. Following service with the Houston and Cunard Lines, he had been employed for the previous seven years as Engineer and Superintendent of Works for the Vacuum Oil Co. His appointment made it unnecessary for the Corporation to employ naval architects and other consultants and all subsequent vessels were designed by him or under his supervision. One of Fry's most memorable duties in 1914 was to prepare the department for the visit of King

George V on 25th March in recognition of the town's elevation to County Borough status. The King and Queen crossed the river to Seacombe in *Daffodil* and laid the foundation stone of the new town hall. The whole ferry fleet was dressed overall and the streets of the town gaily decorated. To Cdr. Fry fell the task of guiding the Ferries department through the difficult war years between 5th August 1914 and 11th November 1918 and for many years thereafter.

The starboard engine of Snowdrop *built by Cammell Laird & Co. in 1910.*   Courtesy T. Morgan

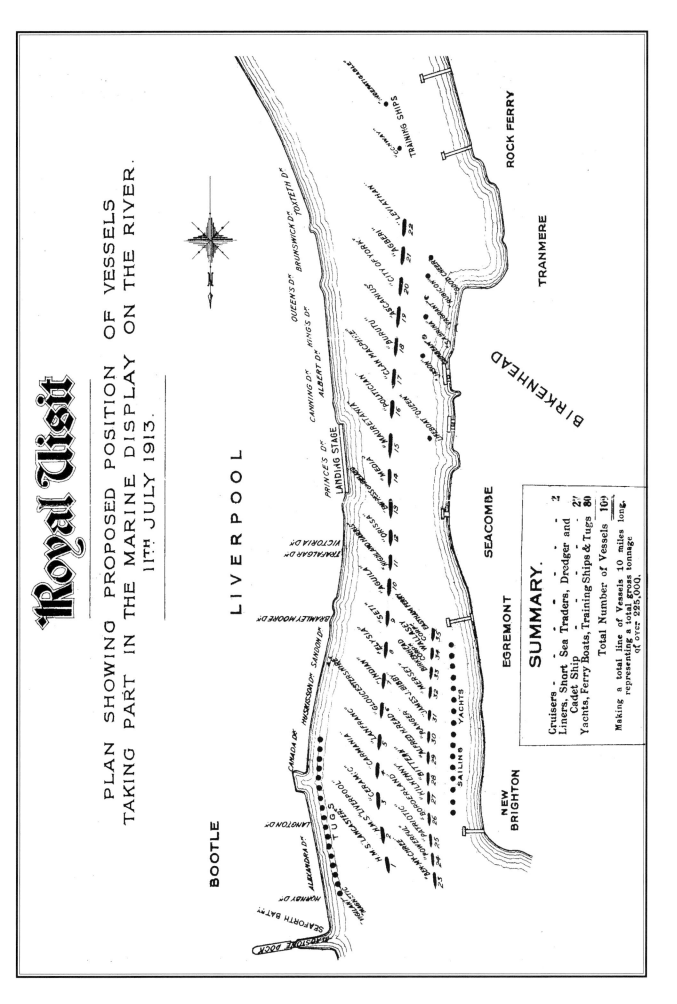

The landward end of New Brighton pier on a busy summer's day with the tram terminus on the right. The luggage boat Wallasey can just be discerned behind the lamp. These vessels, with portable floatable seats arranged on the deck, augmented the New Brighton service on very busy days for many years.

Wirral Archive Service

5 1914-1939

THE Great War of 1914-18 brought many problems which affected day-to-day routine – the loss of skilled staff to the armed forces, the restriction of supplies, the postponement of new boats and an increase in peak hour loadings as more and more people were put on to war work. The Corporation decided to make up the pay of staff in the armed services and the cost of fuel and other materials increased steeply. As more men left, the impossibility of replacing them led to substantial overtime payments. The ferries workshop was soon engaged in turning and fitting work for the government.

Costs and staff shortages were dealt with by curtailing sailings as far as possible on the northern ferries. The Sunday service finished at 9.15pm from 18th January 1915 and from 8th November the 20-minute service was reduced to 30-minutes, saving one boat, with a daily last sailing at 9.15pm. This resulted in 2,000 fewer contracts being sold at Egremont in December 1915, compared with the previous year, as passengers found it more convenient to reach Seacombe by tram. The 10-minute Seacombe service was reduced to 15-minutes off-peak though an attempt to maintain this frequency with one boat was soon abandoned.

Fare Increases

The lower fares fixed in 1914 were not to be enjoyed for long as wartime inflation soon brought increases which were staggered in three stages on 1st July and 1st October 1915 and 1st April 1916, a different group of fares being raised on each occasion. This brought the Seacombe annual contract up to £1. 10s. 0d. (+33%) and New Brighton annual to £2 (+60%). But there was much worse to come. The ferries had now reached the limit of their charging powers under their enabling Act and were forced to apply to Parliament for a new maximum tariff. The Royal Assent was obtained on 16th May 1918 and ordinary fares went up the next day to Seacombe $1\frac{1}{2}$d, Egremont 3d and New Brighton $4\frac{1}{2}$d. However pre-8.0am workmen's tickets at 1d single and 2d return replaced the early morning 1d returns which had been issued for many years but had been confined to Seacombe since 1st January 1913. The new ticket was at first available at all ferries which would have given a reduction for users of Egremont and New Brighton but it, too, was soon limited to Seacombe.

Luggage boat tolls were increased from 1st April 1916 by which time the two boats were handling

New Brighton ferry pier in its heyday with the Promenade pier alongside. The beach and the piers are crowded – note the people watching an entertainment – and either Snowdrop *or* John Joyce *is returning to Liverpool for another load.*

Commercial postcard

500 vehicles per day. Motor cycles had been banned from passenger vessels from 1st March 1915 except when the luggage service was suspended and revised rates for pedal cycles were introduced including a special Seacombe workman-plus-bicycle fare of 2d return before 8.0am.

Reduced fares for children were introduced from 1st January 1913; children under seven travelled free and after that the full fare but this was changed a year later to under 3 free, 3-7 years half fare and full fare thereafter. Machines for half-fare tickets were installed on boats and at terminals and these were, for a time, used also for workmen's tickets but were abandoned as being too slow.

A tender of £27,000 from the Ailsa company of Troon for a new four-cylinder, triple-expansion engined steamer was accepted in January 1915, subject to a government loan being granted but this was refused on the grounds that 'a new steamer was not a pressing necessity on account of war requirements'.

Admiralty Demands

There was a great demand for vessels of all kinds for work generated by the war effort and, in 1916, the Corporation received the first order requisitioning the two paddlers, *John Herron* and *Pansy* which were wanted to carry munition workers on the Thames to Woolwich Arsenal. The Chairman of the Ferries Committee, John Farley, and the manager went to the Royal Dockyard at Woolwich in December 1916 to try to prevent the loss of these vessels which, because of their lower fuel consumption, were still in regular use on the northern passages. After some discussion they agreed to sell *Pansy* for £5,000 or hire her for £15 per day. The Admiralty offered a lower purchase price, condemned by the Council as 'paltry and inadequate' but eventually a price of £4,800 was agreed. With her decks heaped with coal and boarded up against rough seas, *Pansy* left the Mersey on 20th January 1917 and next day ran aground and broke her back on the rocks in Bull Bay, Anglesey. Within five days, *John Herron* was despatched to replace her and eventually reached the safety of the Thames. For the first time since 1822, the ferries were without paddle-steamers.

An attempt to get the Admiralty to purchase *John Herron* was overruled by the War Office Transportation Administration Board and the Corporation was eventually obliged to accept a hire charge of £4 per working day, equal to £511 per year. However compensation of £5,119 was paid for the loss of *Pansy*.

Next, the War Office attempted to commandeer the luggage boat *Seacombe* but this time the deputation was successful in persuading the authorities that the vessel was playing a vital role

Pansy, sister ship to John Herron, *was one of the last paddlers to be placed in service by Wallasey ferries. She was requisitioned by the Admiralty in 1916 but ran aground and was wrecked at Bull Bay, Anglesey on 21st January 1917.*

M. Jenkins collection

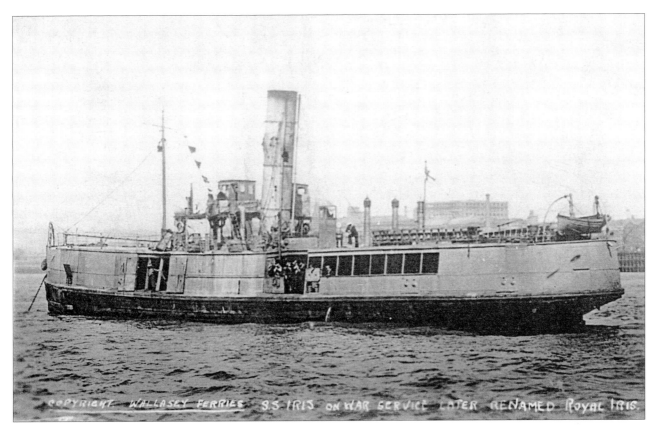

A starboard view of Iris *with armour-plating after the naval action at Zeebrugge in 1918.*

Iris *and* Daffodil *at anchor with a tug after their return from naval service in 1918.*

After their return from Zeebrugge, the two vessels were put on public show in Liverpool before their damage was repaired. Visitors view the promenade deck of Iris. *Note the damaged bridge and the wreath in tribute to the fallen.*

Merseyside Fire Brigade

in transporting essential supplies and, if requisitioned, the task would be left to the 36-year old *Wallasey*, a ship in urgent need of new engines. Early in 1918, the Admiralty requisitioned *Iris* and *Daffodil*. They had been selected for their shallow draught which enabled them to pass through minefields unscathed and their water-tight compartments made them virtually unsinkable. Renamed *Iris II* and *Daffodil IV*, both were prepared for their mission and the journey to Dover by Ferries staff. All passenger equipment was removed and armour plating fitted to vulnerable parts fore and aft. Painted in battleship grey, they slipped out of the river on 12th February crewed by the navy but with Ferries personnel manning the engines so that naval engineers could master their idiosyncrasies. As fleet auxiliaries, they played a prominent part in an attack on Zeebrugge on 23rd April 1918. Sometimes described as the first commando raid, its purpose was to block the entrance to the Bruges canal by sinking three hulks thereby denying the Germans access to their submarine base at Bruges. *Iris* and *Daffodil* landed troops on the Mole protecting the harbour and came under severe enemy fire. Considerable damage was caused to their superstructures and Cdr. Fry persuaded the Admiralty to allow them to be repaired by Ferries staff in Liverpool under naval supervision. When they returned home on 17th May 1918, they were given a tremendous welcome, ships being dressed overall. Both were allowed to berth free of charge in East Canning Dock where they were opened to the public for three days. On 28th May the Council learned that the King had 'acceded to the prayer of the petition of the Corporation' and had commanded that the ferries steamships *Iris* and *Daffodil* should henceforth be named *Royal Iris* and *Royal Daffodil*'. Copies of the King's illuminated letter were exhibited on both vessels and commemorative brass plates were unveiled by Admiral Sir David Beatty at a ceremony in March 1919. The two vessels were rechristened by Mrs. Farley on 30th July and returned to passenger service immediately. After the shell-pitted funnel of *Iris* was taken through the streets of Liverpool for a flag day parade on 31st August 1918, it stood on land south of Seacombe stage until it disintegrated from corrosion during the 1939-45 war. However, the naval engagement was celebrated in Wallasey annually until the 1960s by the Zeebrugge and Walcheren memorial service which took place on the nearest Sunday to St. George's Day on board the current *Royal Iris* or *Royal Daffodil*.

During the absence of *Iris* and *Daffodil*, the ferries were left with only four passenger steamers, *Lily*, *Rose*, *John Joyce* and *Snowdrop* and the Admiralty agreed to finance the daily hiring of the 1899 Birkenhead steamer *Lancashire*, the hire lasting for 164 days. On her return there was a dispute about the hire charges, Birkenhead demanding £42. 1s. 9d. per day. The vessel also required an overhaul and refit which occupied 42 days at a cost of £1,160. Finally, new terms were negotiated whereby Wallasey and the Ministry of Shipping were each to pay half the cost of the refit plus an allowance of £407 in respect of the 42 days in dock; the 164 days were assessed at £9. 14s. 0d. (£9.70) per day making a total of £1,590. 16s. 0d. (£1,590.80). As an insurance policy, in April 1917, Wallasey Corporation came to a three-year agreement with Birkenhead for the hire of a vessel to assist with the summer traffic. As rail fares had been raised to discourage travel, day trips to New Brighton by ferry increased, a fine summer bringing almost five million in 1916-17 but the following year was an all time record with 31.8 million, of which 4.7 million used Egremont and almost seven million New Brighton, record traffic being carried on both Whit Monday and August Bank Holiday 1917, all this being achieved with a much depleted fleet. At times of exceptional demand, calls at Egremont would be suspended, all efforts being concentrated on New Brighton, a source of vociferous complaint from traders at Egremont.

From 1st June 1918, all through ferry-railway tickets except those with the Wirral Railway, were withdrawn in order to discourage non-essential travel. However, on 17th August 1918, the ferries were called upon to transport thousands of American and Canadian troops from Liverpool to New Brighton for a charity baseball game. Many boat loads of singing soldiers were landed and even the luggage boats were filled to overflowing. After the match the New Brighton pubs did well and the return sailings were not entirely without incident! As the war drew to a close, the river was full of ships bringing men home for which no berths were available. Ferry vessels were requisitioned daily to act as tenders, sometimes going out as far as the Mersey bar. On Christmas Day 1918, thousands of Chinese were unloaded in a snowstorm.

Even before the end of the war, coal shortages were causing serious operating problems. From 4th November 1918 all peak hour services to and from New Brighton were suspended, a single vessel steaming hourly to New Brighton between 10.0am and 12 noon and 2.0 and 5.0pm and all day Sunday. At other times one boat maintained a half-hourly service to and from Egremont to which New Brighton contract-holders were taken by an augmented tram service paid for by the Ferries. This proved very unpopular and the normal winter service was restored from 1st December 1918 at one day's notice thus causing considerable friction between the Ferries and Tramways departments, the latter having laid some special pointwork for the augmented service.

The second Snowdrop *(above) and* John Joyce *(below – originally intended to be* Bluebell*) were built on the Mersey by Cammell Laird in 1910. Once again, the promenade deck did not extend for the full width of the vessel and their passenger certificate at 1,563 was almost 200 less than their immediate predecessors* Iris *and* Daffodil *which had full width decks. They had very rounded sterns and remained in service until 1936.*   G. Parry collection

Post-1914-18 War Problems

The war ended on 11th November 1918 and the ferries carried enormous crowds during the special Peace Days. As soon as possible, the Ferries Committee started to tackle the various problems which had been held over; these included renewal of steamers, both goods and passenger, and reconstruction of Seacombe and New Brighton landing stages, the condition of which was giving cause for concern. Nationally, there were serious labour problems and difficulties with coal supplies, the lifeblood of the ferry service. However, the most insidious problem was inflation which accentuated all other difficulties and inhibited their rapid solution. However, costs continued to rise and in September 1920 the basic fares went up again to 2d, 4d and 6d respectively. On 1st April 1921 some fares and all contracts were increased by 33%, though only the Seacombe ordinary fare was increased (to 3d) and the early morning tickets to 4d return. An annual Seacombe contract was now £3, Egremont £3. 10s. 0d. (£3.50) and New Brighton £4; the 24-hour contract doubled in price to £4. 4s. 0d. (£4.20). Increases of this magnitude were a local political hot potato and some concessions had to be found to appease public opinion. The introduction of a weekly contract for 1s. 9d. (9p) at Seacombe, 2s. 0d. (10p) at Egremont and 2s. 3d. (11p) at New Brighton had the greatest impact as it brought the contract system within the means of all. The New Brighton rate was a winter rate and henceforth it became the practice to have different summer and winter rates for monthly and weekly contracts at Egremont and New Brighton. Further concessions were twelve, six and three-monthly juvenile contracts (which were extended to age 18 for students and apprentices in 1926) and a full range of cycle and rider contracts, minimum monthly augmenting an annual facility introduced in 1904. In those days many workers took their cycles with them on the boat; they were required to embark and disembark after all the other passengers with a view to minimising claims for stockings laddered by contact with pedals.

A deficiency of £24,830 in respect of 1920-21 was met from the rates, followed by amounts of £37,890 and £22,003 in the next two years. Inflation having gone into reverse there were significant contract reductions from 1st April 1923 the Seacombe annual falling to £2. 15s. 0d. (£2.75) and the weekly to 1s. 3d. (6p). The Seacombe single fare was reduced from 3d. to 2¹/₂d. but no other fares were changed. There was a further reduction in twelve, six and three-monthly contracts on 1st April 1926 bringing the Seacombe annual down to £2. 10s. 0d. (£2.50) but the monthlies and weeklies remained unchanged and this tariff remained stable until the 1939-45 war inflationary increases.

Pass tickets, available at any time except during the night hours, continued to be sold in packs of twelve, giving a discount on the ordinary fare. Day return tickets between Liverpool and New Brighton were available at certain times, usually after 5.0pm, and inspectors went on board at New Brighton to collect fares or cancel tickets from passengers who did not go ashore. Many years later, similar arrangements were made at Seacombe. There was an unusual arrangement for passengers travelling from Egremont to New Brighton or vice versa. As once they had passed through the turnstile there was no control over the direction they took, they were charged the fare to Liverpool and given a refund of the difference at their destination.

Trade union militancy led to both higher wages and shorter working hours resulting in more men having to be employed to do the same work. Coal shortages, caused by strikes both in the mines and on the railways, sent the cost of coal rocketing and the following comparisons of just three key items in the accounts will illustrate the magnitude of the problem:

Year	Wages £	Coal* £	Repairs £
1913-14	21,322	19,163	14,555
1917-18	25,624	32,993	21,604
1918-19	34,074	41,316	25,381
1919-20	52,205	55,888	31,575
1920-21	67,880	68,366	40,707
1921-22	66,079	72,460	37,960
1922-23	56,443	47,996	27,292

* Includes fuel oil   1921-22 £57,065;
1922-23 £25,536

It should perhaps be mentioned that 'Repairs' in 1917-18 and 1918-19 were at minimum levels because of the shortage of both labour and materials under wartime conditions.

Coal supply problems occupied much management time as it was essential to keep the ferries running. An additional railway siding had been laid into the Seacombe yard where reserves were piled up but in June 1921 these were virtually exhausted, forcing the management to buy in small lots from wherever they could at whatever price. Fuel oil offered an alternative and *Royal Iris*, *Royal Daffodil*, *John Joyce* and *Snowdrop* were converted, the latter being the first to re-enter service on 14th May 1921. It was also proposed to convert the Seacombe hydraulic plant, thus saving 10 tons of coal per week but it is not certain that this was done. Next, it was agreed that *Lily*, *Rose*, *Seacombe* and the two new luggage boats should be temporarily converted to oil. The cost was estimated at £500 per boat giving a manageable total of £3,500 most of which could be paid from a reserve fund. However the actual cost at £7,709 was more than double, consisting of the installation of an oil burner for each boiler but there were savings on stoking costs. Unlike the situation after the 1939-45 War, inflation started to go into reverse in 1922 and the entire fleet reverted to coal a year later by which time the price was below that of oil.

An added annoyance was the Board of Trade requirement that 80% of seats on the vessels should be of the buoyant type and that there should also be more buoyant equipment. Safety had been exercising the minds of government officials for many years. In 1874 every vessel was required to have a lifeboat and 12 lifebuoys, a demand said by the ferries management to be totally impractical and in 1891 life saving equipment had to be provided for 10% of passengers. In 1916, the Board of Trade required 40% of seats to be buoyant and many were replaced. The cost of all this was estimated at £12,400 and a joint approach to the Board was made by Wallasey and Birkenhead as a result of which the ruling was reluctantly set aside provided more lifebelts, life boats and buoyant seats were provided, the work being done during 1919-20. Capt. Fry invented a device for liberating and throwing overboard lifebelts with Holmes lights attached. It was operated by captains pulling a lever on the bridge and was fitted to all ferry boats.

It was fortunate that the lifts and high level goods bridge at Seacombe had been designed to carry railway wagons for this extra strength enabled them to cope with the increasingly heavy traffic. However, by 1920 the whole structure, including the landing stage itself was in very poor condition and the vehicular traffic had increased so much that there were frequent queues, sometimes stretching back along Birkenhead Road to the Four Bridges. As the tide fell, the bridge which was part of the 1880 terminal, being only 150ft long, became too steep for vehicles. The intermittent service provided by the hydraulic lifts and the relatively small area of the stage led to serious congestion and ruled out the use of a second luggage boat at busy times. The floating roadways at Liverpool and Woodside had been made much longer than the passenger bridges by cutting a water inlet in which they floated so that the gradients were reduced. Following a detailed report by Wilton & Bell, consulting engineers, it was decided to build a floating roadway at Seacombe, to enlarge the stage to accommodate two luggage boats and to abandon the hydraulic lifts. Then, on 2nd January 1920, the Council approved in principle an overall strategy for the ferries undertaking, the various projects being prioritised as follows:

1. First passenger steamer.
2. First luggage steamer.
3. New Brighton stage.
4. Extension of vestibule at Seacombe.
5. Extension of Seacombe passenger stage and provision of bridges.
6. Second passenger steamer.
7. Second luggage steamer.
8. Extension of luggage stage.
9. Provision of additional pier and lifts.
10. Provision of floating bridge.
11. Third passenger steamer.

New Brighton Landing Stage Refurbished

Early in 1920, Wilton and Bell advised that two or three pontoons supporting the New Brighton stage needed replacing; they also recommended that the superstructure be completely renewed as patching up the old girders would not be satisfactory. Later that year, in the hope of receiving some financial assistance, the Corporation requested a meeting with the newly-formed Ministry of Transport to discuss the reconstruction of both Seacombe and New Brighton landing stages but the Minister did not think any useful purpose would be served by receiving a deputation. However, the Ministry's Director of Engineering met the general manager and Mr Wilton on 9th November, and a Public Inquiry was held on 7th January 1921 into the Corporation's application to borrow money for the reconstruction work, £45,000 being authorised for New Brighton.

A contract for this was awarded to Sir William Arrol & Co. Ltd at £25,691. 5s. 0d. the intention being for the work to be done during the winter. The ferry would be closed, the bridges removed and the new superstructure placed on the pontoons in time for the resumption of sailings at Easter 1921. However, the contract time was nine months which would have led to a loss of most of the 1921 summer season's traffic. This was economically unacceptable and the consultants advised that if the stresses were reduced by removing the north bridge and some patching was done to the stage, it should be safe until the end of the season, the north bridge being brought back in time for the Easter traffic.

The traditional method of removing and replacing bridges of this kind was to float camels beneath them but, in September 1920, the 100-ton floating crane *Mammoth* had been acquired by the Mersey Docks & Harbour Board and it was decided to make use of this monster. On 2nd December 1920, she sailed down-river to New Brighton accompanied by three tugs with a ferry steamer in reserve. The problem was to maintain the crane in position during the lift. This was achieved by the attendant vessels pushing

The landing bridges were originally floated into position on camels as shown here but acquisition of the 100-ton floating crane Mammoth *by the Mersey Docks and Harbour Board in 1920 enabled the bridge to be carried to its location on the crane's deck. The north bridge at New Brighton ferry is shown being returned to its position after repair on 8th March 1921.*
M. Jenkins collection

the crane against the landing stage. The 140-ton north bridge was successfully removed, taken up river on the crane's deck and deposited on a prepared site on the bank south of Seacombe, the whole operation taking just under six hours. After the winter's patching up of the stage, the bridge was repositioned on 8th March 1921.

On 15th October 1921 the ferry closed for the winter and the north and south bridges were removed on 24th and 25th October. The redundant stage was towed into the West Float on 7th November and work began on dismantling it so that the pontoons which it was proposed to reuse could be completely refurbished. Two new pontoons, measuring 55ft long by 11ft 6in. wide by 6ft 3in. deep, divided into three watertight compartments, were manufactured by Cammell Laird & Co. The dividing bulkheads had to be of sufficient strength to withstand the stresses involved when the stage was grounded at very low tides. The new stage was 242ft long by 45ft wide and the wooden deckhouses, flooring and fenders were constructed by Ferries Department workmen. Instead of positioning the new girders on dolphins and floating the pontoons beneath, the stage was erected on the dockside and launched sideways like a ship. After completion, the stage was towed to New Brighton and moored in position. The south and north bridges were replaced on 8th and 10th March respectively and the ferry reopened on 12th March. The same lifting techniques were used with complete success.

The Post-1914-18 Vessels

The last remaining paddler, *John Herron*, which had lain at Woolwich since the end of 1918, returned to the Mersey on 17th May 1919. It was estimated it would cost the Admiralty £2,100 to recondition her and work began in early July only to stop when it was decided to dispose of her as she lay. She was sold to Cunard for use as a tender in France and later passed to two French companies before being broken up in 1925. The Corporation received £4,100 to cover her hire and partial reconditioning.

In December 1918, tenders were invited for one or two goods boats to be built to a specification prepared by Cdr. Fry. Despite financial problems, it was felt essential to renew the fleet and in March 1921, it was agreed to order two passenger steamers, to be named *The Thistle* and *The Shamrock* but the full Council substituted *John Farley* and *Francis Storey* after Committee chairmen. The two new goods steamers were to be named *Poulton* and *Liscard*. In due course *John Farley* and *Poulton* were disallowed by the Registrar and the names *J.Farley* and *Leasowe* were adopted instead. As most British yards were busy, the manager even visited shipbuilders in Belgium and Holland but without success. Finally he went to Scotland accompanied by the chairman, J. Farley, with a view to sorting out problems with the Ailsa company. The Council had been demanding that Ailsa should honour the outstanding contract and build a passenger ship at 1915 prices; this was manifestly absurd and agreement was eventually reached whereby the company would build two passenger steamers for £149,000, including £24,000 to cover establish-ment charges and a profit margin, an escalation clause being embodied in the contract. This was ratified by the Council on 11th February 1920. At the eleventh hour, it was also decided to order two luggage boats and on 18th February, the tender of John I. Thornycroft & Co. Ltd, Southampton was accepted at cost of labour and materials plus £18,000 per boat for administration charges and profit. A loan of £323,550, the largest in the Corporation's history, was then approved by the government in August 1920 to cover the cost of these four steamers, plus a further £19,400 in respect of the reversionary foreshore leases, the purchase of which achieved a long term economy.

J. Farley and *Francis Storey* were similar in general design and dimensions to *Iris* and *Daffodil*, the promenade deck extending to the full width of the vessels. They were equipped with 4-cylinder triple-expansion reciprocating engines developing 1,400 hp. 'Gunboat' type boilers were supplied by Dunsmuir and Jackson Ltd, Govan. They were certified to carry 1,629 passengers and had framework for awnings over the aft promenade deck. *Francis Storey* was launched on 25th May 1922 and *J. Farley* the following day, trials being undertaken at Skelmorie immediately. It was agreed to accept *J. Farley* incomplete so that she could be used at Whitsuntide, painting being completed on the voyage to the Mersey. The quoted price of £70,720 was reduced to £56,399 because of deflation. *Francis Storey* went into service in August 1922. Being speedy vessels, they were used mainly on the New Brighton service for most of their days. *Francis Storey* served as the cruise vessel with grey hull and yellow funnel in 1934-36.

The Special Committee of Inquiry

The recent substantial losses led the Council to appoint a Special Sub-Committee on 2nd March 1922 'to investigate and report upon the financial policy of the Ferries undertaking, with power, if deemed necessary, to call in expert assistance'. This Sub-Committee met 35 times before presenting its report on 7th May 1923. The Report highlighted a fundamental weakness in municipal trading in that the finances are controlled by a different department into which day to day management

One of the first post-1914-18 war steamers was J. Farley, *built in 1922 by the Ailsa yard. With a full width deck and provision for an awning on the after promenade deck, she was a regular performer on the Seacombe service in her early years until displaced by* Wallasey *and* Marlowe.

has no input. It was clear from the Inquiry's interrogation of Capt. Fry that he had no knowledge of ferry finances, a very hazy idea of how the system of municipal loans worked and, alarmingly, no one had thought there was any need to inform him. The orders for new boats had put the cost of steaming up from 18/6d (92¹/₂p) per hour to 24/- (£1.20) per hour or, in other terms, there would be revenue of about £95,000 against costs of £104,000.

The Inquiry noted that the undertaking had shown a surplus in only three of the previous 14 years and felt that budgeting for a surplus was unrealistic and that any small excess of income over expenditure should be placed to reserve. They first turned their attention to the numbers employed which had risen from 367 in 1910-11 to 537 in 1921-22 and, whilst some of the increase was attributable to shorter working hours, it was believed economies should be made, the objective being a minimum permanent staff augmented by temporary employees when necessary, A large number of apprentices and 'scaler boys' had been employed at low wages to help keep the older vessels in good condition, the manager pointing out that the department's policy had changed from 'if it isn't broken don't mend it' in 1910-11 to one of regular preventative maintenance. Trade union restrictive practices were also blamed for increased numbers. The Sub-Committee was not entirely convinced and it is significant that between 1921-22 and 1922-23 staff numbers did fall by 56 (10.4%) to 481.

The Sub-Committee was surprised to discover that the boats were run without a qualified engineer on board, the rule being that boys who started as trimmers became firemen and then graduated to engine drivers. It recommended that a certificated engineer should be carried on every vessel and that the highest level to which a fireman could aspire should be Assistant Engineer. It was correctly believed that a qualified man would achieve savings on coal and reduce maintenance costs by more sympathetic use of the machinery. This recommendation was adopted before the report was published and confirmed by the Council on 7th December 1922. Four unqualified engineers with 56, 54, 50 and 47 years' service were retired and granted pensions, qualified engineers being recruited gradually over the next year or two. Rev. counters were also fitted to the steamers to reduce excessive wear.

Consultants who were retained to advise on the cost and quality of coal used on the vessels found that the coal being purchased was unsuitable and extravagant and that the best steam coal came from particular locations; the Council was recommended to buy from those sources (which were not publicly named) or from other collieries, the product of which had been tested and found economical. After the Report was received, further tests were carried out on *Francis Storey, Liscard* and *Leasowe* using two boilers instead of three with a view to demonstrating that, in some cases, too much power was being generated.

Attention was next focused on the loss-making goods service and, coupled with that, the practice

Royal Daffodil *in final form with central wheelhouse, is shown passing Barton bridge on a Manchester Ship Canal cruise. Note the frame designed to carry an awning in a final recognition that some cover for upper deck passengers was desirable.*
M. Jenkins collection

of the Ferries Committee of making decisions without any apparent regard to the financial consequences. The goods service had been making increasing losses since 1914 (see Chapter 6), the problem being that, even though the revenue trend was upwards, the cost of providing the service had increased steadily. The purchase of *Liscard* and *Leasowe* added £31,030 loan charges for 20 years whilst estimated income for 1922-23 was only £26,000.

As early as 1912, the Finance Committee had warned the Ferries Committee about their policy of buying expensive new boats but the advice had not been heeded. Capt. Fry said that his instructions were to draw up a report showing how congestion at Liverpool and Wallasey for both goods and passenger traffic could be alleviated and that is what he did but without any reference to the cost of the measures. He insisted that he had never seen any figures of loan charges and that in the past he had 'had his knuckles rapped' for enquiring into such matters. One exchange with Councillor Gordon is of particular interest:-

Coun.Gordon	…I take it the manager is concerned as far as the running expenses and receipts are concerned. I take it that you would be cognisant of the loan charges on such expenditure.
Capt. Fry	No, sir. I have never been at all sure on that matter and I do not know what loan charges are chargeable unless I ask the Treasurer what the loan charges are, who will tell me that it has been dealt with as a financial matter and in the province of the Finance Committee as distinct from the Ferry Manager's office.
Coun.Gordon	You really never had it in mind what the effect of the luggage section of the undertaking would be in getting two ferry boats at peak prices?

Capt. Fry	No, sir.
Coun.Gordon	It is quite a simple question - as manager of the undertaking when making this recommendation you never had your eye, for instance on a pro forma balance sheet?
Capt. Fry	No. I have always looked upon it as my duty to provide a safe and efficient service. One boat was necessary, no matter what it cost.

There was a school of thought that, instead of subsidising the goods service from profits on the passenger service, it should be shown as a charge against the rates in order to concentrate the minds of the Council and the ferries management on the need to exercise strict economies.

If the Financial Inquiry achieved anything, it succeeded in imposing financial discipline in connection with the improvements at Seacombe, though, with hindsight, much of the outlay was wasted in the sense that the Council failed to look ahead and assess the impact that the building of the first Mersey road tunnel would have on cross-river traffic.

The Seacombe Improvement Scheme

As already mentioned, the January 1921 government Inquiry had authorised finance for the New Brighton scheme but the Inspector did not consider that a *prima facie* case had been made for the Seacombe scheme and requested detailed specifications, drawings and estimates. The whole scheme was divided into three phases as follows:-

Work 'A'	New floating goods landing stage.
Work 'B'	New floating roadway.
Work 'C'	Cut and works in connection with floating roadway.

In September 1921, in the interest of unemployment relief, the government offered financial assistance for capital schemes which would not ordinarily have been started at that time. Tenders were invited and that of Cleveland Bridge & Engineering Co. Ltd for £54,101 with completion in 48 weeks was accepted for work 'A'; tenders for Work 'B' and 'C' were likewise provisionally accepted from Sir William Arrol for £54,196 and £31,420 respectively. However, on 7th December 1921, the full Council voted 41:9 in favour of delaying all three projects pending clarification of financial matters, in particular government grants and further delays and deferments ensued. Some work at Seacombe was urgent and a report on the condition of the stage and the hydraulic lifts was prepared by a consultant, Mr E. Cruttwell, MInstCE. His report, received in January 1923, revealed the need for a new 90ft pontoon and several other repairs. It was decided that only safety work should be done.

By 1923 the whole scheme had become much more ambitious and a new 640ft long stage was proposed incorporating a northern extension with an additional passenger berth and a high level bridge. The cost would have been enormous and consultants Wilton and Bell scaled it down to a 485ft long stage which was 170ft longer than the old one, increasing the berths from two to three.

Approval to proceed was given in 1924 but there was a further delay for schemes 'B' and 'C' pending receipt of the report of the Merseyside Municipal Co-ordination Committee on the proposals for a Mersey road tunnel. However, Wallasey was excluded from the scheme because the terms they had laid down proved unacceptable to the other councils involved. Wallasey wished to transfer their loss-making goods service to the Tunnel Committee while retaining the passenger service and limiting their financial liability to 6d in the £ of rateable value. Failure to come to terms about the tunnel turned out to be one of the most expensive blunders the Council ever made.

The Cleveland Bridge Co. assembled the new 485ft stage alongside the Oil Quay in the West Float. It rested on 38 pontoons of which 11 were to be taken from the old structure. Seven longitudinal beams were to carry the deck, the beam nearest the land being a stronger, box section to withstand the stresses from the movement of the two hinged booms which would tie the stage to the river wall. The two existing bridges, which were to be

The forward promenade deck of Royal Iris *with the vessel in dock in Liverpool undergoing rehabilitation after war service at Zeebrugge. Note the painter just visible behind the ventilator and the flotation gear beneath the seats on the starboard side. Later vessels had upper deck seats arranged longitudinally rather than crosswise.*   G. Parry collection

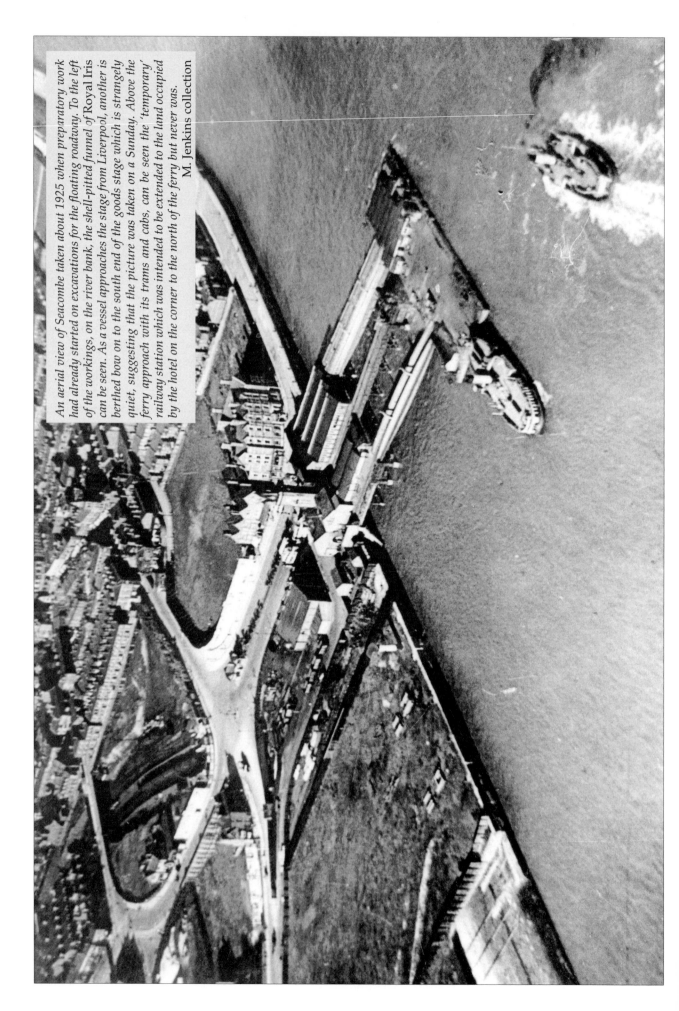

An aerial view of Seacombe taken about 1925 when preparatory work had already started on excavations for the floating roadway. To the left of the workings, on the river bank, the shell-pitted funnel of Royal Iris can be seen. As a vessel approaches the stage from Liverpool, another is berthed bow on to the south end of the goods stage which is strangely quiet, suggesting that the picture was taken on a Sunday. Above the ferry approach with its trams and cabs, can be seen the 'temporary' railway station which was intended to be extended to the land occupied by the hotel on the corner to the north of the ferry but never was.

M. Jenkins collection

retained, rested upon it, their outer ends sliding in and out as the stage rose and fell with the tide. Each new pontoon came by rail from Darlington in three sections; the London & North Eastern Railway had only four suitable wagons which had to be kept moving day and night to keep up with the erection gangs. On Saturday afternoon, 2nd May 1925, the stage, complete with its passenger shelter (of sufficient height to accommodate the double-deck structure envisaged in the future), was towed out into the river. The ferry was closed from 11.0pm, the old stage removed and the new one positioned by 6.30pm on Sunday 3rd, under the personal supervision of the manager. The ferry reopened at 5.0am on Monday 4th May. A special service was run between Liverpool and Egremont (at Seacombe fares) and trams were diverted during this carefully managed and highly successful operation.

Before being positioned, the stage had been equipped with the familiar balanced gangways, two nine feet wide for the main deck and one six feet wide for the promenade deck, enabling more than 1,500 passengers to disembark in an average of $2^3/_4$ minutes. The hydraulic lifts and the old vehicle (south) bridge served the new stage for 18 months until the floating roadway was opened.

On the south side of the terminal a 350ft long

The north boom at Seacombe was one of two which, together with the huge mooring chains, held the stage in position in the river. It is being lifted by the floating crane Mammoth *in May 1925 after the new landing stage had been floated into position.*   T. B. Maund collection

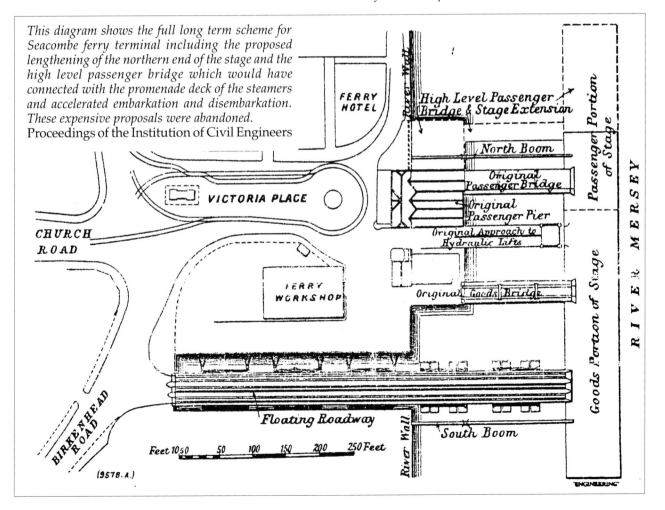

This diagram shows the full long term scheme for Seacombe ferry terminal including the proposed lengthening of the northern end of the stage and the high level passenger bridge which would have connected with the promenade deck of the steamers and accelerated embarkation and disembarkation. These expensive proposals were abandoned.
Proceedings of the Institution of Civil Engineers

inlet was cut into ground which had been reclaimed during the 1876-80 reconstruction. Running sand was encountered and steel sheet piling had to be used to isolate the working area. The cut was lined with concrete. This work was carried out by the Bristol firm of Nott, Brodie & Co. Ltd.

The new floating roadway, also built by Cleveland Bridge, was laid down in this inlet and is fully described in Chapter 6.

The final cost of the work (to the nearest pound) was as follows:

Landing Stage	£ 87,782
Floating Roadway	50,039
Cut	57,649
Covering Passenger Bridge	1,535
Wilton & Bell Fees	10,223
Miscellaneous	874
TOTAL	£208,102
Less sale of old stage	(1,550)
Recoverable items	(408)
GRAND TOTAL	£206,144

Ferries workmen were employed on all three projects and wages of £10,222 are included in the above totals.

The old lifts and hydraulic equipment were sold to local scrap merchants, Robert Smith & Sons for £510 in 1927 and in 1930 the same firm paid £100 for the privilege of demolishing the high level bridge. The goods yard was closed to rail traffic, the Dock Board lines being blocked off in Birkenhead Road, immediately south of the floating roadway. The ferry workshop was converted from steam to electrically driven machinery in 1927 to enable the steam plant to be dismantled.

The reopening of the ferry coincided with the start of the General Strike during which the northern services were suspended and a skeleton service was run at Seacombe manned by officers and volunteers. The strike was called off on 17th May but the coal miners stayed out for several more months and the ferries experienced several difficult months due to a serious coal shortage. What coal there was was expensive and there was a temporary reversion to oil firing on several vessels. The impact on the ferries' finances was severe as seen by comparing fuel costs (coal and oil) for October 1926 of £6,168. 12s. 5d. with those for October 1927 when supplies had returned to normal at £2,012. 5s. 7d.

The New Terminal Building and Workshop

In 1926 a government circular was issued inviting Town Councils to submit estimates for major works which could be started to alleviate unemployment.

Capt. Fry and W. H. Travers, the Borough Engineer, collaborated on a project to replace the ferry terminal buildings and approaches at Seacombe by new facilities better able to accommodate the growth of traffic by offering a swift interchange between buses and boats. The scheme was accepted by the government and the Unemployed Grants Committee offered £27,000 towards the estimated cost of £107,000. Work on the new terminal, which was to be built around Victoria Place, commenced in 1930. It also used the land on the south side between the Floating Roadway and the old coal yard.

The impressive new terminal building was entered through a colonnade 190ft long and 16ft deep behind a vestibule 28ft wide, divided into two parts by a 90ft high clock tower. This acted as a master for all the clocks on the premises and chimed the quarters and struck the hours. It was set in motion by the mayor on 19th August 1932. The Booking Hall, 200ft long and 75ft deep, was double the size of the old one and was designed to handle 500 passengers per minute with the up and down traffic separated by a line of kiosks and booths. The old goods bridge was widened, re-decked and roofed over for use by disembarking passengers, the north bridge being reconditioned and retained for embarking passengers and the roof over the stage was extended down to the south bridge. Separate pay-booths and turnstiles were provided for each direction. Folding shutters behind the colonnade were used as windbreaks in inclement weather. A news stand, tobacco kiosk, toilets and offices were provided.

On the southern side of Victoria Place was a two-storey building in which were housed the ferry headquarters, a post office, bus inspector's office and canteen as well as a two-storey car park for 200 cars. An adjoining single-storey building housed a cycle park. The colonnade continued along the front of this building and under cover loading barriers were provided for 15 buses. On the south side of the floating roadway, a new two-storey ferry workshop was erected by local builder, William Bradshaw, in 1930 at a contract price of £14,835. There was a time clause, stipulating completion within 10 months as the old workshop had to be demolished to make way for the new approach road and car park.

The Booking Hall roof, reconstruction of the south bridge and extensions to the shelters on the floating stage were carried out by Sir John Wolfe and Partners of London, under the supervision of Capt. Fry. The landward buildings, including the new ferry workshops were constructed under the direction of the Borough Engineer. The final cost was below estimate at £98,443.

The new terminal was officially opened by the Mayor at 2.30pm on 10th April 1933. Guests walked

The departure side of the Seacombe terminal building in original condition in 1933 showing the payboxes with turnstiles and contractors' gates. The layout was duplicated on the arrivals side beyond which is the clock tower. Children's 1d ticket slot machines can be seen on the right. Just out of the picture in the background, next to the sweet shop, was a post office, the postmaster being a Ferries employee.

Wirral Archive Service

In the upper view, fully restored after her wartime adventures, Royal Iris *sails towards New Brighton with several hundred passengers during the 1920s. In 1923 she was selected as the first cruise vessel with her hull painted grey, lined out in red, as seen in the lower view. An iron framework was erected on the aft promenade deck to carry a canvas awning to give some protection from the weather. Note the 'W.C.F.' House flag which was normally flown only for special occasions and at holiday times.*

G. Parry collection

down the north bridge on to *Royal Iris II* and afternoon tea was served during a short river cruise. The vessel returned at 4.15pm and the guests took a further half hour to inspect the south bridge, bus terminal and car park. The town could be justly proud of its new integrated transport facility.

New Sources of Revenue

The financial crisis of the early 1920s stimulated efforts to achieve more intensive utilisation of the undertaking's fleet, a high proportion of which was used only in peak traffic conditions. Cash flow was improved slightly by the introduction of weekly contracts from 1st April 1921 at 1s.9d. (9p) at Seacombe, 2s. (10p) at Egremont and 2s. 3d. (11p) at New Brighton. They were not available on Sundays until 1925 by which time, the Seacombe contract had been reduced to 1s. 6d. (7^1/2p). From May 1923, a 1s. (5p) circular ticket was issued between Liverpool and New Brighton, by ferry to Seacombe, tram to New Brighton, then ferry to Liverpool (or vice versa), the ferries taking 8d. and the tramways 4d. They were not very popular and were sold only for the 1923 and 1924 seasons.

In August 1923 a programme of public week-end pleasure cruises was launched, *Royal Iris*, repainted grey with red lining being selected as the cruise vessel. The normal white funnel with black top was retained but later this was painted yellow; the steamer was dressed overall. Structural alterations were minimal but the reputation of the vessel was an attraction in itself. She cruised from New Brighton to Eastham, calling at Liverpool, at 1s. 6d. for adults and 6d. for children. A band and non-alcoholic refreshments were provided but no sailing was to start before 3.0pm on Sundays. The programme was expanded the following August with three cruises on Saturdays and Sundays at 3.0, 5.0 and 7.0pm and two on Wednesdays at 3.0 and 7.0pm the latter being a three-hour dance cruise at a fare of 2s. The sailings were varied to include cruises to the Mersey bar instead of to Eastham where navigation could be difficult when there were very low tides. From 1925 cruises were run daily during the first two weeks of August. From 1926, except for the long Wednesday dance cruise, the cruise season started in June and from 1929, the boat called additionally at Egremont. This general pattern was maintained for many years though extra cruises for special events were run such as those on Coronation Day 1937 at two-hourly intervals to view the liners taking part in a special river pageant.

The dredger *Tulip* had, in the past, been made available to Birkenhead Corporation for dredging at Rock Ferry and it was now hired out on projects further afield. In March 1923, spoil from the excavation at St. Peter's Church site in Church Street, Liverpool was removed from Princes Dock where it had been dumped, at 2s. 3d per ton and, in June, *Tulip* went as far afield as Bangor to pump sand from beneath the pier, at £35 per day plus insurance. Later she went to Port Dinorwic where she was found unsuitable for the work. As she was no longer fully employed, her sale was considered but she remained in the fleet until 1934.

Included in the Wallasey Corporation Act 1927 were powers to provide cycle storage rooms with lockers at Seacombe and this provided an alternative for the passenger who wished to cycle to and from the ferry but who might have problems parking it at his place of employment or wanted to arrive at the office smartly dressed. The rates with locker were 4s. 0d. (20p) for three months, 7s. 6d. (37^1/2p) for six months and 14s. 0d. (70p) for one year. Without locker, the charge was 3d. per day, 3s. (15p) for three months, 5s. 6d. (27^1/2p) for six months and 10s. 0d. (50p) for a year. A similar service was extended to motorists when the new covered ferry car park opened in 1933, combined parking and ferry tickets being issued.

Following the inclusion of Moreton and Leasowe in Wallasey from 1st April 1928, through bus and ferry tickets at 8d. and 10d. were introduced to and from those outlying areas because Birkenhead offered a similar facility via Woodside and from 10th June 1928 a ticket from the Hotel Victoria, in the upper part of New Brighton was issued to Liverpool via Egremont at 10d. (later 9d.); this was not popular and was withdrawn from 1st April 1935 when it was found that only ten had been issued during the previous year. The Moreton and Leasowe tickets were very successful, the numbers issued in the mid-1930s being 149,199 (1934-35), 168,265 (1935-36) and 270,388 (1936-37). Circular tour tickets which included admission to the Derby Bathing Pool and the Promenade Pier were tried out with little success in 1932-33.

During the 1930s, the fares were relatively unchanged though the Seacombe weekly contract was increased to 1s. 4d. and then 1s. 5d. (7p). Both Egremont and New Brighton, where the single fares were 3^1/2d. and 6d., offered 6d. return tickets after 5.0pm though the New Brighton fare was 9d. on Sundays.

Fleet Replacement

Two new large steamers were now planned for the Seacombe service, to replace *Rose* and *Lily*, emphasis being placed on coal economy and the ability to absorb the additional peak hour traffic which followed the increase in the borough's population. A model was made which was specially tested by the National Physical laboratory at Teddington before details were finalised but nothing was done until the Unemployment Grants Committee indicated that a contribution would be made. In the meantime, the full Council demanded a study of the viability of a scheme to recondition *Rose* and *Lily* for five more years' service. However, in January 1926, having chosen the names *Wallasey* and *Marlowe*, the Council accepted the tender of Caledon Shipbuilding and Engineering Co., Dundee for £83,900 and the offer of T. W. Ward Ltd for £1,325 for each of the old boats was accepted. However. the aftermath of the General Strike and the continuing coal dispute was causing difficulty in getting materials and, in October 1926, there was no alternative but to cancel the deal with Ward's and renew the certificates for *Rose* and *Lily*. The trials of the new vessels were successfully completed in early July 1927, the contract speed of 12 knots being reached and *Wallasey* entered service on 19th July followed by *Marlowe* on 30th August.

They had many new features, in particular a beam measurement on the main deck of 47ft 6in, only slightly less than the luggage boats. There were 12 separate watertight compartments and five collision bulkheads and the design offered greatly increased strength in the regions most likely to be affected by collisions. There was a central hand pumping plant, boilers of return tube marine type, steam drying plant, Weir's latest design of condenser with independent dual air pumps and centrifugal circulating pump, exhaust steam feed water heater and Michell thrust blocks built integral with the main engines. But emphasis was placed on the Flettner rudders which were operated without the use of steam steering gear. The system, said to be new to the United Kingdom, was described as a modern adaptation of a system experimented with in the Navy before 1860 and adopted successfully by the German government, at first to steer large Zeppelin airships and latterly by a private firm on numerous vessels. It was manufactured by Harfield & Co., at Blaydon, Newcastle-upon-Tyne under a rigid guarantee and was expected to result in a saving of one ton of coal per ship per day. In fact the results were much better as the average daily coal consumption during December 1927 was 8.54 tons for *Wallasey* and 8.76 tons for *Marlowe*, giving an economy of four tons per day per vessel compared with the next best.

The fixed wooden awning on the promenade deck between bridge and stern was a new feature and other improved passenger amenities included roomier cabins, improved lighting and ventilation and larger lavatories. Passenger certificates for 2,283 (*Wallasey*) and 2,233 (*Marlowe*) were issued. These vessels worked mainly on Seacombe in their prime and gave yeoman service. For the first time,

they were financed from the department's reserves and the government grant which, capitalised, represented 24% of the purchase price.

Ward's were no longer interested in buying *Rose* and *Lily* which were sold to S. Gould acting on behalf of Palmer Bros. of Queenstown (Cobh) for £1,750; the delay in their disposal thus brought the Corporation an additional £850! Both vessels experienced a new lease of life in Irish waters.

More Troubles at Egremont

In 1927 an inspection revealed that Egremont stage was in urgent need of repair and a tender by Cleveland Bridge Engineering Co. Ltd at £28,816 was accepted. The Corporation had hoped to receive an Unemployment Assistance grant but their application for this was turned down together with a scheme for roofing the pier and stage at New Brighton. On 24th January 1928, the Ferries Committee actually recommended the permanent closure of Egremont but a special Council meeting on 13th February referred it back and at another special committee meeting on 21st February it was proposed to go ahead with the repairs. A Joint Transport Sub-Committee was appointed with three Ferries and three Tramways Committee representatives, their task being to explore means of greater co-operation to encourage people to use Egremont. The Finance Committee, who supported total closure, failed in an attempt to defer the repairs at Egremont until the Sub-Committee reported. The work involved reconstruction of the stage and bridge, the latter being widened by 3ft and was intended to be carried out during the winter of 1928-29. However, indecision resulted in closure being deferred until 8th April 1929, the ferry reopening on 26th June 1929. During closure, Egremont contract-holders had been given a refund of one shilling per week or could use New Brighton without extra charge.

Another golden opportunity to close the loss-making ferry station occurred on 28th May 1932 when a large oil tanker, *British Commander* drifted down on to the pier, demolishing several spans and dropping the bridge into the river. However, in the knowledge that the cost of repairs would be borne by insurers, everything was rebuilt. The bridge was placed in position on 17th July and the terminal reopened without ceremony on Tuesday, 1st August 1933, 3,380 passengers being carried on that day. In reality, Egremont had been redundant since the electrification of the tramways, only a vociferous minority ensuring its longevity.

Wallasey *and* Marlowe, *built in 1927 by the Ailsa company at Dundee were the largest passenger vessels to enter Mersey Ferries' service with certificates for 2,233 passengers. They were the mainstay of the Seacombe service for very many years. They had fixed wooden awnings over the aft promenade deck.*
J. B. C. McCann/Pam Eaton

The long pier at Egremont was something of an obstruction to shipping and it was partly damaged on 28th May 1932 by an oil tanker British Commander which drifted following engine failure. The bridge was dislodged but the stage remained afloat. Note the additional cross-bracing fitted to the pillars of the original pier and the rails upon which the running out stage ran.   G. Parry collection

Following repairs to Egremont pier after the British Commander *incident in 1932, the bridge is seen being replaced by the floating crane* Mammoth. *The ferry reopened on 1st August 1933 but was again struck by a coaster* Newlands *on the night of 12th May 1941. This time, there was no rebuilding and the pier was dismantled in 1947.*   G. Parry collection

The Three-Deck Steamers

Attention was then directed to the replacement of *Royal Iris* and *Royal Daffodil*, which were over 30 years old. *Royal Iris* was withdrawn at the end of the 1931 season and sold on 12th October. Unfortunately, the Corporation did nothing to protect the name which was sold with it. A new vessel was designed, to be named *Royal Iris II* the most notable feature being the provision of a third deck, aft of and at the level of, the bridge. The order was placed with Harland & Wolff at Govan with engines to be supplied by D. & W. Henderson. There were a number of mechanical innovations, her triple-expansion inverted three-cylinder engines having specially designed valves; Weir's steam condensing plant and the most modern pumping equipment were fitted. Power was transmitted to four bronze-bladed propellers through Michel thrust blocks and automatically lubricated stern tubes. Three single-ended two-furnaced Scotch boilers, fitted with Hotchkiss-type water circulators had internal steam dryers. This was to be the largest passenger ferry owned though her passenger certificate was for only 2,024, less than *Wallasey* and *Marlowe* which were seven feet longer. The non-smoking (aft) saloon, with Old English style panels and beams in old oak finish was fitted out and decorated by Heaton, Tabb &

Co. of Liverpool, green upholstered seating being covered with antique hide. Portions of the seating were fitted with divisions, providing a number of single seats. A specially commissioned painting of the storming of the mole at Zeebrugge in which her predecessor had taken part and a copy of the King's letter granting the 'Royal' prefix adorned the bulkhead. The forward (smoking) saloon was constructed in oak.

At 151ft long and 48ft 1in in beam her dimensions were close to those of a luggage boat, but her maximum draught compared to *Wallasey* had been reduced by 18in to 13ft, a difficult task achieved with the aid of the National Physical Laboratory, Teddington but essential if she was to be available to work to New Brighton at all states of the tide. Any three of her 21 watertight compartments could be flooded without impairing the safety of the ship. A new feature was the provision of sliding doors on the main promenade deck beneath the bridge so that the commuters, whose regular practice was to march around the deck five or six abreast in an anti-clockwise direction, would be better protected in adverse weather conditions. The smokestack was of greater diameter than those of the earlier steamers. She cost £43,290 and entered service on 10th May 1932 on the Seacombe service, becoming instantly popular with regular commuters. She was often used on New Brighton at holiday times.

Royal Iris II *was the first three deck ferry vessel and was built by Harland and Wolff at Govan in 1932. She was a popular crowd shifter and was renamed* St. Hilary *in 1950. She was sold in 1956 for further service in Holland.*

R. L. Wilson collection

For the 1932 and 1933 seasons, cruising duties were taken over by *Royal Daffodil* which operated with a grey hull lined out in red and a yellow funnel. However, she was the same age as *Royal Iris* and survived only because she was in slightly better condition. An order for her successor was placed with Cammell Laird & Co., at Birkenhead, the old boat being taken in part exchange. She was withdrawn in 1934 and subsequently sold, again with the name, to New Medway Steam Packet Co. with whom she served for four years before being broken up at Ghent in 1938.

A second large passenger vessel, very similar in appearance to *Royal Iris II* was built by Cammell Laird & Co., Birkenhead in 1934. *Royal Daffodil II* was the same length as her sister but two feet narrower at 46ft. Her saloons were built of the finest Burma teak lined internally with oak and, again, there was a 6ft x 4ft painting depicting the Zeebrugge raid. She was visually distinguishable by the wooden shelters over the staircases to the upper deck though these were later removed. Her powerful 1,200hp steam engines gave her a maximum speed of 12^1/$_4$ knots. She cost £44,790 (less £2,515 for the old vessel) and her passenger certificate was for 1,995. In between the two three-deckers, the coal barge was replaced by a new vessel *Emily II*, built by Cammell Laird in 1933. She cost £9,690 and

was delivered on 19th August 1933. Following a change to delivery of coal in sacks which could be tipped into bunkers through a 'coal hole' on deck, she was sold in 1937.

With four large capacity steamers in service, the department decided to dispose of *John Joyce* and *Snowdrop*. Dating from 1910, they were sold at the end of the 1936 season, *John Joyce* going to Cork Harbour Commissioners where she joined *Royal Iris* and survived until 1953. *Snowdrop* went to the London & North Eastern Railway for service between Granton and Burntisland on the Firth of Forth, renamed *Thane of Fife*. Neither vessel was replaced.

Competition by Road and Rail

When the first Mersey road tunnel opened on 18th July 1934 there was considerable concern about the effect it would have on the ferries. Tunnel tolls were about equal to those on the ferries but a speedier journey was possible, 24-hours a day, which was bound to lead to an increase in cross-river trips by car. It was not just the vehicle trips that would be lost as passengers could also travel by car instead of ferry. The undertaking as a whole had been showing a modest profit year by year but the surplus on

Royal Daffodil II was built by Cammell Laird at Birkenhead in 1934 and whilst of very similar appearance to Royal Iris II was not identical, being two feet less in the beam. She is seen en route from New Brighton to Liverpool in her early years. She was renamed St. Hilary in 1957 and sold in 1962.

M. Jenkins collection

the passenger services was just about equal to the loss on the goods service. On 2nd March 1935, a sub-committee was appointed to investigate means of reducing ferry costs and examine the desirability of combining the ferries and bus undertakings as a single transport department. One of their early findings was that between October 1934 and February 1935 the average number of passengers on the New Brighton service had been just 32 per trip with revenue of 5s.3d (26p) compared with costs of 19s.1d (95p) thus establishing a good case for winter closure. In the financial year 1934-35, which included the first nine months of competition from the Mersey Tunnel, the number of vehicles conveyed on the goods steamers was 403,346 compared with 527,508 in 1933-34, a reduction of 121,162 (23%), an average of 332 per day, though carryings still averaged over 1,000 vehicles per day. The extensive use of horse-drawn vehicles, which were excluded from the tunnel, by the Great Western Railway ensured the retention of a nucleus of ferry traffic.

New Brighton Ferry Pier Improvements

The Council believed that there was a need to improve the facilities at New Brighton to enable the huge crowds carried in the peak summer periods to be handled more safely and expeditiously.

Poor bank holiday and summer weather could cause wide variations in passenger figures from year to year as is demonstrated by the figures for 1927-33 reproduced below.

The figures apply to the whole weekends and the contrast between 1932 and 1933 is instructive, 1933 with three fair weekends showing a 44% increase compared with 1932 which had none. In those days August Bank Holiday was on the first Monday in August.

Plans were drawn up for work costing £25,000 comprising renewing some of the girders and most of the diagonal bracing, adding new columns, widening the pier deck and completely rebuilding the booking hall. The original columns were 60ft apart and some new ones were placed between them to halve this distance, others being used to support the widened ticket office. The pier was divided laterally into three separate walkways between the booking office and the shore to allow for two to be used in the prevailing direction of flow. Two were 11ft wide and one was 16ft. Between the ticket office and the bridges there were two separate walkways, each 17ft 6in wide, one up and one down,

It was decided to do this work, partly using ferries staff, during the winter of 1935-36 and the ferry was closed on 1st October 1935; there was, of course, an outcry from the vocal minority of regular users but matters soon settled down and the point had been proved that no serious inconvenience would be caused by permanent winter closure. From 1st October 1936 both northern ferries closed once more for the winter, establishing a regular practice. Strangely there was a steep rise in wages and other costs and one boat was kept tied up at Egremont during the winter and councillors were left wondering if the closure had resulted in any actual savings. Certainly the displaced passengers did not show up at Seacombe where, contrary to expectations, revenue fell by an average of £120 per day in November 1936.

Further trouble was looming. In the same month contracts were awarded for the electrification of the LMS Railway branch to New Brighton causing yet more concern about the effect on the ferries revenue. A direct electric service between New Brighton and Liverpool Central started on 14th March 1938. There was a loss of revenue on all parallel bus services but the effect on the ferry was harder to ascertain as

		Bank Holiday Weather		
Year	Easter	Whit	August	No. of passengers
1927	Fair	Dull	Fair	933,177
1928	Fair	Dull	Fair	990,447
1929	Fair	Fair	Dull	934,540
1930	Dull	Fair	Dull	856,041
1931	Dull	Dull	Fair	829,652
1932	Inclement	Dull	Dull	739,183
1933	Fair	Fair	Fair	1,065,277

only the northern end of the borough was served by the railway. An estimate of £5,000 per annum from railway competition was made. There was a fall of some 200,000 passengers at New Brighton in 1938-39 but it was more than regained in the following year. But travel patterns of regular passengers were changed as many workers in Liverpool who had used the ferry now found it possible to come home by train for lunch, the extra travel costing nothing if a season ticket was purchased. The withdrawal of the Seacombe-West Kirby train service no doubt resulted in the loss of a few passengers at Seacombe though through bookings to and from the London and North Eastern Railway service from Wrexham continued. The railway booking office on George's landing stage remained open at least until the outbreak of war in 1939 and possibly later.

From the seasonal resumption of the northern ferries on 3rd April 1938, only weekly and monthly contracts were issued. The spiralling decline of Egremont was highlighted when only 541 passengers used it on Whit Saturday 1938.

Capt. W. H. Fry, RNR, general manager since 1913, retired on reaching the age of 65 in February 1939. He had been honoured in 1933 when he was appointed a Freeman of the City of London for services to the Honourable Company of Master Mariners of which he was a founder member. He was not to enjoy retirement for long as he died on 18th February 1940.

The Council appointed as manager at a salary of £850 x £50 to £1,000, Lt.Cdr. L. D. Price, RNR, Harbour master, pilot master and quay manager at Wisbech for the past eight years. He had been an apprentice and sea-going officer with P. & O. Line from 1922-30 followed by master of a private yacht. He had considerable experience of maintenance and repairs of ships, piers, landing stages, workshops and machinery and was an acknowledged expert on coal economy. He was destined to guide the ferries through the difficult war years and the challenging peace which followed.

Francis Storey, *sister ship to* J. Farley, *is shown with grey hull and yellow funnel as the cruise vessel in 1934. She went to the Navy as a net defence vessel in 1942 and after returning to the Mersey was sold to Cork Harbour Commissioners in 1951 and renamed* Killarney.

G. Parry collection

The Seacombe luggage boat Wallasey and a Woodside vessel load at Liverpool in 1911 as the Royal Liver Building nears completion. Note the scaffolding on the towers and the absence of Liver Birds.

G. Parry collection

6 THE LUGGAGE BOATS

ON the Mersey, vehicular or goods boats were always referred to as 'luggage boats'. Braithwaite Poole echoed local opinion in a pamphlet he wrote in 1860 complaining of the lack of facilities at Seacombe and Egremont for the handling of merchandise of any description. On deciding to settle in Egremont, he had been forced to send his household goods by way of Tranmere ferry where the proprietors employed three men, three carts and three horses to deliver anywhere in Birkenhead and Wallasey. There was no means by which intending visitors could send their luggage in advance for collection at Seacombe. Poole advocated the introduction of a 'luggage' or goods service once the ferries were taken into municipal ownership in August 1861. The Seacombe boats had for centuries transported agricultural produce and live animals but this had never involved porterage or delivery.

The passenger boats were first used for conveyance of goods but in February 1862, *Elizabeth*, which had been declared unfit for passenger traffic had its decks cleared at a cost of £247 and became Wallasey's first dedicated 'luggage boat'. A scale of charges covered every conceivable consignment from live animals to expensive household furniture. *Elizabeth* made three daily trips, the last leaving Liverpool at 4.0pm, with an extra trip on market days at 5.30am from Seacombe. Horses, carts and light luggage were conveyed on passenger boats until 6.0pm.

Traffic increased but so did costs and the elderly *Elizabeth* was losing 18s. 2d. (92p) per day; she was withdrawn at the end of April 1863 and replaced by a new arrangement whereby two boats covered both passengers and goods. The first (usually *Wild Rose*) sailed from 5.30am to midnight carrying only passengers while the second (either *Wallasey* or *Thomas Wilson*) carried passengers at peak times but goods only from Seacombe at 11.0am, 1.0 and 3.0pm and from Liverpool at 10.30am, 2.0, 3.30 and 7.0pm. This practice of carrying goods, animals and passengers on the same boat survived for nearly 20 years and was an obvious health hazard. In hot weather the stench was overpowering and, especially in rough weather, animals frequently fouled the deck. The crews were expected to keep the decks swilled and scrubbed but, with other duties to perform, this was easier said than done.

In order to separate goods from waiting

The luggage boat Wallasey *is seen tied up at Seacombe in its last days in service. Built at Preston and based on the Birkenhead steamer* Oxton, *she plied the river from 1882 to 1925. The picture was taken at half-tide as the goods bridge is at a useable angle; the high level bridge can just be discerned behind. In the background is the clock tower which housed the hydraulic machinery and Seacombe Ferry Hotel.*

M. Jenkins collection

passengers, the hull of *Elizabeth* was anchored off the end of Seacombe running out stage in March 1864, the centre part being used by passengers, one end for coal and the other for goods. She remained there until moved to New Brighton in October 1865. There was often congestion at Seacombe on market days when scores of hampers would be loaded on to the 5.30am boat; on arrival at Liverpool unloading was hindered by large numbers of labourers en route to their work at Birkenhead docks demanding an immediate departure for Seacombe to avoid losing pay. Low rated cargoes such as bricks, cement, hay and domestic coal were often carried in an iron flat, (similar to a coaling flat) purchased in 1863, towed by a passenger vessel. Deliveries were made to all three terminals.

In February 1867 Wallasey Local Board published a comprehensive list of tolls for conveyance of goods, cattle, carriages etc. The list reveals the wide variety of goods as well as something of the life-style of the times. Some examples follow:-

Ale & Porter, per hogshead	4d (1.66p)
Spirits, Wine, Pipe, Puncheon or Tierce	1/6d (7.5p)
Bicycle	2d (0.83p)
Perambulator	1d (0.42p)
Cart (loaded or empty) with two horses	1/9d (8.75p)
Adult corpse accompanied by four men, to New Brighton	6/- (30p)
Hearse and four horses	5/- (25p)
Child's coffin (empty)	6d (2.5p)
Chimney tops	1d (0.42p)
Fire grates	3d (1.25p)
Ice, per cwt	2d (0.83p)
Mussels, per bag	1d (0.42p)
Pigs, dead or alive	1d (0.42p)
Sofa	3d (1.25p)
Lump of salt	$\frac{1}{4}$d (0.1p)

Tallow, per cwt	1d (0.42p)
Guano, per ton	2/6d (12.5p)
Wool, per bale	8d (3.33p)

The Dock Board cooperated in the Local Board's effort to improve facilities by increasing Wallasey's footage on the Liverpool landing stage thus facilitating the advertising of regular departures from the south end of Prince's stage instead of the north end of George's stage. A small hut was erected and freight and luggage clerks were employed on both sides of the river. From 2nd December 1867 a new parcels service was advertised aimed at providing speedy deliveries between all parts of Wallasey and the Liverpool railway termini in conjunction with the Liverpool Parcels Delivery Company. James Hall, who still handled the traffic on the Wallasey side, published his tolls in 1869 viz:-

To any part of Seacombe, Poulton or Liscard – the same as the ferry toll. As far as the old gates in Field Road, Upper Brighton – half as much again as the ferry toll. Into Upper Brighton – double the ferry toll.

In August 1870, the Board franchised their parcel business to J. Hall for £49 per annum together with their van and two horses for £40; in 1875 the business passed to another local haulier, Henry Bryant. These improved facilities gradually persuaded residents to send their merchandise via Seacombe instead of Tranmere or Woodside which had offered a superior system of collection and delivery.

However, the luggage boats were rarely full; in 1867 there were three daily crossings from Seacombe and four from Liverpool. As well as goods, these sailings handled the majority of livestock. In a cost-cutting exercise in the winter

This picture was also used in Volume 1 but it is the only view of an early purpose-built luggage boat, this being Birkenhead's Oxton on which the design of Wallasey's Sunflower was loosely based. Note that a high proportion of the merchandise was sent loose, involving porterage and, doubtless, breakages and loss.

of 1868-69, goods were not handled between 8.0am and 11.0am so that the second vessel could be devoted solely to passenger traffic at the time of peak demand and from 22nd October 1868, the morning sailings were cancelled allowing all the ferry services to be run with three vessels. This pattern continued until June 1873 when an early boat at 4.30am was run on Wednesdays and Saturdays for the conveyance of market garden produce. It operated in July, October and November but was withdrawn on 22nd November due to poor patronage. In August 1873 it was decided that, in future, parcels would be carried only on the luggage boat.

The policy was to cascade the goods boats from the passenger service when they were no longer considered fit or were nearing the end of their lives. In 1864 *Tiger* worked her last few months this way; *Wallasey* was demoted to luggage duties on 26th May 1864, a role she fulfilled until 1st December 1867 when she sank during a violent storm. Her place was taken by *Thomas Wilson* which also continued to work a limited number of early passenger trips from Seacombe. Despite suffering many mid-river failures during which she was coaxed into action by her tenacious captain, Richard 'Foggy Dickie' Fenby, she soldiered on, until her passenger certificate was withdrawn in March 1877. She made her last luggage crossing

on 24th July 1877. Many carters and draymen recalled Fenby bellowing down the speaking tube to his engineer, Richard Davies, every time the steam shortened and watching Davies come on deck to insert a crowbar through the grating allowing him to lever the crank round for a fresh start. She was succeeded by *James Atherton* which, although in poor condition, maintained the service until 31st March 1880.

During the weeks following the fire which virtually destroyed George's Landing Stage on 28th July 1874, the luggage boats were suspended and all commodities were towed across in flats. At the height of the fire, the crew of *Thomas Wilson* persuaded the proprietor of Simpson's refreshment room to save his furniture and fittings by carrying them on board. A partial service was restored during the winter of 1874-75 but the full service was not resumed until April 1876 when the landing stage came back into use. Development in Wallasey was hampered during this time as it was difficult to obtain building materials in any quantity.

The Seacombe Goods Terminal

As part of the new Seacombe ferry works, it was decided to provide for a much expanded goods traffic. This was to be completely separated from

Wallasey, the first broad beamed luggage boat unloads at Seacombe landing stage. The goods bridge with advertisements for Russell's Watches is clearly visible but the gradient is too steep for several horse-drawn carts which are making for the goods lift on the right. The superstructure on this vessel occupied more space than on the later vessels.

Priestley & Co.

the passenger service. As explained in Chapter 3, having studied the floating roadways at Liverpool and Woodside, the manager, William Carson, changed his mind and settled for a fixed goods bridge which would be useful for about five hours (and longer for light traffic which could negotiate the gradient at low tide) in every tide and two hydraulic lifts. This was estimated to be cheaper as the cost of maintaining an incline would be incurred whether or not there was traffic whilst the cost of working the lifts would be incurred only when revenue was being earned.

It is not clear whether the idea originated with Carson or the Ferries Committee but the belief that there was a potentially lucrative traffic in moving railway wagons across the river led to the planned incorporation of rails and capstans on the approaches (including the hydraulic lifts) and landing stage and on the early purpose-built goods boats. Members of a ferry sub-committee went to Scotland to observe the steamers which carried railway wagons between Granton and Burntisland. The movement of single wagons was envisaged, using a series of winches, capstans and turntables on a tortuous path from the railway sidings in Birkenhead Road down to the stage. End-loading of the vessels was adopted with an embayment at Seacombe landing stage and the southern end of the ferry approach was designed to be laid out as a railway goods yard. It is surprising that so much money was sunk into this project when there had never been any suggestion that matching facilities would be provided at Liverpool as the Dock Board was positively hostile to the scheme. As it happened, there was already an embayment built into the Liverpool stage, born of the mistaken belief that the luggage boats would have difficulty in

berthing without one. However, the Woodside boats had never used it so the Dock Board agreed to install a large balanced gangway to facilitate end-loading.

It was thought that, with improved facilities, the existing small parcels service could be developed into a lucrative source of revenue. A report said 'A Receiving Place in Liverpool and two or more daily deliveries in Cheshire should be established to create this income which would be nearly all profit as boys can be taught to do the work'.

The specification for the first purpose-built luggage boat, *Sunflower* required her to be capable of carrying 100 tons; her deck height was not to exceed 6ft when light and her draught was not to exceed 5ft unladen. Her dimensions were 140ft 2in by 26ft 2in by 9ft and her hull was divided into seven watertight compartments. She had a large overhang fore and aft rendering her deck almost circular and if her load was badly distributed she would develop a severe list. Her speed was to be not less than nine knots. She made her first trial trip from the Seacombe luggage embayment on 19th January 1880 as a result of which alterations were made to one end of the vessel. Her first revenue-earning trip was on 1st April 1880 when the service was transferred to the new stage; a two-hourly service was operated. On 29th April work began on removing the rails from her deck, her place on the service being briefly taken by *James Atherton* which was sold for scrap soon after. Despite assurances that *Sunflower* was working well, it soon became apparent that she was unsuitable for the traffic.

Birkenhead's first purpose-built luggage boat, *Oxton* had entered service in 1879 and a second vessel, *Bebington* had been added in 1880. They were designed by J. Taylor and had clear decks except for a central 'island' which included the smokestack, bridge and ticket office. They were extremely manoeuvrable side-loading double twin-screw steamers and proved very stable, even in rough weather. Taylor offered to design a boat for Wallasey but it was turned down on the grounds that end-loading was required. However, tenders were immediately invited for a vessel to be very similar to *Oxton* but incorporating end loading. The order went to the builders of *Bebington*, Allsups of Preston at £11,350.

The new boat, named *Wallasey*, was launched on 10th September 1881 and entered service in February 1882. As built she had no gangways only openings on both sides closed by sliding doors. Forward, the deck was slightly ramped downwards towards a pair of doors which swung inwards. Gangways were installed on the landing stages. She had a passenger certificate for 100. She was an immediate success and traffic increased rapidly. In the year ending 25th March 1880 tolls at Seacombe were £743, a year later £1,743 and by 1885 over £3,000. Negligible amounts were still handled at the northern ferries, there being occasional special luggage boat sailings for exceptionally heavy loads. Demand at Seacombe resulted in an increased service from 15th November 1880 with early boats on Saturdays and weekday sailings up to 5.0pm from Seacombe and 5.30pm from Liverpool; a month later the service was extended by a further two hours. Early morning sailings were essential to market people and others but loadings were light and it was decided to convert *Waterlily* to a combined passenger and goods boat so in March 1883 her forward cabin was removed clearing a space for vehicles and animals, the whole conversion being done in seven weeks by Grayson's yard at a cost of £2,130.

The master and crew of *Wallasey* became experts at viewing the waiting traffic as they approached the stage and mentally positioning them on the vessel to spread the load in the most efficient way.

The end-loading embayments were not a success and by September 1883 the Seacombe one was showing structural weaknesses. It was decided to fill it in but the work was not done as Birkenhead Corporation objected to the prospect of *Wallasey* unloading broadside on at the north end of George's stage, claiming it was their exclusive berth. The Dock Board concurred so both embayments had to remain in use. However, when the Board became anxious to fill in the embayment, they agreed to pay £175 to convert *Wallasey* to broadside loading only. The work was done during October 1888, *Waterlily* handling the traffic in the meantime. Liverpool embayment was finally filled in in 1894, the Board having given one day's notice on 12th March that work would start and that the Seacombe boats must somehow share one berth with those plying to Woodside.

As a result of increasing traffic and improved availability of vessels, the luggage service was stepped up to half-hourly in 1895 but the facilities at Seacombe could not handle the traffic quickly enough and the frequency had to be modified to 40 minutes. In 1901, the Council decided to acquire a second purpose-built luggage boat, the successful tenderer being Cochran of Annan. This vessel, named *Seacombe* was of similar design to *Wallasey* but five feet wider at 50ft. She was launched on 28th September 1901 and entered service in January 1902, the builders being fined £1,250 because the stipulated speed was not reached. As traffic increased, congestion caused by waiting carts became a problem on both sides of the river. With only one berth at Seacombe, there was nowhere for vehicles to queue to enable a vessel to be loaded

Seacombe, *the second wide beam luggage boat was placed in service in 1901 when traffic had increased considerably. She was over five feet wider than* Wallasey *so able to carry a greater load. She was broken up in 1929 when* Perch Rock *took her place on the service.*
The Collingwood Collection

The controversial embayment at the south end of Princes landing stage was built as it was thought that the broad-beamed luggage boats would have difficulty in getting away from the stage in bad weather. The end loading gangway was built for the Wallasey boat Wallasey *which was equipped to carry railway wagons. The embayment was filled in during 1894 at Dock Board expense.* Wallasey Tramway Preservation Group

A busy scene in 1925 at the foot of the floating roadway on Liverpool landing stage. One of the two Birkenhead berths is unoccupied and the Seacombe berth further north is occupied by Seacombe. *The passing New Brighton boat is* Snowdrop *or* John Joyce. Liverpool City Engineer

The end of the High Level goods bridge at Seacombe with lift attendants posing for the camera. The south lift is at the upper level waiting to receive a vehicle while the gate is across the entrance to the north lift which is at the stage level.

M. Jenkins collection

quickly. The ferries management again raised the question of a floating roadway in February 1902 but the idea was rejected because, within the length available, the gradient would have been 1 in 16 at low tide. However, approval was given to spending £11,530 on the installation of a modern hydraulic system to work the existing goods lifts. Work began in April 1903 and included the filling in of the disused embayment in the Seacombe stage and the building of an improved approach to Birkenhead Road. It was not finished until August 1904.

During the installation of new hydraulic machinery to work the lifts, carts were hauled up the goods bridge by teams of horses provided by local cartage contractors, R. & J. Evans. There were occasional accidents as carters struggled to guide their teams into the lifts and also when persuading reluctant horses to board steamers tossing and pitching in stormy weather. In January 1906 there were two serious accidents, one in which a carter was killed while attempting to calm a terrified horse and another when one horse of a team stumbled and fell between the vessel and the stage.

Wallasey was taken out of service in September 1906 and fully overhauled, new boilers being fitted by Rollo & Co. She re-entered service on 12th December when *Seacombe* was released for her annual survey.

In the first decade of the 20th century, traffic increased by 50% and the provision of a regular two-boat service was under active consideration. For one week, commencing 18th December 1911, an experimental two-boat 15-minute service was run between 8.0am and 7.0pm but a census revealed that although 405 additional cash-paying

vehicles had been carried, the numbers of vehicles of credit account customers had decreased by 63. The additional revenue was only £20. 14. 9d. (£20.74), far below the sum needed to cover the cost of the extra boat. The Corporation's Finance and General Purposes Committee had their feet much more firmly on the ground than the Ferries Committee and a report was made by the Chairman of the former in 1912:-

'The luggage traffic result is all too obviously unsatisfactory if examined in detail. ... there was a loss of £1,732 without a penny piece being charged for management and establishment expenses, loan charges or renewals contribution. ... A proposal is before you to add a new luggage boat. In the interests of the borough, efficient means of transit for goods must, of course, be provided but it would appear that unless some radical change be effected in the boat-building policy of the Committee, both the Luggage and Passenger departments will seriously affect our finances. ... While our goods receipts remain constant, the annual cost of conducting the traffic is rising and will still further increase if the building of expensive types of boats is to be persisted in. My observations as to the financial effect of adopting the recent boat-building recommendations are these:-
"... If three new boats* are obtained, as proposed, it means raising the all-round cost of steaming to about 24/- (£1.20) per hour whereas the ferry receipts cannot stand anything over 18/6d. (92^1/$_2$p) per hour (the cost of the '[John] Joyce and Snowdrop)"'.
* Two passenger and one luggage.

The Finance Committee was rightly warning the Ferries Committee against the policy of building

N.B.—The Corporation are not required to carry on board their Boats any aquafortis, oil of vitriol, naphtha, benzine, petroleum, gunpowder, lucifer matches, nitro-glycerine, or any other goods of a dangerous nature. Any person sending or conveying by the Ferry Boats any such goods without distinctly marking their nature on the outside of the package containing the same, and giving notice in writing of nature of such goods to the master of the boat, book-keeper or other servant of the Corporation with whom the same are left, at or before the time of sending or taking on board, is liable to a penalty not exceeding £100 for every such offence, and such goods may be thrown overboard.

A person sending any such goods under a false description is liable to a penalty not exceeding £500.

Persons committing any breach of the Rules of the Explosives Act, 1875, with respect to the packing of Explosives, are subject to penalties not exceeding £20 in each case.

NOTICE.—If any person knowingly or wilfully refuses or neglects to pay his Fare or Toll for using the Ferry when the same is payable, every such person will be liable to a penalty not exceeding forty shillings.

H. W. COOK,
Town Clerk.

Oct. 29th, 1915.

County Borough of Wallasey.

TOLLS & CHARGES

For the Conveyance of

VEHICLES, GOODS, &c.

SEACOMBE FERRY, EGREMONT FERRY,
AND
NEW BRIGHTON FERRY.

From April 1st, 1916, and until further notice

(Cancelling all previous Lists).

Charles Birchall, Ltd., Printers, 17, James St., L'pool.

Any Articles not particularly enumerated hereon as per special arrangement.

The Corporation are not responsible for the handling or storing of any articles or things carried by the Ferry Boats.

The Tolls above mentioned for the conveyance of Vehicles or Animals include the Fare for the Driver or Drover.

An additional charge will be made for overhanging loads on the following scale:—

5 feet and under 10 feet ...	6d.
10 feet and under 15 feet ...	9d.
15 feet and under 20 feet ...	1s.
Over 20 feet	2s.

The Goods Steamers are not allowed to sail with the gangway or gangways down without special permission from the Ferries Manager.

Double Tolls will be charged on Bicycles, Handcarts, Parcels, &c., carried by the Night Boats between the hours of 12·40 a.m. and 4·30 a.m., inclusive.

For Rates for special trips per Goods Boats apply to:—

WILL. H. FRY,
FERRIES MANAGER.

expensive, heavy boats unless contract charges or tolls were raised or a rate of at least 4d. in the £ was levied until 1923. However, in the aftermath of a campaign by the Dock Board to encourage livestock traffic which caused Birkenhead to reduce tolls, from 31st January 1913, charges for livestock were reduced – cattle from 6d. to 4d. and sheep from 1s. 6d to 1s. per score. Between 1st April 1916 and 22nd February 1916, 5,288 cattle, 86 sheep and 193 pigs were carried.

However, the Council realised that if traffic continued to grow, a two-boat service would be an absolute necessity so they sanctioned the purchase of a new luggage boat, possibly to be oil fired, to replace the 30-year old *Wallasey*. The outbreak of war in 1914 caused this to be postponed for seven years. In the same year, to speed up turnround, both goods vessels were fitted with steam-operated gangways, powered by separate donkey-engines, and a steam-driven winch was installed at the head of the road bridge to haul up the heaviest loads when the gradient proved too steep for the horses.

During the war, traffic fluctuated with increased usage in 1916 which was not maintained. With the war at an end, there was a tremendous explosion of traffic leading to even longer queues and waits of two or three hours were not uncommon. These costly delays became a cause celèbre and added considerable impetus to the proposed under-river tunnel proposals. Although the Seacombe goods ferry was in competition with Birkenhead's Woodside passage, the operating conditions were quite different. Since 1868, Woodside had benefited from a floating roadway provided by the Dock Board thus making loading and unloading much more efficient. Furthermore there was a much greater flow of industrial traffic; in 1915-16 Woodside carried 428,881 vehicles compared with Seacombe's 185,291. In 1915, Birkenhead abolished all rebates (discounts) for credit account holders, with one exception, describing the practice as 'a pernicious system which should not be tolerated and utterly against the interests of the Birkenhead ratepayers'. The exception was the Great Western Railway which, despite the fact that its rails ended in Birkenhead, carried on an extensive business in Liverpool where it had several receiving and delivery depots. Until 1922, a declining proportion of this traffic was barged across the river but most was conveyed by cart using the goods ferry. The Great Western retained their reduced rebate at Woodside until June 1918 when the system was finally abolished.

The Ferries' management saw this as a wonderful opportunity to increase their revenue and, despite the inferiority of its infrastructure, persuaded the Great Western to switch its traffic to Seacombe. Rebates were also extended to other customers at the rate of 25% on a volume of £300 per month. In September 1920, the rebate was increased to 30% on this volume and, a month later, to $32^1/_2\%$ on £350 and $35^1/_2\%$ on £400 per month. The GWR qualified for this maximum rate and the Finance Committee's advice to stop these discounts was ignored by the Ferries Committee. Their effect on the revenue is clear from the following summary:-

Year ended 31 Mar	Gross Receipts £	Rebate £	Net Receipts £
1919	2,550	638	1,912
1920	3,448	862	2,586
1921	4,940	1,500	3,440
1922	6,228	2,211	4,017
1923	7,315	2,597	4,715

The Committee had failed to realise that, as long as Birkenhead paid no rebates, they needed to offer only a minimum reduction, say 5%, in order to secure the traffic and, by the end of 1925, probably as a result of pressure from the Finance Committee, they were thinking in terms of no rebate on receipts of under £2,500, $7^1/_2\%$ on £2,500-5,000, 10% on £5,000-7,500 and $12^1/_2\%$ on £7,500-10,000. This was taken back for reconsideration and discussions with Birkenhead, a formula being proposed whereby each higher rate applied only in respect of the incremental traffic. The Ferries Committee's lack of understanding of the financial consequences of their decisions is clear from the following statistics for the years 1916-22. Only the profitability of the passenger services prevented the department from virtual bankruptcy.

Year ended 31 Mar	Receipts £	No.of Vehicles	Loss on Trading £
1914	10,703	160,000	1,228
1915	10,969	170,000	3,559
1916	12,019	185,291	8,049
1917	14,385	172,297	7,165
1918	12,373	149,071	9,454
1919	14,908	168,876	13,060
1920	19,097	213,449	20,367
1921	21,863	210,939	22,987
1922	26,109	230,991	28,154
1923	26,642	242,880	13,927
1924	32,641	273,523	
1925	34,513	283,399	
1926	35,403	293,603	

Rebates were abolished from 30th May 1923 and the Great Western railway traffic was lost as rates were equal to those at Woodside which was nearer than Seacombe to Morpeth Dock goods station but traffic continued to increase.

Two new luggage boats commissioned in 1921 set a new standard for the vehicular ferry which was to last until its closure. *Liscard* and *Leasowe*, built by J. I. Thornycroft & Co. at Southampton, were longer at 146ft 3in than their predecessors and, at 50ft 1in beam were about the same as the 20-year old *Seacombe*. Each was equipped with a flying bridge, making for an uncluttered deck which aided vehicle manoeuvrability. They were designed to meet the challenge of the great increase in traffic in the post-war years and were speedier than the earlier vessels. The two-boat service was introduced on 30th September 1921, the 40-year old *Wallasey* being kept in reserve; in 1923 her use as a coal barge was considered and rejected so she was finally broken up in 1925. The new fast boats enabled the traffic to be handled more expeditiously though the limitations of the lifts and bridges and the lack of space on the landing stage still governed the rate of despatch at Seacombe. The lengthening of Liverpool landing stage in 1922 to provide two berths for the Woodside goods boats eased matters there; hitherto the Woodside boats had been allowed to use the Seacombe berth when the Wallasey boat was not alongside but inevitably there were occasions when the berth could not be cleared in time.

The decision to order two instead of one new luggage boat played havoc with the Ferries' finances, particularly as they were large, sophisticated and expensive. They cost £213,445 and, although they were not paid for when post-war inflation was at its peak, interest rates were high and loan charges totalled £21,650 per annum for 20 years. Of £500,000 6% Corporation stock issued at 95^1/$_2$%, 62% was used for ferry purposes.

For the use of the Dock Board's facilities for carrying vehicles and goods traffic, the ferry operators paid a percentage of the gross tolls. Birkenhead paid 25% for the use of floating roadways and two landing stages on the Liverpool and Cheshire sides, all provided by the Dock Board but, as early as 1891, they had negotiated a revenue ceiling. Wallasey, who provided all their own facilities on the Cheshire side paid 16% on all tolls with no ceiling. In January 1923, they rather belatedly discovered that Birkenhead was getting a better deal and the Dock Board was approached with a view to securing a reduction. The Board agreed to continue the same percentage with a ceiling of £4,000 on the tolls for a period of eight years with effect from 7th July 1923. This effectively reduced the percentage to 11-12% which fell further as traffic increased. From 1st April 1923, the passenger and goods accounts were separated.

The luggage boats were manned for 24 hours and the night watch was kept busy on various housekeeping tasks. The vessel was cleaned and scrubbed from stem to stern, the decks being treated with sand and water to remove all traces of animal waste matter, the bulk being removed as it was dropped and thrown overboard. The brasses were lightly polished and the windows cleaned.

In the summer of 1925 a trial luggage boat service, primarily for private cars, was run on Sundays for two months. In the aftermath of the General Strike, Sunday services were suspended during the coal shortage in June 1926.

The Floating Roadway

The extended Seacombe landing stage and floating roadway was part of the overall modernisation of the ferry terminal described in Chapter 5. The floating roadway which measured 590ft long and 45ft wide, was the largest structure of its kind. It floated level on a 29ft tide and grounded for its whole length on concrete beds at low water. It was built in five linked spans secured to the stage and shore by six suspended spans. Each of the spans was supported on eight steel pontoons placed transversely in the river and fore and aft in the cut. The superstructure comprised a series of eight girders and, owing to the racking effect of the heavy loads which the structure had to carry, steel construction was considered to be too rigid, the girders being built up from Oregon pine logs which were specially imported in order to get the desired length without splicing.

The new southern part of the stage could accommodate vehicles of 30 tons weight with a maximum axle weight of 20 tons. Unlike the Liverpool and Woodside twin-track roadways, the Seacombe floating roadway had three lanes so that, when vehicles were discharged from the boat, the fast traffic could make use of the centre carriageway and the slow traffic the south side, the third being reserved for down traffic. The wheel tracks were made up of half-inch steel plates with wood block horse tracks between them. The roadway was officially opened by Lord Derby and brought into service for public use on 23rd October 1926.

The floating roadway revolutionised the handling of vehicular traffic. It was the job of the Mate to plan the stowage of vehicles so as to get the maximum number on board without creating a problem for unloading at the other side. As the boat approached the landing stage he would view the waiting vehicles and, in his mind's eye, plan the order in which he would call them for embarkation knowing exactly where each one should be stowed on board. At quiet times, vehicles could run straight off the floating roadway on to the vessel. There were still problems at low tide when horses hauling heavily loaded carts needed assistance and, from the opening day the local

Sister ships Leasowe and Liscard were built by Thornycrofts at Southampton in 1921 and were much faster than their predecessors despite their crabwise passage across the river. Flying bridges minimised intrusion upon the deck space. The gangways were power operated. Leasowe was scrapped in 1948 but Liscard went to Denmark where she was converted into a salvage vessel named Lisca.

G. Parry collection

Liscard lies in Egerton Dock, Birkenhead with her derrick still on deck after wartime service unloading aircraft fuselages and wings from ships in mid-river. Her hydraulic gangways have been removed. Note the deck surface, designed to give horses' hooves a good grip.   G. Parry collection

contractor, Charles L. Warren, supplied two 'pull-up' horses and drivers at £1 per day per horse and per man for a period of three months at the expiry of which tenders were invited for the service.

Some Liverpool-Wallasey traffic had used Woodside because of its three- or four-boat service and the floating roadways at both sides and much of this now transferred to Seacombe where the fast boats and new facilities provided a speedier journey. A late theatre boat, aimed at attracting the increasing numbers of affluent private car owners, was tried from October 1926 but discontinued due to poor support in March 1927. From 23rd April 1928, the finishing times of the goods service were extended to 10.0pm on weekdays instead of 3.0pm on Saturdays and 8.0pm on Mondays to Fridays. A regular hourly Sunday service between 10.0am and 9.30pm commenced on 20th May. A half-hourly service between 10.30pm and midnight was given a two-week trial for visitors to Blackpool Illuminations in September-October 1930. Increased tolls were generally charged on Sundays.

The greater use of private cars created a new class of regular user and books of 12 tickets were sold from 1927 at 15 shillings (75p) for cars up to 12ft

long or 12 hp and £1. 2s. 6d. (£1.125) for cars up to 14ft long or 14 hp. Books of prepaid tickets were also sold for passengers travelling in cars.

In 1927 both Birkenhead and Wallasey appointed sub-committees to discuss collaboration between the two goods ferries. Birkenhead's floating roadway was 60 years old and needed repairs which could not be done while it remained open for traffic. Wallasey proposed a charge of £150 per week or 10% of the gross tolls for use of their floating roadway and the latter option was agreed on 2nd November. These arrangements were put into practice in January 1928 when Woodside floating roadway was closed for repairs from 6.0pm on Saturdays 21st and 28th January to 6.0am Mondays 23rd and 30th. On each occasion a combined service was run using three Birkenhead and two Wallasey boats. Birkenhead also agreed to lend a luggage boat to Wallasey in the event of an emergency during the next five years or until the opening of the tunnel. It seems that Wallasey Council was not altogether comfortable with this arrangement. *Liscard* and *Leasowe* were only six years old and were adequate for the normal service but the ageing *Seacombe*, built in 1901, was the only back-up and was reaching the end of her useful life. On the face of it, she could be withdrawn without replacement and a Birkenhead boat hired when necessary. The Council preferred to stand on its own feet and, despite the financial implications, ordered another expensive replacement vessel of similar design to *Liscard* and *Leasowe*. Named *Perch Rock*, she was built by the Caledon company of Dundee, being launched on 25th January 1929 and entered service soon afterwards. She was destined to be the last boat on the goods service when it ceased on 31st March 1947.

The First Mersey Road Tunnel

With hindsight it can be said that neither Birkenhead nor the Wallasey Corporations foresaw the effect the opening of the tunnel would have on the cross-river traffic. There was, of course, a considerable amount of horse-drawn traffic and many handcarts which were barred from the tunnel and steam-wagons, of which there were still a great number, and vehicles carrying dangerous goods such as petroleum products were barred. But the tunnel's very existence generated new traffic and led to many firms accelerating the changeover from horses to motors. Wallasey had been running a 20-minute service needing two vessels between 6.40am and 8.0pm, continuing with a one-boat half-hourly service, until 10.0pm from Liverpool. On Saturdays the half-hourly service started at 3.15pm but this had been deferred until 4.15pm by July 1934 when the tunnel opened. An hourly Sunday service had operated from 9.30am until 10.0pm from Liverpool but this was augmented to run half-hourly from 8.45am. Both the half-hourly and hourly services required only one boat so the extra cost was not high.

Whilst traffic at Woodside quickly reduced to little more than 10% of the pre-tunnel level, Wallasey was not so badly affected and the daytime frequency was stepped up to 15-minutes. This could still be achieved with two boats, the turn-round at Liverpool being greatly assisted by the elimination of congestion on the floating roadway and stage. The early morning service was improved with a 5.40am departure from Seacombe on Tuesdays, Fridays and Saturdays and 6.10am on all weekdays. By summer 1936, the 15-minute service was running from 6.0am to 8.15pm. However, the Sunday traffic which had consisted almost entirely of private cars was soon abandoned. This timetable, augmented by special very early market boats when required, continued until the outbreak of war in September 1939.

Overleaf: *A comparison of the goods tariffs for 1st April 1916 and 18th July 1934 (the date the first Mersey Tunnel opened) demonstrates how the tunnel tolls influenced those of the ferry.*   M. Jenkins collection

The spacious decks of the last three luggage boats are typified by this view of Perch Rock *during her trials in 1929.*
Allsup & Co.

VEHICLES, HORSES, &c.	SEACOMBE. Goods Boat Service (Return) Ordinary Rate.	SEACOMBE. Goods Boat Service Empty V'hicle Rate.	SEACOMBE. Pass. Boat Service	NORTH FERRIES. Egremont.	NORTH FERRIES. New Brighton.
	S. D.	S. D.	S. D.	S. D.	S. D.
Ass and Man	0 6	—	—	—	—
—— and Cart	1 0	0 6	—	—	—
Bassinette, Mail Cart or Go-cart (including Passenger)	0 2	—	0 2	0 3	0 4
Bath Chair (includ'g Passenger)	0 3	—	0 3	0 4	0 5
Bicycle (including Passenger)	0 3	—	0 3	0 4	0 5
Calf	0 2	—	—	—	—
Cart (2 wheels), 1 Horse	2 0	1 0	—	—	—
Cab or Hansom, 1 Horse	1 3	—	—	—	—
Coach, 2 Horses	3 0	—	—	—	—
Cattle, per Head	0 6	—	—	—	—
Dog and Passenger	0 2	—	0 2	0 4	0 6
Float (large), 1 Horse	2 6	1 3	—	—	—
—— (small, 1 Horse	1 6	0 9	—	—	—
Handcart	0 6	—	—	—	—
Hearse, 2 Horses	5 0	—	—	—	—
Horse and Man	0 6	—	—	—	—
——additional	0 6	—	—	—	—
Light 4-wheel Phæton or Carriage, 1 Horse	2 0	—	—	—	—
Lorry or Waggon, 1 Horse	2 0	1 0	—	—	—
——(exceeding 18 ft. long,) 1 Horse or 2 horses	3 6	1 9	—	—	—
Mourning Coach or Brougham	2 6	—	—	—	—
Motor Bicycle	0 4	—	0 4	0 5	0 6
——Bicycle & Trailer or Side Car	0 6	—	0 8	0 10	1 0
——Car, not exceeding 11 ft in length over all	1-0 ~~0 8~~		~~1 4~~	~~1 6~~	~~1 8~~
——Car, not exceeding 14 feet	1 6	—	—	—	—
——Car, exceeding 14 feet	2 0	—	—	—	—
——Char-a-banc	4 0	—	—	—	—
——Delivery Van, small	1 6	0 9	—	—	—
——Delivery Van, large	2 0	1 0	—	—	—
——Hearse	5 0	—	—	—	—
——Omnibus	3 6	—	—	—	—
——or Steam Lorry or Wagon	3 0	1 6	—	—	—
——or Steam Lorry & Trailer	6 0	3 0	—	—	—
——or Steam Furniture Van (or Lift Van)	4 0	2 0	—	—	—
——or Steam Furniture Van and Trailer	6 0	3 0	—	—	—
——Taxi Cabs	1 6	—	—	—	—
——Tractor Engine	4 0	—	—	—	—
Oil Tank Wagon, 1 Horse	2 6	—	—	—	—
Organ, 2 Wheels	1 0	—	—	—	—
Sheep or Pig (dead or alive)	0 1	—	—	—	—
——in droves, per 100	7 6	—	—	—	—
Trap, 1 Horse	1 0	—	—	—	—
Truck, small	0 3	—	—	—	—
——large	0 6	—	—	—	—
Van, Furniture, 1 Horse	3 6	1 9	—	—	—
—— Parcel Delivery (2 wheels), 1 Horse	2 0	1 0	—	—	—
—— Parcel Delivery (4 wheels), 1 Horse	2 6	1 3	—	—	—
—— Undertaker's, 1 Horse	2 0	—	—	—	—
Wa'gonette or Omnib's, 4 Horses	5 0				
—— 3 Horses	4 0	—	—	—	—
—— 2 Horses	3 0	—	—	—	—
—— 1 Horse	2 0	—	—	—	—
Wheelbarrow	0 4	—	—	—	—

Return tickets available on day of issue only.

GOODS, PARCELS, &c.	SEACOMBE. Goods Boat Service.	SEACOMBE. Pass. Boat Servi.	NORTH FERRIES. Egremont.	NORTH FERRIES. New Brighton.
	S. D.	S. D.	S. D.	S. D.
Ale, Porter, or Vinegar, per Hogsh'd	0 5	—	—	—
—— per Barrel	0 4	—	—	—
—— per ½-barrel.	0 3	—	—	—
—— per ¼-barrel.	0 2	—	—	—
—— per Case, according to size	2d to 6d	—	—	—
Apples, per Barrel	0 3	—	—	—
Bacon, per Bale	0 4	—	—	—
—— per Truss	0 3	—	—	—
—— per Side	0 2	—	—	—
—— per Cwt.	0 1	—	—	—
Axles, per Pair	0 2	—	0 3	0 4
Baskets or Boxes, per Bundle, according to size	2d to 6d	—	3d to 6d	4d to 8d
Beef, per Quarter	0 3	—	—	—
—— per Side	0 6	—	—	—
Besoms, per Bundle, accord'g to size	2d to 3d	—	3d to 4d	3 dto 6d
Biscuits or Bread, per Cwt.	0 2	—	0 2	0 2
Butter or Margarine, per Tub, Firkin, Kiel, Box, or Cask	0 2	—	0 2	0 2
Candles, per Box	0 3	—	0 3	0 4
Canned Goods, per Case	0 2	—	0 2	0 2
Carpets, per Bdl., according to size	2d to 6d	—	3d to 6d	4d to 8d
Cement, per Cwt.	0 2	—	—	—
Chairs, per Bundle, accord'g to size	1d to 6d	—	3d to 6d	4d to 8d
Cheese, per each	0 1	—	—	—
Chips, or Firewood, per Package	0 2	—	0 3	0 4
Cockles, or Mussels, per Bag	0 1	—	—	—
Coffee, per Bag, not exceed'g 56 lbs.	0 2	—	—	—
Corpse	5 0	5 0	5 0	5 0
Dried Fruit, per Bdl., ac'rd'g to size	2d to 6d	—	3d to 6d	4d to 8d
Earthenware or Hollow Ware, per Crate or Hogshead, ac'rd'g to size	4d to 1s	—	—	—
Eggs, per Quarter-case	0 2	—	—	—
——per Half-case	0 4	—	—	—
——per Case	0 5	—	—	—
——per Box	1 0	—	—	—
Empties (Returned), per Barrel, Cask, or Milk Can	0 1	—	0 1	0 2
——Drums	6d – doz	—	—	—
Firegrates	0 6	—	—	—
Firebars, Hardware, &c., per Bundle not exceeding 1 Cwt.	2d to 6d	—	—	—
Fish, per Basket	0 2	0 2	0 3	0 4
—— per Box	0 3	0 3	0 4	0 5
—— per Barrel	0 4	—	—	—
Flour, per Barrel or Sack	0 3	—	—	—
——per Bag, not exceeding 140lb	0 2	—	—	—
Fowl, per Crate (dead or alive) according to size	4d. to 8d	—	—	—
Fruit, per Case, Box, or Crate, according to size	2d to 4d	—	—	—
Furniture, per Package, ac'rd'g to sz	4d to 1s	—	—	—
Geese, Fowl, or Poultry, per Score	1 0	—	—	—
Glass, per Box	0 2	0 2	0 3	0 4
——per Crate, according to size	4d to 8d	—	—	—
——per Crib	1 0	—	—	—
Croceries, per Box, not exceed. 112 lbs.	2d to 4d	—	—	—
Hamper, small	0 2	0 2	0 3	0 4
——large	0 3	0 3	0 4	0 6

GOODS, PARCELS, &C.	SEACOMBE. Goods Boat Service.	SEACOMBE. Pass. Boat S'vice.	NORTH FERRIES. Egremont.	NORTH FERRIES. New Brighton.
	S. D.	S. D.	S. D.	S. D.
Lard, per Firkin or Pail	0 2	—	—	—
——per Barrel	0 3	—	—	—
Milk, per Can	0 2	0 2	0 2	0 2
——per Tankard	0. 3	—	—	—
Mineral Waters, per Case, ac'rd'g to size	2d to 4d	—	—	—
Molasses, per Hogshead	0 6	—	—	—
—— per Puncheon	1 0	—	—	—
Nails (Bag or Keg), per Cwt.	0 2	0 2	0 2	0 2
Nuts, per Bag or Box, ac'rd'g to size	2d to 6d	—	—	—
Oakum, per Cwt.	0 2	—	—	—
Oats, per Case, according to size	2d to 4d	—	—	—
Offal, per Bag (conveyed only by Goods Steamers)	0 2	—	—	—
Oil, per Barrel	0 6	—	—	—
Paint, per Drum, according to size	2d to 4d	—	—	—
Paper, per Bundle, ac'rd'g to size	2d to 3d	—	3d to 4d	3d to 6d
Parcels, Baskets of Fruit, &c., or Box, not exceeding 20lbs. wgt. ea. nor £3 in value	0 2	0 2	0 3	0 4
Petroleum, per Barrel	0 6	—	—	—
Piano, Harmonium, or Barrel Organ	1 0	—	—	—
Pitch, per Cwt.	0 2	—	—	—
Provisions, Salted, per Tierce	0 5	—	—	—
—— per Barrel	0 4	—	—	—
—— per Keg	0 2	—	—	—
Rabbits, per Case or Box	0 2	—	—	—
Rushes, per Bundle	0 2	—	—	—
Salt, Wheat, Barley, Oats, Potatoes, Rice or Beans, &c., per Bag	0 2	—	—	—
—— per Sack	0 3	—	—	—
Sheet Iron, Tin, &c., per Bundle, not exceeding 1 Cwt.	3d to 6d	—	—	—
Soap, per Cwt.	0 2	—	—	—
Spirits or Wine, per Hamper, small.	0 3	—	—	—
——per Hamper, large	0 6	—	—	—
——per Quarter-cask	0 4	—	—	—
——per Hogshead	0 8	—	—	—
——per Puncheon	1 4	—	—	—
——per Basket, Case or Jar	0 2	—	—	—
——per Octave	0 4	—	—	—
Sugar, per Bag, small	0 2	—	—	—
——per Bag, large	0 4	—	—	—
Syrup or Treacle, per Case, according to size	2d to 4d	—	—	—
Tallow, per Cwt.	0 2	—	—	—
Tar, per Cwt.	0 2	—	—	—
Tea, per Chest	0 3	—	—	—
—— per Half-chest or Quarter-ch't	0 2	—	—	—
Timber—Spokes, Handles, Hammer Shafts, &c.	2d to 6d	—	—	—
Turpentine, per Barrel	0 6	—	—	—
Yeast, per Crate or Basket, according to size	2d to 4d	—	—	—

NOTICE.—The above Tolls and Charges are payable to the Collectors of the Corporation on the Ferry Premises or on the Ferry Steamers.

Tariff 1st April 1916

MOTOR VEHICLES.

Description of Vehicle.	Laden s. d.	Empty s. d.
Ambulance	2 0	—
Bicycle (including passenger)	0 6	—
" & Sidecar (1 passenger)	0 8	—
" (2 ")	0 10	—
" (Trader's) Sidecar	0 9	—
Car - Not Exceeding 8 h.p.	1 0	—
" 12 h.p.	1 4	—
" 16 h.p.	1 8	—
" Exceeding 16 h.p.	2 0	—
Car - 3 Wheels - 2 Seater	1 0	—
Chara (or Motor Bus) - 14 Seats	2 6	—
" " but not exceeding 26 Seats	3 6	—
" " Exceeding 26 Seats	5 0	—
Furniture Van	3 0	2 0
" (and Trailer)	3 6	3 8
Hearse	1 6	1 6
Lorries - Not Exceeding 1 Ton	2 0	2 0
" 2 Tons	2 6	2 0
Exceeding 2 Tons but not 4 Tons	2 6	2 6
" 4 Tons	3 0	3 0
" " and Trailer	5 0	3 8
Six Wheelers:—Not exceeding 4 tons	3 0	2 0
Exceeding 4 tons	5 0	3 8
Scammell Cob under 5 tons	2 6	2 0
Steam Roller	5 0	—
Tank Waggon	3 0	2 6
Taxi	1 6	1 6
Tractor Not exceeding 2 tons	1 0	—
Tractor (exceeding 2 but not 4 tons)	3 0	2 6
" " " and Trailer	2 0	—
" " 4 tons	3 6	2 6
" " " with Trailer	3 0	2 6
Vans:—Not exceeding 12cwt.	5 0	3 8
" 20cwt.	1 0	1 0
" Exceeding 20cwt.	1 6	1 6
" " and Trailer	2 2	2 2
" Undertakers' " and Trailer	5 0	3 0
	2 6	—

HORSE DRAWN, Etc.

Description of Vehicle.	Laden s. d.	Empty s. d.
Bath Chair (including Passenger)	0 3	—
Barrel Organ	1 0	—
Bassinette, Mailcart, and Passenger	0 3	—
Bicycle (including Passenger) or Trader's	0 3	—
Goods Vehicles—Not Exceeding 12 cwt.	1 0	1 0
" Exceeding 12 but not 20 Cwt.	1 6	1 3
" Exceeding 20 Cwt.	2 0	2 0
Hackney Vehicles —Not Exceeding 4 persons	1 6	—
" —Exceeding 4 but not 8 persons	2 0	—
" —Exceeding 8 persons	2 6	—
Hearse and 2 Horses	3 6	—
Handcart	0 11	—
Tricycle—Trader's (Small) and Passenger	0 6	—
" " (Large)	0 8	—
Truck (Small)	0 4	—
" (Large)	0 8	—
Van—Undertaker's	2 6	—
" Furniture	3 0	2 0
Wheelbarrow (and Man)	0 6	—
Horse (additional)	0 6	—

LIVESTOCK.

	Laden s. d.	Empty s. d.
Ass or Mule,	0 6	—
Calf	0 3	—
Cattle—Per head	0 2	—
Sheep or Pig (each)	0 2	—
" (in droves)—per 100	9 2	—

NOTICE.—The above Tolls and Charges are payable to the Collectors of the Corporation on the Ferry premises or on the Ferry Steamers.

Maximum Weights:—**Liverpool:** 4 wheels, 12 tons. **Wallasey:** 30 Tons, or (per Axle) 20 tons.
6 " 15 "

The Rates for transport of Vehicles on Sundays and Bank Holidays following 9th July, 1934, will remain as on week-days.
For Contract Rates and other information, please apply to General Manager's Office, Seacombe Ferry.

Tariff 18th July 1934

County Borough 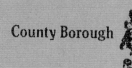 of Wallasey.

TOLLS & CHARGES

For the Conveyance of

VEHICLES, GOODS, &c.

SEACOMBE FERRY,

EGREMONT FERRY,

AND

NEW BRIGHTON FERRY.

From 11th September, 1922, and un
further notice

(Cancelling all previous Lists).

Charles Birchall. Ltd.. Printers. 17. James St.. L'p

County Borough of Wallasey.

TOLLS & CHARGES

For the Conveyance of

VEHICLES, GOODS, &c.

BETWEEN

LIVERPOOL

AND

SEACOMBE FERRY

(per Vehicular Service)

From 18th JULY, 1934, and until
further notice.

(Cancelling all Previous Lists).

Wallasey Printers Ltd., 63, Borough-road, Wallasey.

A 1920s aerial view with the Wallasey goods boat Seacombe *at the stage and a Birkenhead vessel approaching. The passenger end of the stage is unusually deserted.*   Liverpool City Engineer

The End of the Goods Ferry

Wallasey Corporation signed a 10-year contract with the GWR in 1937, an action which they later came to regret. In 1939, the ferry carried 364,000 vehicles yielding gross revenue of about £30,000. Quite early in the war, two of Birkenhead's luggage boats were requisitioned for use as cranes for lifting aircraft fuselages and wings from the vessels which had brought them across the Atlantic and landing them at Liverpool for onward transmission to Speke for assembly. They were soon joined in this work by *Liscard*. Wallasey had no difficulty in maintaining the service with the two remaining vessels and Birkenhead hoped that Wallasey would come to their rescue if anything happened to their remaining steamer. However on 16th July 1941, the latter was also requisitioned and the Woodside vehicular ferry service ceased on 21st July. Birkenhead tried to persuade the government to order Wallasey to lend them a vessel but Wallasey, with the prospect of increased traffic, was not inclined to be cooperative and the powers that be considered Seacombe would now suffice to cater for all remaining goods traffic.

The service was busy during the war and in December 1943 the contractor supplying horses for the pull-up service on the floating roadway was given permission to erect a stable on the stage, probably because of the danger of leading horses on the blacked-out streets. However, despite the fillip given by wartime conditions, the goods ferry averaged losses of £15,000 per annum every year from the opening of the tunnel in 1934 and in 1943-44 the deficit rose to £33,796. The Corporation decided that there was no alternative but to close it down permanently and applied for the necessary parliamentary powers. These were granted by the Wallasey Corporation Act, 1945 but the ferry had to continue in operation until the expiry of the GWR contract on 31st March 1947. The Mayor travelled on the last, virtually empty, boat and various speeches were made as the goods ferry passed into history.

Liscard was returned at the end of the war, reconditioned at government expense and sold to Danish owners in 1946 for £10,000. *Leasowe* was sold for scrap in 1948 for £1,850 but *Perch Rock*, which worked the service alone in its dying

Seacombe ferry from the air in the last days of the goods ferry just after the 1939-45 war. Perch Rock *departs for Liverpool very lightly loaded and one solitary vehicle makes its way up the floating roadway. Note the four air raid shelters on the ferry approach and several others on the land behind Seacombe Ferry Hotel.* M. Jenkins collection

days was retained. She was only 18-years old and had a passenger certificate for 1,500. There were schemes for using her on the New Brighton service or converting her into a cruise vessel or 'floating ballroom'. Like other luggage boats before her, she helped out on New Brighton on very busy days with buoyant seats arranged on her deck but no money was spent on her. She was kept until December 1953 when she was sold for £8,800 to Swedish owners for ferry service between Denmark and Sweden.

Whereas the Woodside goods ferry generated large profits for Birkenhead Corporation before the tunnel came (and the Mersey Tunnel Joint Committee bore the losses thereafter), Wallasey's vehicular service was always a financial millstone.

Woodside had the advantage of being at the end of the main road from Chester and benefited from a subsidised floating roadway from 1868; Wallasey depended on local traffic and its 1880 infrastructure was clumsy and expensive to operate and maintain. The town's floating roadway was built and installed at its own expense in 1926 when the tunnel was already under construction. If Wallasey had agreed to participate in the tunnel scheme on the same terms as Birkenhead, it is safe to assume that the 1926 improvements at Seacombe would have been scaled down considerably and the ratepayers would have benefited in that the grievous ferry losses over the remaining years of municipal ownership would have been borne by the Tunnel Joint Committee.

This picture of the three-lane Seacombe floating roadway may have been taken during the last week of the service in March 1947 as the vessel at the stage is bedecked with flags. Note the joints between the segments of the floating structure and the wooden tracks between the metal wheel-guides, which are well-worn by thousands of horses' hooves. The building on the left is the two-storey car park which was showing signs of neglect after years of little use during the 1939–45 war.

Wirral Archive Service

Royal Daffodil II partly submerged off Seacombe landing stage after being struck by an enemy bomb on 8th May 1941. She was raised 13 months later and returned to service in June 1943.
M. Jenkins collection

7   1939-1957

THE immediate effects on the ferries of the outbreak of war on 3rd September 1939 were the replacement of the 10-minute Seacombe service by a 15-minute service. This saved the department very little as the same two boats were needed; its main purpose was to enable the connecting buses to meet the requirements of fuel rationing. The New Brighton and Egremont service was completely withdrawn and the immediate effect of these curtailments was reflected in the revenue for September 1939 which was £8,608 compared with £12,820 in 1938. A 10-minute service was restored from 7.0am to 10.0am and 4.0 to 7.0pm from 1st November 1940 but there was a reversion to a 15-minute service in April 1941 by which time enemy air raids had resulted in a partial depopulation of the town. There was also the need to observe the blackout restrictions by dimming and hooding the lights in the saloons. The so-called 'phoney war' with no major activity persisted until the summer of 1940 and some relaxations were granted, a limited service being permitted to New Brighton. After the first daylight air raids on 31st August 1940, the whole fleet was painted all-over grey to reduce visibility from the air.

The ferries made little demand on imported fuel sources and they provided some relaxation for war workers when other means of transport were severely restricted. The provision of a direct service from Liverpool to New Brighton obviated difficulties which would have arisen at Seacombe as fuel rationing precluded the augmentation of bus services to New Brighton. A service to New Brighton was provided at Easter 1941.

The Air Raids

Air attacks started in August 1940 and gradually increased in frequency and intensity. Every endeavour was made to maintain the Seacombe service but there were times when safety demanded that the boats be berthed at the stages until things calmed down. During some attacks, mines were dropped by parachute into the river and the service was suspended on safety grounds until minesweepers had removed the danger. The first of these occasions was on 13th September 1940 and this was repeated on 13th March 1941. Buses were diverted to the Mersey Railway in Birkenhead and a special service ran through the tunnel at certain times.

On 7th May 1941 *Marlowe*, berthed at Liverpool stage, was narrowly missed by a high explosive bomb and on the following night, *Royal Daffodil II* was directly hit on the starboard side of her engine room, 60ft of her inner side being wrapped round the engine 'like a tarpaulin'. She sank in her berth with a slight list and the service had to be carried on from the centre berth, using narrow portable gangways. Despite the severity of the explosion, none of the crew was hurt, though one man was blown out of the engine room with the loss of his denture. A great many ships had been sunk by the Luftwaffe that week and salvage equipment was at a premium; three attempts to lift her using inadequate equipment were made in an effort to avoid her filling with silt but these were unsuccessful because of the failure of the pumps. It was over a year before the Dock Board was able to lend modern equipment and the vessel was successfully raised on 2nd June 1942 by Ferries staff under the direct supervision of Cdr. Price. She was a sorry sight when she floated to the surface with powerful pumps at work and tugs in attendance, bereft of funnel and mast, smothered in marine growth and with some 300 tons of mud and silt aboard. She was towed by the paddle tug *Troon* to a drying out berth by Morpeth river wall where it was found that the starboard engine was completely destroyed and mud could be removed only by taking off some of her bottom plates.

At this time the Admiralty was anxious to requisition two of the smaller ferry steamers for 'secret duties' which would have made the operation of the ferry service very difficult. Thus the work of restoring *Royal Daffodil II* to serviceable condition was given high priority and she was taken to a Grayson, Rollo and Clover dry dock. The lack of seasoned hard timbers and general shortage of materials and skills made it impossible to restore her saloons to their original condition and she assumed an austerity with what was described at the time as an all-steel interior which remained with her for the rest of her time on the river, re-entering service on 2nd June 1943, just one year after being raised.

Ferry Boats at War

The 'secret duties' for the Admiralty were later revealed as use as Net Defence vessels, laying and maintaining underwater nets to protect against enemy torpedoes and mines. *Francis Storey* was taken in 1942, followed by *J. Farley* in 1943 when the return of *Royal Daffodil II* to service was imminent. The former remained in the

Mersey but *J. Farley* worked both at Milford Haven and on the Clyde. They were under naval command but with Ferries department crews. At the end of the war, the Admiralty paid the following tribute to their service:-

'On the conclusion of the War, it gives me much pleasure to express appreciation of the services rendered by Commander L.D. Price, R.N.R., General Manager, Wallasey Ferries, and by the Masters and Crews of the *Francis Storey* and *J. Farley* throughout the four years and $2^1/2$ years respectively that they have been employed on duties with this Department.

The manner in which these vessels have been maintained in a state of constant readiness for duty and the spirit of helpful co-operation which they have constantly shown in furthering the work in hand, is most creditable to all concerned.

It is requested you will be good enough to convey to Commander Price and the Masters, Chief Engineers and crews of these two vessels, appreciation of the work they have done and, in the case of the *Francis Storey* which they are still doing for the Net Defence Department.

Yours truly (Signed) W. H. Mackenzie, Rear Admiral.'

Prior to air raids in 1940-41, a luggage boat would be sent down river carrying smoke canisters which were released near the estuary to provide a smoke screen over much of Liverpool. Both Birkenhead and Wallasey luggage boats were used as fire-fighting vessels, doing valuable service when fires were raging in the docks. In 1941 *Liscard* was requisitioned and fitted with a large derrick and, in company with two Birkenhead luggage boats, was used to unload aircraft sections and land them at Liverpool prior to assembly at Speke.

Ferry vessels were frequently called upon to act as tenders for troop ships which were unable to tie up at the landing stage; sometimes this involved trips to the Mersey bar. During the air raids, *Royal Daffodil II* was sometimes called upon to stand by laden troopships in mid-river ready to evacuate troops in the event of a direct hit by a bomb, a duty which, thankfully, was never necessary.

Egremont pier was once more demolished by a drifting steamer, *Newlands*, on 13th May 1941; the service was already suspended and the Council finally decided that it would not be resumed after the war. The stage was broken up at Tranmere but the pontoons were retained, some being used later at New Brighton. The remains of the pier were dismantled and the stone slip blasted away in 1947-48 by the Demolition and Construction Co. for £3,000 of which half was paid by the Ministry of Works. The terminal building remained in use for other purposes until the early 1980s. The balanced

gangways were stored and two were sold to Birkenhead in 1955.

Economic Effect of the War

The blackout and the air raids had a serious effect on carryings in the years 1940-41 and 1941-42 as only essential journeys were made during the hours of darkness and, as air attacks intensified and widespread damage was caused, Wallasey became seriously depopulated as people and their jobs moved to safer areas. Passengers carried were the lowest for 40 years and serious financial losses loomed. In October 1941 the Ministry of Health agreed that the Reserve Fund should be kept intact for post-war replacement of assets and indemnified the ferries against losses not exceeding £20,000. This was insufficient and £80,000 was taken from the rate fund over two years. New Brighton sailings were severely restricted in 1941-42 but an improvement in the fortunes of war from 1943 onwards led to much better summer services, for example, a late Saturday boat at 11.30pm from New Brighton to Liverpool during the summer of 1943 which was severely criticised as imposing a severe strain on late transport facilities from Liverpool Pier Head. Over the three holidays in 1944 New Brighton carried 617,959 passengers; at the August Bank Holiday weekend 354,262 passengers (excluding contractors) were carried on the Wallasey ferries of whom 242,812 passed through the New Brighton turnstiles, requiring four boats. The service, due to close for the winter on 1st October, was kept running on Sunday afternoons until the end of the month. The relaxation of restrictions and strong support by the public turned an estimated deficit of £21,770 for 1943-44 into a profit of £35,121. It was an optimistic sign when, in June 1943, the strike and chimes of Seacombe ferry clock, which had been silenced in 1939, were restored.

Post-war Rehabilitation

At the end of the war *Liscard*, looking very down-at-heel, was reconditioned at no expense to the department and, in view of the decision to close the goods service, was sold to Danish owners for about £10,000 being converted by them to a salvage vessel named *Lisca*. *Leasowe* was reserve vessel for the goods service until it closed in 1947, being sold for scrap for £1,850 in August 1948. *Perch Rock* was used for a time as a relief passenger steamer as described below.

Francis Storey and *J. Farley* were reconditioned at Admiralty expense in 1946 and went back into service, *J. Farley* being converted to oil firing, fitted

After wartime service on boom defence gear J. Farley was rehabilitated and converted to oil burning. Here she is seen approaching Liverpool stage to take on passengers for a special cruise to watch the launching of HMS Ark Royal in 1951. She was sold the following year.

J. B. C. McCann

with the Wallsend-Howden Pressure System. With the rapid increase in the price of coal following nationalisation of the mines, oil more and more being seen as a viable alternative to coal. In addition to service to New Brighton she undertook a number of Manchester Ship Canal cruises. *Francis Storey* was used as a relief boat for New Brighton and was eventually sold to Cork Harbour Commissioners on 8th February 1951 for £7,500 and renamed *Killarney* while *J. Farley* fetched £12,000 when sold in January 1952.

Royal Daffodil II was a further conversion to oil fuel on the pressure jet system in 1947, the installation, comprising Wallsend-Howden Duplex pumps and heaters and a Worthington-Simpson transfer pump, being supplied by the Wallsend Slipway and Engineering Co. Ltd. The plant was fitted by A. Rutherford & Co. Ltd of Birkenhead. The oil bunkers held 47.7 tons. *Marlowe* was converted later the same year. The changeover to diesel was expected to improve efficiency and reduce manpower. A coal-fired steamer took 24-hours to prepare and flexibility in the level of service was possible only by keeping a spare vessel crewed and in steam in the tideway. With diesel power, sudden fluctuations in demand could be swiftly met.

The Post-War Boom & Cruising

As people threw off the travel restrictions of the war years, public transport benefited from a post-war travel boom nationwide. In the summers of 1945-46 the New Brighton steamers attracted over four million passengers. Passengers peaked at more than 21 million in 1946-47 thereafter falling annually for the remainder of the department's separate existence. As a victory celebration, a week of evening Dance Cruises by *Royal Daffodil II* was announced between 18th and 23rd September 1945, the Ferries Committee generously donating all receipts to hospitals and local charities. The venture proved tremendously successful, and all tickets (1,000 per night) were sold out well in advance. On the final night, part of the proceedings was broadcast on the BBC Home Service.

All previous records for New Brighton ferry were broken at Easter 1946 when 230,732 passengers were carried over four days plus 117,575 at Seacombe. No fewer than 116,231 passengers were carried to and from New Brighton on the Monday when two luggage boats and a hired Birkenhead steamer augmented the fleet.

Encouraged by the success of the cruise programme in 1946, it was proposed that *Perch Rock* should have a full overhaul and then have two decks added. The former main deck was to provide bar and lounge facilities, the middle deck was to have a cafeteria, palm lounges and rest rooms while the third deck would have been used for dancing. During the wonderful summer of 1947, she was used on the New Brighton service with a passenger certificate for 1,600, floatable seats being placed on deck which was covered by an awning. However, she worked on only 40 days in 1946-47 and 20 days in 1947-48, her use being confined only to occasions when there would otherwise have been serious overloading for which the Corporation could have been prosecuted. It was felt, too, that she presented a poor image and there was evidence of passenger resistance so her conversion plans were abandoned. She was sold to Swedish owners for £8,800 on 17th December 1953, seeing further service as a vehicle and passenger steamer named *Betula*.

For the 1946 summer season a regular cruise programme was launched, a good class dance band playing for about two thirds of the time with a commentary from the Captain on points of interest on the river being used to fill in. These cruises lasted two hours and were priced at 2s. 6d. (12^1/$_2$p) for adults and 1s. 6d. (7^1/$_2$p) for children; a licensed bar and buffet was available. They were run on three afternoons and evenings per week the Saturday evening cruise being for adults only at four shillings (20p); on the other days the vessel was chartered by such large firms as Pilkingtons Glass, Napier's and British Enka. Although *Royal Daffodil II* was licensed for 2,000 passengers on service, numbers were limited to 1,000 when cruising. The scope of cruising was extended to include trips up the Manchester Ship Canal to Manchester, undertaken by *J. Farley*. The eastbound journey with commentary from the bridge, was made on a Saturday and at Pomona Docks, Manchester the vessel was met by fleets of buses to convey passengers either to the city centre or to Belle Vue, the passengers returning to Merseyside by bus from Piccadilly in the evening. On the Sunday the cruise worked in reverse, Manchester people being conveyed to New Brighton by boat and returned by bus in the evening. Cruising became an integral part of the department's activities and during that superb summer of 1947 *Royal Daffodil II* carried 120,000 cruise passengers, including 20,000 on private charters.

In 1949, advance bookings were so heavy that some charters had to be refused and the decision was taken to order a new vessel of revolutionary design, planned specifically for cruising but suitable for ferry service if required. Cruise passengers increased in numbers annually up to 1951-52, following the delivery of the new boat after which a slow decline set in. Each winter, the Cruise Master made extensive publicity tours of the catchment area – industrial Lancashire, West Yorkshire, the Potteries and West Midlands.

All three decks of Royal Daffodil II *are packed with happy trippers as she prepares to leave Liverpool for New Brighton during the Festival of Britain in 1951.*   J. B. C. McCann

Royal Daffodil II *was the post-war cruise boat until the arrival of the new* Iris. *She is seen approaching Seacombe just prior to her withdrawal for a second refit. Note the canvas shrouds to shelter the promenade deck which was used for dancing.*   J. B. C. McCann

Increased revenue was soon outpaced by costs. By 1949 medium quality coal cost £3.25 per ton compared with the 1939 price of £1.20 for the best quality coal and wages had almost doubled. From 1948-49 the ferries showed a trading loss, rising steeply from £5,546 in 1949-50 to £39,513 the following year and contributions from the Rate Fund were made annually, increasing from £10,000 in 1951-52 to £100,000 in the final years of Wallasey Corporation ownership. The belief that all would be well following the closure of the loss-making goods service on 31st March 1947 was soon confounded.

Although the facilities at Morpeth Dock which provided winter moorings and some repair facilities were inexpensive, it took a long time to get a vessel in or out as, in the early days of the war, the Dock Board had permanently closed the Morpeth Channel entrance to the Birkenhead docks. Boats proceeding to and from the Morpeth Dock were obliged to pass through three movable bridges and the double lock of the Alfred channel, incurring much unproductive time.

The Radar Installation

One of the major problems experienced by the ferries were the thick fogs which made even the short Seacombe passage hazardous. In these conditions the $7^1/_2$-minute crossing could occupy up to 45 minutes causing serious delays. Radar had been developed secretly during the 1939-45 war and, as the Clean Air Act was still some years in the future, Wallasey ferries decided to experiment to see if radar could be used to improve reliability and safety during spells of poor visibility.

Radar was still in its infancy and there were many practical difficulties to be overcome. None of the shore-based instruments proved suitable and a Cossor ship's instrument was installed in the clock-tower at Seacombe, a scanner being mounted on top of this tower, high enough to avoid all adjacent objects. In case of power failure a stand-by generator was purchased and vessels were equipped with radio telephones, masters receiving verbal advice from the land-based operators. During the winter months the station was manned continuously by three men working shifts.

The system was established in September 1947 and was the first installation of its kind in the world. It was so successful that 95 per cent of normal services could be run with complete safety in the densest pea-souper. In 1948, Wallasey agreed to supply radar facilities to Birkenhead for £600 per annum and four of their steamers were equipped with radio telephones. This was a rare example of co-operation between the ferries undertakings of the two boroughs.

New equipment installed in the radar station was officially opened on 28th July 1949 by Rt. Hon. Alfred Barnes, Minister of Transport. It is of interest to note the extent to which it was operational. Figures for 1953-54 during which it was manned for seven months (September to March) show that it was used for 39 days during which there were 55 'occasions for operation'. In total there were 193 operations and as the wages were £746, the cost of each operation was £3.17s.5d. (£3.85). The equipment was updated by Cossor in 1958.

Fleet Replacement

In 1948, the Corporation decided to order a new vessel of revolutionary design specifically for cruising but suitable for use on ferry service if required. Dr. A. M. Robb, Professor of Naval Architecture at Glasgow University, was engaged as a consultant and a specification was drawn up for a diesel-electric vessel to be built of Siemens Martin best quality steel throughout. A speed of $11^1/_2$-knots was required for ferry service with additional power in reserve. The main propulsion machinery was to comprise four diesel engines working at constant speed, each driving a main and auxiliary generator, the main generating direct current on an approved system to two propulsion motors mounted directly on the respective propeller shafts. The generating machinery and auxiliaries were to be situated amidships and the propulsion motors and exciters aft. Normal service was to be maintained with three generator sets, the fourth acting as a stand-by and power reserve for extra speed and enabling maintenance to be carried out with the vessel in service. Generator sets were to be coupled electrically so that any one or any combination of two, three or four could deliver current to the propulsion motors to enable two propellers to be driven ahead or astern simultaneously at the same speed or independently in opposite directions at different speeds, or be stopped independently of each other. The vessel was to be capable of control from the bridge or from the generating room by means of a changeover switch. A speed of 12 knots was to be guaranteed.

The vessel was to be named *Royal Iris* and the successful tenderer was W. Denny & Bros.of Rosyth. The design was different from any previous ferry vessel, the bridge being much further forward and the three decks were named 'main', 'shelter deck' and 'sun deck'. There was no conventional funnel, just two exhausts placed well aft. There was a dance floor and a fish and chip restaurant, the whole of the appointments being luxurious. The power units comprised four Ruston & Hornsby 6VEBXZ diesel engines, pressure charged with Napier exhaust turbo blowers,

Type of Vessel	Approx. Passenger Capacity	Date of placing order	Probable date of delivery	Approx. Cost £	Vessel for sale
Diesel- electric[†]	2,500	8.48	1. 4.1951	256,000	*Perch Rock*
Royal Iris	2,000	1.10.1949	1. 4.1950	70,000	Conversion to straight diesel.
Diesel	1,050	1.10.1949	1. 5.1951	126,000	*Francis Storey*
Diesel	900	1. 9.1953	1. 3.1955	*	*J. Farley*
Diesel-electric	2,250	1. 1.1956	1. 9.1957	*	*Wallasey*
Diesel-electric	2,250	1. 1.1956	1. 9.1957	*	*Marlowe*
Diesel	2,250	1. 1.1961	1. 6.1962	*	*Royal Daffodil II*

[†] Already being built. * Too far ahead to make a reliable estimate.

developing 540hp at 500 rpm. The auxiliaries were powered by two 5XPHZ engines. Marine diesel oil was used necessitating heating to remove any suspended water before centrifuging. The two Metropolitan Vickers propulsion motors developed 720hp each @ 215rpm when on four generators and 540hp at 195rpm on three. Other equipment was supplied by General Electric.

By 1949 the average age of the fleet was 22 years, far too high, and a report drawn up by the general manager set out a possible replacement strategy over the following 12 years. This is summarised in the table above.

The strategy outlined in the report was for the three diesel-electric vessels to maintain the Seacombe service and cruising, including time off service for surveys. Of the four straight diesel vessels, the two smaller ones would have a greater speed and all four would be available for New Brighton, the Seacombe night service and supplementary cruising. It was intended that the conversion of *Royal Iris* from coal to diesel would

increase speed by one knot and that the replacement for *Francis Storey* should be 1.5 knots faster. The retention of the latter and her conversion to straight diesel had been approved subject to a ceiling of £38,000 but the cost far exceeded this amount and the proposal was abandoned. The diesel boats required refuelling at Dingle oil jetty or Herculaneum only about once a week and each vessel would be replaced by the stand-by boat while this was done.

A suggestion that the New Brighton service should be suspended between Easter and Whit was rejected as it was feared traffic lost to rail might never be regained. There was a further suggestion that a small ex-Admiralty launch could cover 'one-hour cruises and other purposes', the manager suggesting that the expected cost of £11,000 could be obtained as a ten year loan though 'this sum could, in my view, be comfortably cleared off in 3-4 years'.

This proposal was acted upon quite quickly, a second-hand wooden twin-screw motor vessel

The motor launch Wallasey Belle *was bought second-hand in November 1949 with a view to making economies on the night and off-peak services but it was a financial disaster being laid up in 1950 and sold at a substantial loss in September 1953.*

T. Turner collection

The general layout of the cruise ship Royal Iris was demonstrated by this publicity leaflet which was sent to prospective charterers.   M. Jenkins collection

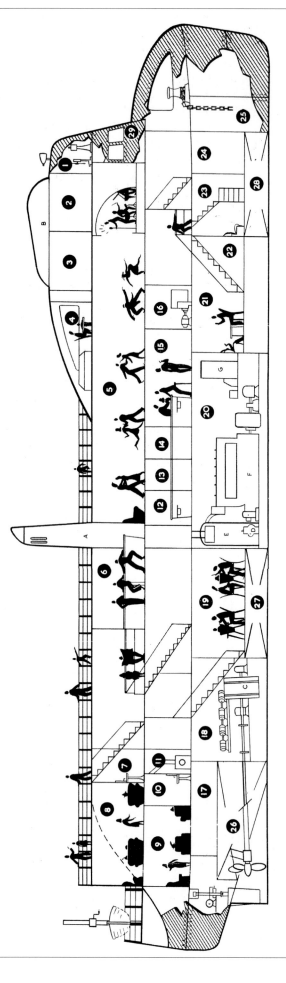

ROYAL IRIS

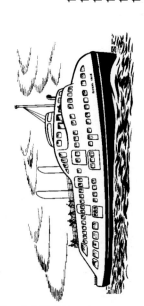

1. Navigation Bridge (with searchlight above) (Full bridge control)
2. Chart Room
3. Captain's Room
4. Modern Tea Bar
5. Pillarless Dance Floor, with Stage and Dressing Room at rear
6. Ice Cream and Cocktail Bar
7. Toilets
8. Ladies' Rest Room and Toilets
9. Ladies' Rest Room
10. Toilets
11. Air Conditioning Unit
12. Bar Counter (with Wash-up Sinks etc.)
13. Bottle Store for Bar Service
14. Additional Bottled Beer Storage
15. Buffet Counter (with Wash-up Sinks etc.)
16. Air Conditioning Unit
17. Cool Beer Storage (below water line)
18. Motor Room (with Exciter Sets and Propulsion Motors)
19. Fish and Chip Saloon
20. Main Diesel Generator Room and Controls
21. Smoke Room for Passengers
22. Smoke Room Bar
23. Crew's Accommodation
24. Engineer's Cabin
25. Anchor Chain Locker (below Windlass)
26. Water Ballast Tank
27. Fresh Water Tank
28. Fresh Water and Ballast Tank
29. Observation Saloon for Passengers
A. Funnels for Exhaust System
B. Dummy Funnel (contains Fresh Water Service Tank)
C. Propulsion Motors driving Twin Screws
D. Electric Driven Compressor
E. Domestic Heating Boiler
F. Main Diesel Generator Set (four in number)
G. Switchboards and Control Panel

named *Channel Belle* being purchased in November 1949 from J. Bolson & Sons, shipbuilders, of Poole, Dorset for £14,500. Built by Johnson and Jago, Leigh-on-Sea in 1944, she was engined by the Gray Marine Motor Co. At first it was proposed to rename her *Gay Venture* with *Crocus* or *Snowdrop* as alternatives but *Wallasey Belle* was chosen instead. She made 450 crossings on the lightly-loaded Seacombe night service when hot soup and tea were served. She occasionally appeared on off-peak sailings but proved totally unsuitable, the slightest swell inducing an unacceptable motion. In 1950, she was kept busy with short cruises up-river to see the new aircraft carrier *Ark Royal* on the stocks at Cammell Laird's yard but at the end of that season she was laid up in Morpeth Dock with a broken crankshaft and eventually sold for £1,250 in September 1953 to a Mr A. P. Martin of Heswall for use at Torquay, ending this sorry and expensive interlude.

With hindsight, the optimism expressed in the Fleet Replacement report seems, to say the least, misplaced but it should be remembered that the Mersey ferries were an institution and they played an important part in the lives of thousands of Wallasey residents. Sentiment, which played almost as important a part in decision making as economics, continued to do so for another two decades. Although in 1948-49 the ferries had carried more than two million fewer passengers than in the previous year, that was still almost a million more than in the year before that and the downward trend would not begin to show for another three or four years. The extraordinary fact is that, despite the experience of the past, the committee and the council still favoured expensive solutions instead of realising that there was money to be saved by providing less elaborate but nevertheless suitable vessels for workaday ferry duties. The hope of an arrangement with Birkenhead for some kind of triangular service, if only at night, was never realised while the two boroughs were rival ferry owners.

The launch, on 5th December 1950 of *Royal Iris* heralded the new diesel-electric era which required the marine staff to undergo much intensive training. Delivered on 28th April 1951, she attracted considerable attention in the river, her streamlined superstructure being finished in cream and green. Her first cruise was on 2nd May and she was very swiftly dubbed 'the floating fish and chip shop'. She was licensed for 2,296 passengers on ferry service and 1,000 for cruising. Post-war inflation had increased her cost from an estimated £256,000 to £450,000, more than ten times the cost of *Wallasey* and *Marlowe* combined! The proceeds from the sale of *Wallasey Belle* and *Perch Rock* were used to reduce the *Royal Iris* debt.

The next deliveries were the two smaller diesel vessels proposed in the replacement programme

Leasowe approaches New Brighton stage in June 1956. One of two vessels commissioned in 1951 and built by Philip & Son at Dartmouth, they were unpopular on the Seacombe service as the absence of a forward gangway door added considerably to embarkation and disembarkation times.

J. B. C. McCann

Egremont *was sister to* Leasowe *and is seen tied up at the Seacombe berth at Liverpool. This vessel had a passenger certificate for 1,432 persons and was withdrawn in 1975 for conversion into a club on the River Dart.*   G. Parry

though their passenger capacity, at 1,472 (ferry) and 700 (cruising), was rather higher than originally suggested. Named *Leasowe* and *Egremont*, they were built on the Dart by Philip & Co. and powered by Crossley Bros. diesel engines developing 1,280 hp; they were 133ft 7in long and 34ft 1in wide. Gross tonnage was 311, exactly half of the *Royal Iris*. These twins departed from traditional design to the extent that the forward section of the promenade deck was covered and glazed and there was only one gangway door aft on each side. Catering facilities were built in so that they could be used for cruising; catering was later provided on the New Brighton service. Costing £140,000 each, the pair entered service in 1951 and 1952 respectively, *Francis Storey* and *J. Farley* being sold, the former, renamed *Killarney*, joining the Cork Harbour tender fleet.

Seacombe was subsequently operated by one large and one small boat. There was some public criticism, mainly because the absence of the forward gangway door on the new vessels hindered embarkation and disembarkation during the peak hours; nevertheless the policy was affirmed in February 1952. To improve passenger flow at Liverpool, the upper deck stairway and gangway unit was rebuilt early in 1953 to project 3ft further on to the stage thus reducing the steepness of the stairs.

The department now had a reliable, economical and reasonably modern fleet and no further replacements were needed until *Wallasey* and *Marlowe* completed 30 years' service in 1957. In view of the financial situation, *St. Hilary* (late *Royal Iris*) was sold in March 1956 to Dutch owners, being converted into a car ferry. It was decided to order one new vessel, sell *Marlowe* and send *Wallasey* to Harland & Wolff for a complete refit at a cost of £52,198 which, by completion, had increased to £62,401.

Royal Iris II underwent two renamings, to plain *Royal Iris* on 1st July 1947 and to *St. Hilary* on 14th March 1950. A proposal to convert her to diesel power was turned down and she was sold on 9th February 1956 to Provinciale Waterstaat Zuid Holland for £17,000 being converted into a car ferry named *Haringvliet*.

The new vessel, the last to be acquired by Wallasey Corporation, was built by James Lamont & Co. and engined by Crossley Bros., developing 1,360hp. She was given the name *Royal Daffodil II*, the earlier vessel of that name, whose passenger certificate had been altered to 1,982 on ferry service and 850 for cruising in 1955, becoming the second *St. Hilary* in October 1957. The use of that name on two vessels of similar appearance at different times will doubtless be a source of confusion to historians for many years. During the new vessel's trials at Port Glasgow in April 1958, the general manager thought the exhaust noise was excessive and asked to be put ashore by tender so that he could listen from the shore. As a result, additional silencers

Leasowe *berthed in Morpeth Dock, Birkenhead. These vessels were the first to have a small covered forward saloon on the promenade deck.* G. Parry

Wallasey *was reprieved and extensively refurbished in 1958. She is shown, fitted with a mainmast in accordance with marine regulations, approaching Liverpool landing stage on 25th May 1961. She was the last steam ferry vessel on the Mersey, being finally withdrawn in 1964 after 37 years service.* J. A. Peden

In the immediate post-1939-45 War period much maintenance work was done at the ferry berth in Morpeth Dock, Birkenhead and this view shows the changeover of vessels; Wallasey entering the river from the Alfred Channel entrance to the East Float while Royal Iris makes her way to Morpeth.
R. L. Wilson

Lt. Cdr. L. D. Price, RNR, general manager, Wallasey Corporation Ferries 1939-63   Wirral Archive Service

were fitted and the vessel left the Clyde at 1.0pm on 19th April, anchored in Rothesay Bay for the night and arrived off New Brighton at 9.40pm on 20th April. Her river acceptance trials were completed at 7.30pm on 21st and she entered service at Seacombe at 9.15pm that night. Her fuel consumption was less than $1^1/_2$-tons daily. It is of interest to note that on 12th September 1958, Wallasey agreed to train Birkenhead's ferry engineers on diesel engines, so that they could have some experience before their first diesel boat, *Mountwood* was commissioned. The new diesel was a full size three-decker, measuring 143ft 1in long and 46ft 1in wide. Her gross tonnage was 609 and her passenger certificate permitted the carriage of 1,950 passengers. There were two gangway doors per side.

The elderly and infirm had always experienced some difficulty in climbing the Seacombe south bridge especially at low tide and in 1951 the department purchased a one-ton Morrison Electricar chassis from Austin Crompton Parkinson Electric Vehicles Ltd. A special body was built by ferries staff, consisting of two outward-facing slatted wooden bench seats divided by a luggage shelf. This accommodated 14 persons and was parked on the stage near to the gangways,

The date of this photograph is uncertain; it shows the interior of the machine shop in the Ferries Workshop with overhead shafting and belt drives. The clutter and unswept floor and the fact that it was allowed to be photographed in this condition, suggests a lack of pride on the part of management.
Wirral Archive Service

A port side view of Royal Iris *cruise boat of 1952. Despite her nickname of 'the fish and chip boat' she soon gained a place in the hearts of Merseysiders and there was genuine sorrow when she was sold when further repairs were uneconomic.*

Wirral Archive Service

providing a service up the slope for one penny (1d) for those who needed it.

The Search for Economies

From this point onwards, the story is one of constant retrenchment and, at the same time, is a dreadful condemnation of municipal arrogance and incompetence for which the unfortunate ratepayers paid heavily. At no time was there any coherent policy for contraction and the Council, just like its predecessors in the 1920s, made expensive decisions on the flimsiest of evidence. A quaint, over-protective affection for the boats took precedence over economic realities.

At Seacombe, the early morning, late evening and Sunday frequency was reduced from 15 to 20-minutes from 29th October 1951, establishing a pattern for several winters. This saved very little as two boats were required for the peak traffic when 1,100 passengers were still being carried on some sailings. The requirement for a third boat, tied up in the tideway, to be manned reduced any saving. In the winter of 1953, the Sunday afternoon service was increased to 15-minutes to connect with an increased bus service but the Motor Bus Department was ordered to pay half the extra cost of running a second boat between 2.30 and 9.30pm.

In November 1951 the Borough Treasurer reported on the finances of the Ferries and suggested various internal economies. Further toll increases were proposed and it was decided that, subject to a cost ceiling of £88,000, *St. Hilary* should be converted to diesel and retained in service for another 15 years. Tenders were invited but action was repeatedly deferred and the work was never done. In retrospect, although there were mounting calls on the rate fund, little urgency was shown and great resistance to change was demonstrated by the management who wrote airily in reports of the advantages of living in Wallasey and 'a service to the residents of the borough' as if this could be justified at any cost.

Councillors showed little understanding of the economics of the ferries undertaking which were different from those of the buses. The ferries were much more capital intensive but their 'vehicles' were capable of absorbing large numbers of additional passengers without any extra cost. They were rarely filled to capacity so any traffic gained by concessionary fares was potentially profitable provided that the core traffic was not eroded. The ferry terminals were enormously expensive, requiring continuous costly maintenance and the need for ensuring safety of passengers was of paramount importance.

Profitability depended on reducing costs to the minimum and increasing revenue to the maximum. The economics of the Wallasey ferries differed considerably from those of Birkenhead as a much higher proportion of Wallasey traffic was seasonal and dependent on the weather, making it difficult to estimate in advance. With demographic changes and greater availability of jobs in Wirral, this proportion grew annually, being estimated at 78% by 1957. All New Brighton traffic and most of cruising came within the latter category. Even at Seacombe, there was a substantial discretionary element. It followed that, when fixing fares, great thought needed to be given to how much the traffic would bear as the demand by the discretionary traffic was much more elastic than that of the business traffic at Seacombe.

The ferries' problems were becoming increasingly politicised and, because of the deteriorating financial position, the Council appointed a Special Economy Committee, chaired by Councillor J. Boucher, a retired borough treasurer, early in 1952. They submitted several reports and recommended the sale of *St. Hilary* (1) to save £6,000 and increasing cruise fares to raise a further £4,000. An enquiry into the establishment also took almost two years to report on the feasibility of eliminating some administrative posts and even then consideration was deferred by the full Council. Much unnecessary paper work was being done. For example, monthly, but not weekly contracts needed an application form for no better reason than it was established practice. Accounting was also being duplicated by the ferries office and the borough treasury. The Committee drew attention to the fact that 31 inspectors and collectors were required to man Seacombe ferry over a weekly period purely because of the separation of embarking and disembarking passengers in a building designed more for municipal pride than for practical purposes. Price Waterhourse & Co.

had drawn attention to this wasteful practice in a report in 1926 but it had been ignored. It took until 1963 to eliminate this practice as explained in Chapter 8.

There was Council opposition to anything seen as a threat to reliability on the New Brighton service but the sale of one vessel was approved in the December, the possible sale of a second being deferred for a year. The Ministry of Transport was asked to approve new maximum tolls in 1951 and some fares were increased almost every year up to 1957. Various cheap fare offers proved ineffectual as they tended to erode the existing revenue to a greater extent than they attracted new custom. A 2d. cheap evening fare at Seacombe was replaced by a 6d. evening return in 1953 but that was withdrawn after only five months and early season cheap returns to New Brighton had little success. Eventually it became cheaper to travel from New Brighton or Wallasey Village to Liverpool by rail than by ferry or a combination of bus and ferry and the gap tended to widen. From 1st June 1953, a range of weekly bus and boat contracts, was based on a ferry contract of 2s. 6d. (12$\frac{1}{2}$p) which had been previously reduced from 3s. (15p). To this was added the full bus fares but the results were disappointing and these tickets were withdrawn from 1st April 1954.

The bridge and controls of the cruise ship Royal Iris *of 1952.*

Metropolitan-Vickers

Attention was given to the theory that loss of traffic at Seacombe was partly attributable to the length of time between departure of the boats from Liverpool and the departure of buses at peak hours. From 13th April 1953 boat departures were altered from the 5s to 0s past the hour, bus timings remaining on the 0s. Buses were to wait for boat passengers no matter how long the delay might be but, if it was not longer than three minutes, the bus crews were urged to make an effort to get back to Seacombe on time. It did not work out and bus delays of five minutes were not uncommon. In September, bus arrivals and departures were retarded by three minutes, this resulting in a busmen's work to rule and dissatisfaction from passengers who just missed the boat to Liverpool. There was a reversion to the original method on 4th January 1954.

In 1951, the New Brighton service ran at least half-hourly from Easter to October and in May 1952, two 'express' boats ran in the morning and one in the evening on Mondays to Thursdays in an unsuccessful attempt to regain commuter traffic. Thereafter between Easter and Whitsun, the New Brighton service was operated in accordance with demand with a basic one-boat hourly service which could be boosted to a two-boat half-hourly headway or, during fine weekends, to three-boats on a 20-minute service. There was much debate about the economics of retaining a vessel just to provide this third boat. It was pointed out that crowd control on the landing stages was difficult and overcrowding was an offence which could lead to prosecution. If the department could show that it was endeavouring to cater for the demand by bringing the third vessel into service, it had some defence but this would not be the case if it provided a service which was clearly below the demand. An unwelcome additional cost was the need to fit mainmasts to all vessels as a result of new navigational regulations at an average cost of £250.

There was a welcome boost in revenue in 1955 when a tugmen's strike led to *Royal Daffodil II* and *St. Hilary* (2) being used as tenders for liners unable to tie up at the stage. Various courses of action were proposed including the reduction of the fleet to just five vessels. New Brighton was seen as profitable and essential for the well-being of traders which undoubtedly was true as later events proved. The reduction of the Seacombe service to one of 20-minutes which could be worked by one boat, was seen as impracticable owing to high peak hour loadings. It was reasoned that reliance on *Royal Iris* as a relief boat for New Brighton would prevent advance cruise bookings being taken.

The diesel-electric *Royal Iris* proved very economical; a survey after four years' service showed a saving of £25 per day compared with the older steam vessels. On ferry service *Royal Iris* used two tons of diesel per day compared with 6.3 tons of 'boiler fuel' i.e. heavy marine oil.

When the new *Royal Daffodil II* was ordered at a cost of £235,000, this sparked off a campaign led by one Rupert Seal for the total abandonment of the ferries; he argued that, since 1863 they had cost the town £448,673 but had put back only £97,292 into public funds. He favoured electrification of the Seacombe branch railway which had been excluded from the 1938 scheme, arguing that, despite the circuitous route, a train could give a weatherproof service to the centre of Liverpool in less than 20 minutes. However, the sentimental attachment to the ferries was too strong for logical financial arguments to prevail. It may have been coincidental that there was an attempt to sabotage the old *Royal Daffodil II* in Morpeth Dock on 9th January 1956, the bilge injection valve in the engine room being opened. Pumping parties worked for 24-hours to save her. The night watchman was given one guinea (£1.05) for his prompt action in raising the alarm!

The Suez crisis at the end of 1956 led to fuel rationing and some reductions in ferry services on Sunday mornings and late evenings, with a 20-minute service at Seacombe until normal conditions were restored in April 1957. The rate of increase in costs was alarming especially fuel which had increased by 40% since 1955, 26% being caused by the Suez crisis though prices fell again in 1957. Rates on ferry properties had increased sixfold since 1939 from £3,000 to £18,000 and uniform clothing fourfold. A partial fares increase in July 1956 eliminated all adult concessionary fares on the New Brighton service, the 1s. 6d. (7$\frac{1}{2}$p) day return and 9d. (4p) evening return being abolished. These measures had a disastrous effect on the New Brighton traffic and a partial reinstatement was made despite the general manager's plea to give the new arrangements more time. He blamed the weather! August Bank Holiday traffic over three days was reduced by 30% compared with the previous year. A further proposal to increase fares led to a Public Enquiry conducted by Lt. Col. F. G. Tucker for the Minister of Transport. Rupert Seal alleged that some councillors had business interests in New Brighton and had asked the Chairman of the Finance Committee not to raise the fares though this was denied. He accused the Council of having no clear ferry policy saying 'never in the history of modern public transport had so many paid so much for so short a journey at so slow a speed' and pointing out that the rate per mile was twice as much as on a luxury liner. He wanted New Brighton and cruise fares increased and Seacombe left as it was. Nevertheless, the Minister approved the proposals and fares went up once more on 31st March 1957, increased revenue being estimated at £18,000.

The Birkenhead steamer Thurstaston *approaches Liverpool stage from Woodside while Wallasey departs for Seacombe, with New Brighton boat beyond on 14th September 1957 which was 'last tram day' in Liverpool.*

J. A. Peden

8 THE LAST MUNICIPAL YEARS

THE Wallasey Corporation Act, 1958 conferred many different powers on the Council and one short section was devoted to the ferries. The most interesting clause was section 158 which stated 'for the removal of doubt', that the Corporation had power to suspend any of their ferry services as they might think fit. Furthermore, with the consent of the Minister of Transport and Civil Aviation, they may permanently discontinue and abandon any of their ferry services. The remaining clauses made provision for the protection of officers and their emoluments and laid certain obligations on the Corporation to ensure that, in the event of abandonment, the residual infrastructure did not become a hazard to navigation.

Sec. 156 removed any obligation to carry anything other than passengers and authorised a night fare between 11.30pm and 6.0am but not exceeding one shilling in addition to the ordinary day fare. Authority was granted to receive tolls for landing and embarking passengers other than from their own vessels, a clarification of an existing practice. The law regarding concessionary fares was brought into line with recent legislation affecting buses and subsidies could be taken from the rate fund in compensation for revenue so lost.

There was no intention to act on these powers at that time but the opportunity had been taken to include these provisions in a general Bill rather than incur the expense of seeking a separate Bill later. In a belated recognition that a very high proportion of journeys commenced by one mode and continued on the other, in May 1958 the Ferries and Motor Bus Committees were amalgamated as the Passenger Transport Committee but the two departments remained separate.

Marlowe was withdrawn after the 1957 season and sold for £6,000 to the British Iron & Steel Corporation on 23rd February 1958, being dismantled at Preston by Thos. Ward & Co. No buyer could be found for *Wallasey* and eventually she was reconditioned at a cost of £62,401 in 1958. By 1963, when she was withdrawn from ferry service, she was the last steam ferry boat on the river and was sold to Heyghen Frères, Antwerp for £5,150 on 31st December 1963, eventually leaving the Mersey in February 1964.

In November 1958, the chairman of this committee, Alderman J. P. Ashton, recognising the seriousness of the situation, drew up for discussion a list of seven possible courses of action:-

A stern view of St. Hilary *in dry dock.*   A. S. Clayton, Online Transport Archive

1. Close New Brighton, dismantle stage and bridge, convert pier for other purposes, discontinue cruising and reduce the fleet from six to four vessels.
2. Curtail New Brighton service to run at Easter and Whitsun holiday periods and mid-June to mid-September as per traffic requirements.
3. Reduce fleet by one vessel. Curtail cruising at peak holiday times in order to provide a three-boat service to New Brighton.
4. Reduce Seacombe service in winter to 30-minute off peak, 20-minute peak service, requiring one boat. (No saving unless reserve boat could remain in dock, risking disruption of service.
   In summer curtail off-peak service except when New Brighton running.
5. Close Seacombe off-peak service during winter months and provide a bus service to Hamilton Square Stn. or Woodside.
6. Close night service at Seacombe.
7. Close Workshops at Seacombe, dismiss all staff, survey and running repairs to vessels and stages to be carried out by outside firms.

All Ashton's recommendations were rejected. However, in 1959 the Council did engage business consultants Urwick, Orr & Partners Ltd 'to make an objective investigation of all pertinent factors affecting patronage, revenue and expenditure and from this investigation to determine the most advantageous policy to be followed and the alternative arrangements to meet this policy'.

The consultants made a very thorough job and, on the basis of 1958-59 revenue and expenditure, settled the argument about the viability of the sixth boat which was employed for 24 days on the New Brighton service. It was proved that the contribution made to revenue was greater than the expenditure so the retention of the second *St. Hilary* was justified even though she was the most expensive boat to run. An exercise was carried out showing that if Seacombe alone had been operated with three boats and all other activities cancelled, there would have been a loss of £83,538 for the year compared to the actual loss of £56,735. Seacombe was the loss-maker at £69,722 whilst New Brighton showed a profit of £1,055 and cruising £11,932 of which 53% came from catering.

The decline of New Brighton as a resort was a strong contributory factor to the loss of ferry patronage as an air of dereliction with empty shops and theatres did nothing to attract visitors. Furthermore, erosion had destroyed parts of the beach which, in the past, had been a big attraction for day-trip family parties. The rise in car ownership raised the sights of trippers who were able to travel further afield. Various suggestions were made for competing with the railway by reducing fares and increasing the speed of connecting buses but licensing and operating difficulties for the bus undertaking made these impracticable. The amateurish approach to publicising the cruising activities was strongly criticised as were the old fashioned methods and

Royal Daffodil II was the last new ferry boat to be built for Wallasey Corporation, entering service in 1958. She was licensed to carry 1,950 passengers and reverted to the traditional design with two gangway doors but retained the forward saloon on the promenade deck. She became surplus to requirements and was sold to a Greek line in 1977. R. L. Wilson

A reminder of the foggy days of yesteryear as Egremont *approaches Liverpool landing stage. Note the upper level gangway and the spotlights aimed at the gangways.* J. B. C. McCann

lack of adequate control in the workshops where the machine tools were said to have only scrap value. There was still duplication of paper work in the Ferries and Borough Treasurer's offices. This was typical of municipal trading enterprises in which there was resentment that the Treasurer had the last say on financial matters so the departments set up their own paper trail in parallel. The scheme for a slipway in the Cut was firmly knocked on the head as, apart from parliamentary authority being required for offering services to outside firms, the going rates were too low to pay even the loan charges on the necessary work. Finally they pointed out that, compared to other activities, the salary levels paid to management and senior ratings were far too low for the degree of responsibility exercised. One of the most radical proposals was the letting out of the ground floor of the covered garage as a motor showroom and workshop and conversion of the workshop yard into a car park.

After months of discussion, in an effort to reverse the loss of ferry traffic, the Motor Bus and Ferries departments at last agreed to issue a comprehensive range of discounted weekly through contracts but the issue of further day returns was not approved; the scheme came into effect on 31st May 1959. Tickets were sold at the ferry from 4.0pm on Thursdays; there were two types – 10 journey available over five days and 12

journey available over seven days. Separate tickets were issued for men and women to avoid transference, this having been standard practice for ferry contracts for many years. The tickets were targeted at people originating their journeys in the parts of Wallasey where the railway was a serious competitor but, to avoid anomalies, they also had to be available from other parts of the borough. In the week preceding their introduction 4,951 weekly ferry contracts were sold and in the first week of the new issue, the total was 4,932 of which 2,206 were bus and ferry contracts. There had been no increase in passengers and some had benefited by a reduction in fare. The finances of neither undertaking were in a position to be able to give 10% discounts. It was too little too late and the through contracts were discontinued from 2nd October 1960.

In the summer of 1959, the hourly New Brighton service was run by *Egremont* or *Leasowe*, the second boat usually being *Royal Daffodil II* with *Wallasey* and *St. Hilary* (2) in reserve, to provide the third boat on New Brighton when necessary. Seacombe was usually run by one of the small diesels; the gross cost of running one boat for a year was estimated at £35,512. The occasional Ship Canal cruises were usually worked by *Egremont* the place of which could be taken by *St. Hilary*. Terms for hiring Birkenhead boats were agreed in February 1956 but were rarely implemented.

The contribution from the rates for each of the years 1956-57 and 1957-58 had been £30,000 but in the next three years the undertaking was supported annually by £70,000; in the following two years it fell to £65,000 but rose to £75,000 in 1963-64 and then to £100,000. Even with these massive injections, a deficit was carried forward each year. The number of passengers continued to fall having halved from its immediate post-war level by 1960-61.

Birkenhead, at the behest of the Mersey Tunnel Joint Committee who supported their service financially, had wisely decided to replace its night boats on 13th May 1956 with a bus service through the tunnel, operated jointly with Liverpool Corporation. The new arrangements had worked well and there was further discussion about the future of the Seacombe service. As usual, there was resistance to abolition but, in the end, common sense prevailed and the almost empty night boats ran for the last time on 10th September 1962. Initially, a feeder bus was run between Liscard and the main Birkenhead tunnel entrance until about 2.30am but this was so poorly patronised that it lasted only until 20th January 1963.

In a radical move, the off-peak day service at Seacombe was reduced from a 15 to a 20-minute headway, worked by one boat. The peak hour service was now often worked by two small boats and a light awning was provided for *Egremont* to reduce overcrowding on the main deck. These sailings remained in force for the remainder of Wallasey Corporation's ownership of the ferries. The advent of the one-boat off-peak service at Seacombe released *St. Hilary* (2) and she went for scrap in August 1962, fetching £7,000. To avoid the need to pay a crew on the stand-by vessel, a berth had been obtained in Trafalgar Dock which was easily accessible at any state of the tide. This facility was lost in 1955, causing a return to Birkenhead. A weekend berth was found in Waterloo Dock in June 1962. To reduce staffing levels, since 1957 the north bridge at Seacombe had been used for both embarking and disembarking passengers in winter and from 13th August 1963, use of the south bridge was discontinued throughout the year, saving £1,500, though it was retained for vehicular access to the stage. Departmentally, this was known as 'one sided working'. It is believed

This replica of Royal Iris *was mounted on a Leyland PD1 bus chassis and used on the annual publicity tour of the north and Midlands from 1963. It was also used in passenger service on the New Brighton promenade in summer.*

R. Marshall

154

Egremont seen on trials on the River Dart before delivery to Wallasey in 1951. Egremont and Leasowe were sleek in lines but flawed by the omission of the forward gangway doors.   M. Jenkins collection

that the Morrison Electricar was withdrawn at the same time.

For several years, the Cruise Master made a winter promotional tour of the undertaking's main catchment areas, Lancashire, West Yorkshire, the Potteries and West Midlands and, in 1963, a replica of *Royal Iris* was built on a Leyland bus chassis. A very creditable likeness was obtained by departmental staff and much favourable comment was made, especially when it was occasionally used in summer service on the promenade at New Brighton.

Reorganisation

In a search for further economies, the Council decided that the Ferries and Bus departments should be amalgamated into a single Passenger Transport Department. Following the early retirement of the ferries general manager, Comdr. L. D. Price, the general manager of the Corporation's bus undertaking, G. G. Harding, was appointed Passenger Transport general manager on 10th September 1963 and was asked to prepare plans for full integration. His preliminary proposals were approved by the Council on 3rd December 1963 and were put into effect gradually during the next few months. There was, therefore, no formal date for the amalgamation of the two undertakings.

Apart from management overheads, it is difficult to say exactly what economies were achieved as there was staff resistance to integration and it was said at one time that the carriage of ferries stores on a bus department lorry would be sufficient to bring both undertakings to a standstill! In due

course wage increases granted to bus workers were extended to ferries floating staff. The combined undertaking continued to incur heavy losses caused by social changes, in particular increasing car ownership and the arrival of television, causing the closure of theatres and cinemas which all but eliminated the once profitable evening leisure traffic. Although Wallasey was an extreme case, the same factors were affecting public transport throughout the land so it was doubtless with some relief that Wallasey Corporation welcomed the provisions of the Transport Act, 1968 which were destined to relieve it of the responsibility for both the ferries and the buses.

The Ferry Terminals – Seacombe

The safety of the travelling public was always uppermost in the minds of the Council and maintenance of the terminals and landing stages was essential if the ferries' proud safety record was to be continued. During the war, shortages of labour and materials had resulted in maintenance of the infrastructure being restricted to essentials but the pre-war policy of keeping everything in tip top condition stood the undertaking in good stead and repairs could be limited to make-do-and-mend which would not have been acceptable under normal conditions.

The north bridge was rehabilitated in 1951-52 at a cost of £6,500. The landing stage was supported by 38 pontoons, enormous 90ft long riveted iron tanks, divided into four watertight compartments and coated with bitumen. From time to time they were struck by floating debris and, of course, had to withstand massive tidal forces which gradually wore the metal away. The buoyancy of the stage was not affected unduly by withdrawing one pontoon which could then be welded or patched in dry conditions and then put back. This was the general method used until 1955. In that year 10 pontoons were renewed followed by another eight in the next five years or so and all these were welded and had seven compartments so that the effect of a leak in one section was less serious. New pontoons were placed in a suitable dock and towed to the ferry. They were expensive items, many being supplied by Cammell Laird & Co. or Francis Morton of Garston though some were sent by rail from Rowhedge of Colchester. Lairds' tender for five pontoons in 1955 was £16,385.

The Floating Roadway

Just as facilities at Seacombe had expanded to meet demand between 1880 and 1926, so the terminal would contract during 1955-66 as demand dwindled and costs escalated. Following abandonment of the goods service, the three-berth Seacombe stage was simply too long. Since March 1947, the southern end was used only for berthing vessels undergoing maintenance or repair and occasionally in stormy weather. The floating roadway was now used only for deliveries of coal, food and drink for the cruises and other materials to the stage, minimal repairs being done to keep it in a safe condition. Consultants had reported in March 1954 as a result of which tenders were invited for its dismantling in July, the contractor being paid no fee but given the materials salvaged. The south passenger bridge was to be used for vehicle access and the Dock Board were asked to allow bunkering at the north end of Woodside stage but, as they failed to reply, it was agreed to ascertain what needed to be done to strengthen the bridge to accept 20-ton loads. Meanwhile, the floating roadway had to be maintained but only in June 1955 was a contract awarded to Horseley Bridge and Thomas Piggott Ltd, Tipton for £10,062. 4s. 0d. to strengthen the bridge in the winter of 1955-56 to enable dismantling the roadway to start in May 1956. Matters did not work out like that, the contractor undertaking to finish the bridge only by October 1956.

The elements then threw a spanner in the works as, on 28/29th December 1955 heavy seas and gales started to break the roadway up. Fearing that the south passenger bridge might collapse, 75 men worked night and day to make the roadway safe, part of it being cut away. The tender of R. S. Hayes Ltd was accepted for removing the roadway, the first half being floated to Egremont on 28th March and the second half on Good Friday 30th March 1956; they were cut up on the plateau south of the terminal building. The contract time was twice extended and the job was finished in February 1957. Wilton and Bell, civil engineers, were engaged to investigate whether the floating roadway cut, 355ft long and 77ft wide, could be put to some useful purpose. There were initially three ideas, a dry dock (£163,000), a wet dock (£114,000) or a slipway (£76,000). It was thought that money would be saved on dry dock fees by doing the annual survey of the ferries vessels and some general maintenance and repair work there, the proximity of the workshops being particularly useful. One of the problems was that of access as the new construction would have been behind the stage and, after rejecting the moving of the stage northwards, it was proposed that the southern boom should be moved north of the cut, at an additional cost of £14,000, enabling vessels to manoeuvre behind the stage. This would still have been a tricky operation with disastrous consequences if absolute control of the vessel was lost. Unless there was a serious collision, the fleet needed a dry dock for only about 36 weeks annually, and it was hoped that the facility could be let out on a commercial basis for the remainder of the time.

Wilton & Bell pointed out that by far the least expensive means of dealing with the cut was to fill it in and use it as a car park, two schemes being drawn up costing £35,000 for an open area or £82,000 for a two-storey covered building. The report was received in May 1958 but no immediate action was taken. Later there was talk of building a marina in the cut but in April 1962 a footbridge was placed across it to give access to a new car park adjoining the Workshops which was opened on 1st June.

In 1963-64 consultants D. V. Buck & Partners were first engaged to report on the shortening of the Seacombe landing stage and then on the department's properties in general. It was found possible to reduce the length so that it could be supported on 26 instead of 38 pontoons and, as 20 pontoons needed to be replaced over the next five years, there was a clear saving of the cost of 12 pontoons, estimated conservatively at £48,000 plus the finance charges. Against this, the cost of removal was put at £33,500 after allowing for the scrap value of the severed structure. However, if the stage were shortened, expenditure on pontoon replacement over a 20-year period was estimated to be £32,000 instead of £80,000. The stage was duly shortened by 150ft at the southern end by Carter-Horsley (Engineering) Ltd of Liverpool. Work started on 9th November 1964 and was completed on 5th January 1966, the final cost being £37,597. 7s. 7d.

The consultants estimated that, provided

Welders and others at work on replacing plates in the north bridge at Seacombe. Note the massive columns which support the terminal building and the floating roadway visible in the background. The rudimentary wooden stage and safety rope would doubtless give a present day Health & Safety inspector palpitations!   Wirral Archive Service

appropriate protective maintenance of the infrastructure continued, the cost of maintaining the Seacombe terminal as a whole would be £149,000 over 20 years but slightly more than half of that sum would be incurred within the first five years as urgent repairs were necessary to the stage keelsons and cladding and to the bridge bearings and roofs. They were also of the opinion that at the end of that period (1984) the stage and bridges would have reached the end of their economic lives.

It was apparent that the undertaking was in no position to incur such sums so only essential work was done. Expenditure on maintenance (excluding storm damage) in the mid-1960s is shown below.

Understandably, priority was given to Seacombe, the all the year round 'main line' and the ultimate demise of the New Brighton service was assured by the Council's inability to pay for the maintenance of its pier.

New Brighton

Several pontoons from the redundant Egremont stage are thought to have been salvaged and used as replacements. All were of riveted construction with five compartments each. As at Seacombe, repairs to pontoons were scaled down in 1955 after which nine of the 18 were replaced with riveted

	1963-64 £	1964-65 £	1965-66 £	TOTAL £
Seacombe landing	11,112	13,002	13,456	37,570
New Brighton landing	4,357	7,182	1,606	13,145
Liverpool landing	807	653	726	2,186
Buildings & plant	3,889	3.888	2,843	10,620
Mooring & chain booms	4,028	771	946	5.745

Royal Daffodil II *approaches Seacombe landing stage beneath a lowering sky with the Liverpool waterfront in the right* *background.*
R. L. Wilson

mild steel structures. The new pontoons were slightly deeper than the earlier ones which, in time, led to some distortion. Because of its position at the mouth of the Mersey, New Brighton was probably the most exposed landing place of its kind in the country and, because it was situated at the end of a 600ft long pier extended by bridges, its moorings could not be attached to the land, as at Seacombe, but were secured to dolphins or anchored into the river bed. Again, unlike Seacombe, the river bed was subject to much movement of sand and there was a tendency for chains to become buried leading to tightening and breakage, resulting in total loss of the chain. To overcome this problem, a technique was devised for attaching buoys to the chains which prevented them from sinking. Whilst this was effective with north-south chains, it could not be used for the east-west chains as navigation would have been impeded by the buoys.

On 11/12th September 1957, a severe storm caused much damage and there was concern about the condition of the bridgehead at the end of the pier. Wilton and Bell were asked to recommend what work was necessary to make good the structure for the next 20 years. The bridges were hinged to the bridgehead and designed to slide on the stage, the attachments allowing for the twisting action of the tide in severe weather. The stresses on the bridgehead were considerable and the survey revealed evidence of much corrosion. The problem was exacerbated by the unequal lengths of the bridges - 157ft 6in (north) and 174ft 6in (south) - an arrangement which had been adopted to enable the stage to take a position in line with the mean flow of the tide. But on occasions the two bridges behaved differently, one resisting a thrust while the other was countering a pull. The

consultants recommended that new reinforced concrete piers should be built around the existing 1935 piles which were still in excellent condition and the bearings were redesigned so that the bridgehead was relieved of the loads and forces to which it was subjected by the two bridges but bore only the loads of the approach pier. They also suggested that the bridges should be of equal length or replaced by one bridge but these solutions were rejected. The original design was rejected by the Dock Board marine surveyors as likely to cause erosion of the foreshore, a subject upon which Wallasey Corporation had many times complained so new but costlier proposals were accepted. The work was considered so urgent that it was started before loan sanction was obtained in order to avoid interfering with seasonal traffic. The new bridgehead was built in 1958 at a cost of £12,000.

The wrought-iron north bridge was replaced by a new £42,000 steel structure, 17ft wide, in 1959-60; the construction was heavy to allow for the wracking strains imparted by the pitching and rolling of the stage during storm conditions. It was assembled on a West Float quay at Poulton. The south bridge was strengthened at the same time, all the work being done by the Butterley Co. of Derby at a cost of £54,368. During the replacement of the bridges in a south-easterly wind, the giant floating crane *Mammoth* was tied to the stage which was displaced to the north; the work of repositioning took several days. The bridges were officially opened by the Minister of Transport, Ernest Marples, who was also the local M.P., on 8th April 1960. On 11th January 1962 during a severe storm, the north bridge was lifted from its shore end pintle, collided with the south bridge and fell into the river. There were fears that the stage would be carried away on the 31ft tide and tugs *James Lamey*, *Marie Lamey* and the Dock Board salvage vessel *Salvor* stood by. The south bridge was lifted and taken to Seacombe landing stage on 15th. At first it was thought that two new bridges would be needed but the north bridge was repaired for £12,000 by the Butterley Co., who quoted £28,541. 13s. 9d. for a new south bridge. In view of the need to get the ferry working for the summer season, standing orders were suspended and the contract awarded without tenders being invited. The new south bridge was placed in position on 12th July 1962 at a total cost of £64,881 most of which was eventually recovered from insurance. Consultants recommended the replacement of several beams in the pier structure and extra bracing between the piles, maintenance cost over the 20-year period being estimated at £99,000 of which £64,100 was to be incurred during the first five years. Although the landing stage and bridges would clearly serve beyond the 20-year period, it was predicted that the pier structure would be life-expired at the end of that period.

In view of their past record, perhaps it is not surprising that, while spending large sums of money on restoring New Brighton ferry pier, the Council were, at the same time, considering closing it down. They first considered withdrawing the ferry service in 1961 when over 1.5 million passengers were carried and it was still adjudged profitable so it was not until November 1964, when the impact of the consultants' report had been absorbed that the first serious proposal was made. This brought forth the expected outcry from local shopkeepers and hoteliers who formed a New Brighton Ferry Defence Committee. However, from 1962 a further problem had manifested itself as changes in the river bed caused more serious silting beneath and to the north of the stage. The moorings were altered and new buoys fitted to keep the stage in the deepest water. As several of the old Liverpool docks were being filled in, the Dock Board was approached to see if the silt could be used for in-filling but the verdict was that the sand at New Brighton was too fine. During most of the 1960s, the service became increasingly unreliable with groundings and sudden curtailments becoming depressingly frequent. In November 1965, the Mersey Tunnel Joint Committee offered to allocate £10,000 per annum towards maintenance and dredging costs at New Brighton but the estimated cost was £25,000 which simply was not available and, if it had been, there was no guarantee that the silt would not return in a very short time. The ferry was soon a pale shadow of its former success as passengers continued to drain away in their thousands. A severe gale on 17-18th March 1968 damaged the pier and stage and carried away a pontoon which was washed up on Waterloo shore; it was moved to Birkenhead docks on a low loader. By the end of the decade, a work-to-rule by ferries staff often made it impossible to run the New Brighton service, which depended on overtime and

The second St. Hilary, *formerly* Royal Daffodil II *shows off her 46ft beam as she leaves Liverpool for Seacombe.*

Pam Eaton

A late 1960s aerial view of Seacombe after removal of the Floating Roadway but before the shortening of the landing stage. Note that the railway station has gone, having been replaced by housing in the background.　　M. Jenkins collection

rest day work to a large extent, even when there was sufficient depth of water.

The unreliability had a knock-on effect on cruising as passengers who had booked to join at New Brighton arrived to find the ferry closed. Free buses were laid on to take passengers to Seacombe but the uncertainty took its toll and added to the revenue loss resulting from new Life Saving Appliance rules introduced in 1965 which required vessels plying on the open sea to carry life jackets and other equipment. This was considered too expensive so *Royal Iris* was unable to go beyond New Brighton lighthouse.

The management was ever on the lookout for new opportunities and in May 1964 *Royal Daffodil II* sailed to Llandudno to act as tender to the Swedish cruise liner *Kungsholm*. At the end of 1968, Menai Bridge Urban District Council asked if the Wallasey Ferries would be interested in providing a seasonal cruising service thence to Llandudno, the previous operator, P & A Campbell of Cardiff, having withdrawn. A detailed assessment was made and it was intended to use *Egremont* which

would have required minimum alterations. New types of life belts and jackets would have been needed and it was thought that a certificate for 650 passengers would be forthcoming, allowing the vessel to operate in an area bounded by Liverpool, Barrow, Holyhead and Menai Bridge. The master would have needed a Board of Trade Home Trade Master's certificate and Mersey and Menai Straits pilot's licences. It was proposed to recruit the crew in North Wales and, apart from two stewardesses, to allow them to live and sleep on board. Landing charges at Menai Bridge (7d per passenger) and Llandudno (one shilling) were negotiated. The fleet had been reduced to the extent that some arrangement had to be made with Birkenhead to hire a vessel when necessary and the whole scheme fell through because of the high rates demanded which would have made the job uneconomic.

The Passenger Transport department was reorganised administratively on 2nd September 1969 but, three months later it ceased to exist altogether, as described in the next chapter.

9 THE MERSEYSIDE P.T.E. YEARS

FROM 1st December 1969, the passenger transport services of Liverpool, Birkenhead and Wallasey Corporations were taken over by the Merseyside Passenger Transport Executive (MPTE) under the terms of the Transport Act 1968. The PTE was responsible for day to day operations to a policy laid down by the Passenger Transport Authority (PTA) the members of which were appointed by the local authorities within the designated areas. Merseyside was one of four PTA/PTEs formed at this time but the only one with responsibility for ferry services.

The PTE took over seven vessels, three from Birkenhead (*Mountwood*, *Woodchurch* and *Overchurch*) and four from Wallasey. Between 1st April and 30th November 1969, the Wallasey ferries had incurred a deficit of £418,842 and, in addition, the PTE was bound by law to compensate the three operating local authorities for severance charges of £163,895. As soon as possible the ferries departments of Birkenhead and Wallasey were merged, the Seacombe workshop being closed, all work being done at Woodside under the control of a Divisional Engineer (Ferries). The floating staff were brought under the control of a Divisional Marine Superintendent, all controlled by a Ferries Superintendent, Mr C. B. Sandland who died in October 1971; he was replaced by his deputy, H. E. Campbell who was designated Ferries Manager.

Royal Daffodil, for which the original name had been regained from the General Steam Navigation Co. in July 1968, was equipped with a new public address system to provide facilities for educational cruises for which a publicity drive was mounted resulting in 23,000 passengers being carried in 1971, compared with 3,500 on this type of activity the previous year. Specialist reports were obtained about *Royal Iris* and approval obtained from the PTA for a £68,000 refurbishment programme carried out by Harland & Wolff during the winter of 1971-72. This was despite the outstanding debt on the vessel being £56,000 which would generate capital charges of £13,000 for the next seven years; this figure would increase by £9,500 for the next ten years. The current loss on cruising was £25,000 p.a. It was suggested to the Executive that 'the Authority may consider that the estimated deficit is a reasonable price to pay for a unique recreational amenity'. The vessel was no longer to be used on ferry service and it was hoped that cruising could be expanded. The chip shop was replaced by a 'tea room' and the layout of the bars and leisure facilities was completely revamped. The green and cream external paintwork was replaced by a new blue and white livery. Results

for 1972 were encouraging, 148 public and 111 chartered cruises being operated; in addition *Royal Daffodil* undertook 62 educational cruises conveying 21,312 children. *Royal Iris* was berthed at Liverpool landing stage and served lunches. In 1973, a new north docks cruise by *Leasowe* was devised. In the 15 months ending 31st March 1975, cruising was carried on with the following results:-

	Cruises	Passengers
Royal Iris evening public cruises	47	4,374
Royal Iris Monday to Friday afternoon public cruises		18,473 adults
Royal Daffodil Sunday afternoon public cruises	83	11,757 children
Royal Iris private charters	172	49,612
Educational cruises	42	19,341
Manchester Ship Canal cruises	9	3,847 adults
		4,726 children

The radar equipment, now over 20 years old, was replaced in 1970, a new base station being installed at Seacombe. In addition to normal contact with the base station, provision was made for masters to communicate direct in an emergency with the PTE's communications centre at Hatton Garden, Liverpool. Work on the filling in of the cut for the floating roadway was completed in 1972 and additional car parking provided on the site. A problem of integrating the ferry fleets was the difference in gangway spacing between Birkenhead and Wallasey vessels and, as the former were the youngest, it was decided to alter the positions of the gangways at Seacombe and Liverpool to the Birkenhead standard, this work being completed in 1974.

The Bill to restructure the Dock Board as the Mersey Docks and Harbour Company was deposited in Parliament in the 1971 session, one of its provisions being the repeal of the requirement to maintain the Liverpool landing stage for the ferries. The PTE was advised that a charge of £77,000 per year would be made for the right to use the stage which was in poor condition. Discussions between the parties resulted in an agreement by the PTE to pay 25% of the cost of a new stage and a monthly sum for maintenance. The stage was designed with two ferry berths at the south end and an Isle of Man berth with vehicular access at the north end. The pontoons were to be fabricated in concrete to the Harbour company's design. Work started on 16th July 1973 on the demolition of the old structure, the ferries being temporarily banished to the south end of Prince's landing stage with a pedestrian bridge across the floating roadway cut. This was an inconvenient location and contributed to a further fall in patronage. Services resumed from the new stage on 13th July 1975 but, following severe storm damage, services were suspended from 3rd January 1976, restarting from the Isle of Man berth on 12th. Then this section was affected by further storm damage on 20th and services were not recommenced until 11th February from Prince's landing stage. There they remained until the concrete stage was back in commission on 13th April 1976. A direct tunnel bus service was run between Seacombe and Liverpool but Woodside passengers were directed to the underground railway. These disasters had less effect on patronage at Seacombe where about 400 daily passengers were lost but at Woodside regular passengers fell from 4,000 daily to 1,900. The grounding of the stage in January 1978 because of insufficient dredging caused yet more disruption.

Closure of the New Brighton Service

The PTE used a suction pump at New Brighton to remove sand from beneath the stage and prevent further damage to the pontoons. This was successful but extra repairs were necessary to replace fractured members of the south bridge. Sailings continued to be restricted to $3^1/2$-4 hours either side of high tide because of the siltation problem. This led to public doubt about the service despite an extensive press advertising campaign and a Freefone telephone information service. Alarm was being expressed at the effect of the ferry's deteriorating service on the economy of the resort and the local Hotels and Catering association claimed that the number of people directly or indirectly employed in the catering and amusement trades had fallen by 90% since 1965. The fire which destroyed the Tower building in 1969 was another serious blow. Passengers declined from 290,000 in 1970 to 216,000 in 1971. Uninhibited by sentiment, the PTE commissioned reports about the future of the service and a special Committee was set up to consider the matter. They recommended total closure of the service at the end of the 1971 season and the last boat ran on Sunday 26th September. *Leasowe* worked the service on the last two days, doing eight hourly trips on the Saturday and nine on Sunday, the last departure from New Brighton being at 7.40pm. This policy was accepted by the PTA, maintenance at New Brighton being scaled down to the absolute minimum. A Public Enquiry was held by an Inspector of the Department of the Environment during February 1972 and the Minister's approval of closure was announced on 25th August 1972. A major factor was the opening of the second Mersey road tunnel between Liverpool and Wallasey on 28th June 1971 as New Brighton was brought within a few minutes' drive for the increasing numbers of private motorists. A frequent bus service was run between the city centre and New Brighton from the opening day.

Some hopes had been raised when Hoverwork Ltd, an Isle of Wight-based hovercraft operator, showed interest in establishing a service on the Mersey. Although the public jumped to conclusions and assumed that a New Brighton-Liverpool service was proposed, the whole coastlines between Seacombe and Hoylake and between Otterspool and Crosby were surveyed. In October 1972 there was a trial of a 38-seat SRN6 craft with members of the PTA, PTE and Wallasey councillors on board and whilst there was optimism, the small capacity of the craft and the difficulty of maintaining a service in a heavy swell rendered the scheme impracticable. An evaluation of a service between various places on the Wirral coast and Liverpool Airport was made but no more was heard of the proposals.

The economic consequences of the closure were publicly demonstrated in November 1972 when the leisure firm, Fortes Ltd, who had leased the New Brighton promenade pier from the Corporation in late 1967 and spent £200,000 on improvements, announced that they were pulling out as the closure of the ferry was 'the last straw'. The consequences for New Brighton were disastrous with unemployment rising at a time when the trend nationally was downwards. There was a ceremony at Wallasey Town Hall on 7th May 1973 when the brass fog bell from New Brighton landing stage, weighing 280lb. and suitably inscribed, was handed over to the Mayor. It took four ferry hands to carry the bell up the main staircase of the Town Hall. Four days later, the floating crane *Mammoth* lifted the two bridges and placed them upon the stage, already cleared of the passenger shelter, which was towed to Egerton Dock, Birkenhead for breaking up. Demolition of the ferry pier commenced on 17th September 1973, being completed in October 1974. When the promenade pier followed in 1977, it marked the end of a saga spanning almost a century and a half.

With the closure of New Brighton, the two small ex-Wallasey boats were redundant. *Leasowe* went in February 1974 to Greek owners for £34,000; she was renamed *Naias II* but *Egremont* was not sold until 3rd August 1975, being subsequently converted into a floating clubhouse at Salcombe, Devon where she remained for many years. *Royal Iris* had a narrow escape when fire broke out in the engine room during her survey on 12th January 1975. There was extensive damage to electrical equipment, many internal fittings were damaged and it was necessary to replace the carpets on the main deck.

A New Transport Authority

From 1st April 1974 the Passenger Transport Committee of the newly-formed Merseyside County Council became the transport authority and had to face up to the deteriorating financial state of the ferries. Simultaneously, all the Wirral local authorities were merged to form the Metropolitan Borough of Wirral. Passengers on the Wallasey services had declined from nine million in 1960 to 2.2 million in 1974, matched by the decline at Birkenhead from 6.9 million to 1.9 million. Consultants reported to the effect that there was no justification for continuing the ferries and, as the current year's loss was about £800,000 and the Council had continued the policy of the original PTE in developing and extending the rail network, the Committee voted to close them down. However, amid a storm of popular protest, the County Council voted to continue the service on a reduced frequency.

The Seacombe fare had increased from 9d. to 1s. in January 1971 and was decimalised to 5p in February 1971; thereafter fares followed the pattern of increases on the buses and trains. Weekly contracts were replaced by multi-journey tickets in October 1974 when automatic turnstiles were installed at Seacombe. Fares were increased twice in 1975, from 5p to 8p on 14th July and to 10p on 2nd November. Intermodal zone tickets were introduced throughout the passenger transport area from 29th October 1978. The peak hour 10-minute service was finally discontinued from 1st April 1975, the one-boat 20-minute service running all day on weekdays.

Losses reached £879,000 in 1974-75 and by 1976-77 had increased to £1,264,000. Passengers on all services had declined from 35.5 million in 1920 to 19.3 million in 1955, 16.2 million in 1960, 7.2 million in 1971 and 3.3 million in 1976. Three of the metropolitan boroughs which had never had any interest in the ferries – Sefton, Knowsley and St. Helens – resented having to share the losses which were covered by the transport precept and thought that the full cost should be borne by Liverpool and Wirral. Some action was essential to stem the losses and, in the 1976-77 Parliamentary session, the Merseyside Passenger Transport Bill was presented by Eric Ogden, MP for West Derby, to give the PTE power to discontinue ferry services and introduce penalties for overriding on the buses. Whilst the PTE had inherited the powers granted in Wallasey's 1958 Act, these did not cover Woodside and, following the integration of the ferries, the closure of Seacombe alone was insufficient to stem the losses. Meanwhile, in 1977, the Leader of the County Council told

The ex-Birkenhead vessel Overchurch, *with white funnel, passes the south end of Liverpool landing stage. This was built to the standard Birkenhead gangway spacing and the gangways at the former Wallasey landing stages had to be respaced to accommodate the three ex-Birkenhead boats.*

R. L. Wilson

Overchurch passing Chester Road swing bridge, Warrington on 23rd September 1984 on a Cooperative Wholesale Society charter cruise along the Manchester Ship Canal from Manchester to New Brighton.   R. L. Wilson

transport interest groups that the future of the ferries lay in leisure cruising. In the event, the Bill was talked out in a $2^1/_2$-hour speech by David Hunt, MP for Wirral West, to the delight of the Friends of the Ferries, a pressure group founded in 1974. Local MPs were also successful in having a proposed clause empowering local authorities to discontinue ferry services after a public enquiry deleted from the government's Transport Bill in 1977.

Integration of the Wallasey and Birkenhead services was completed following the destruction by fire of the Woodside workshops and the loss of most of the stock of spare parts in May 1980. New workshops and stores were already being built at Seacombe and the administrative offices were moved there in March 1981. Passengers at Seacombe had fallen to little more than 1.5 million in 1978 and after a boost to cruising in 1973 and 1974, enthusiasm seems to have been lost and only 33,000 passengers were carried in 1978. The 19-year old *Royal Daffodil* was declared surplus to requirements and sold for £55,000 in 1977 to Greek owners who renamed her *Ioulis Keas II*. From 6th April 1981, both Seacombe and Woodside were reduced to a basic 40-minute headway worked by one boat, additional peak hour trips being provided by *Royal Iris* which still offered an attractive lunch-time restaurant service, tied up at Liverpool landing stage. *Woodchurch* was laid up. Eventually it was realised that the 40-minute service was self-defeating and from 28th November 1983, she was brought back into service

and the off-peak and Saturday frequencies on both the Seacombe and Woodside services were doubled to 20-minutes (30-minutes on Sundays), requiring one boat on each service and one in reserve. In 1984 the promotion and marketing of ferry leisure services was handed over to the County Council's Tourism Committee, operational control remaining with the PTE. Services in 1984 benefited from two special events. For the Liverpool Garden Festival, a landing stage was built up-river at Otterspool and between 3rd May and mid-October, a special service was run from Liverpool via Woodside to Otterspool for 25p. The depth of water at Otterspool restricted the service to high tide and only between two and five trips per day were possible. *Overchurch*, painted in a somewhat garish red, white and blue livery, was mainly used on this special service, an unexpected revival of the South End ferry of the 1860s. The second event was the Tall Ships Race from 1st to 4th August when 250,000 passengers were carried, the Woodside service being suspended for eight hours on 4th so that all the vessels could be used as grandstands for the Grand Parade of Sail. Notwithstanding these bonuses, the loss in 1984-85 was still £2,115,000.

These were the days of strong political divisions on Merseyside and *Royal Iris* was used in the campaign for the retention of Merseyside County Council, sailing all the way to the Thames where she was moored as close to Westminster as she could get, emblazoned with suitable slogans. However, the County Council was abolished and

Mountwood loaded to the gunnels at the time of the Tall Ships' Race in August 1984. The slogans were in support of a campaign against the abolition of the Merseyside County Council.   Merseyside PTE

Royal Iris *in PTE red, white and blue livery in Albert Dock, Liverpool in June 1985. This vessel travelled to London to demonstrate against the dissolution of Merseyside County Council.*   J. B. Horne

The north bridge and boom being supported on jacks pending the arrival of the new Seacombe landing stage in September 1999 and the new stage in position with a work boat still in attendance.
A. D. Maund

The south bridge at Seacombe supported on jacks and ten days later with Mountwood *berthed at the new landing stage on 24th September 1999.*
A. D. Maund

the ferries once more came under the control of the PTE, comprising representatives of the five metropolitan boroughs, Liverpool, Wirral, Sefton, Knowsley and St. Helens. Fears that the deregulation of bus services would seal the fate of the ferries were unfounded and, although there are many more bus services through both tunnels, they have taken patronage mainly from the railway. A subsidiary company, Mersey Ferries Ltd, was formed by the PTE as an arm's length operating subsidiary and, with the need to replace or refurbish the fleet at great expense looming, L & R Leisure plc were engaged as consultants to recommend how to adapt the ferries to a purely tourist role. It was decided to refurbish *Mountwood* and *Woodchurch* and, from 1st April 1990, a half-hourly triangular ferry service was initially run by *Overchurch* between Woodside, Seacombe and Liverpool, operating clockwise in the morning peak and thereafter anti-clockwise, with a 45-minute Sunday service. This was subsequently amended to an hourly off-peak cruise, the vessel sailing further up and down river on each circuit; the half-hourly peak service was retained. Ancillary attractions include an aquarium and

children's play area at Seacombe and a restaurant at Woodside. Gift shops were opened at all three terminals. These cruises proved very popular and, in addition, special trips to Manchester and through the Liverpool north docks were undertaken from time to time. The 43-year old *Royal Iris*, the last ex-Wallasey boat, was now redundant. She was eventually sold in 1993 to a consortium interested in turning her into a floating night club at Cardiff. This project failed and the unique vessel, now in a sorry state, was gently decaying on the Thames at Woolwich in 2002.

As the end of the century approached, a strategy was needed for fleet renewal as two of the vessels were almost 40 years old and, *Overchurch*, the newest was only two years younger. It was decided that a radical refurbishment of *Overchurch* presented the best value for money and application was successfully made to the European Development Fund for a financial contribution. The work was carried out by Lengthline in Manchester, with consultancy services by Graham and Woolnough Ltd. As rebuilt, the vessel has two spacious through

The new landing stage at Seacombe features this unusual tubular A-frame construction. The north bridge, visible in the picture is used for both embarking and disembarking passengers, the south bridge being used only for vehicular access for maintenance or revictualling. The close up view, taken from an approaching vessel,shows the foot of the north bridge and the balanced gangway.   T. B. Maund

saloons, both with catering facilities, one on the main deck and the other on the promenade deck above. Extra space on the main deck was given by removing the forward gangway doors, similar to *Egremont* and *Leasowe* of 1951. New Wartsila NSD 700kw engines and generators were installed by Wartsila NSD (UK) Ltd in June 1999. The boat returned to the Mersey bearing the time-honoured name *Royal Daffodil*.

With the fleet problem alleviated for the time being, a decision had to be made about Seacombe landing stage as, despite heavy expenditure on remedial work during the previous two decades, its condition was such that the choice was between complete renewal or total abandonment. After much discussion, installation of a new stage was authorised by the PTE. The stage, measuring 102m x 20m wide by 6m deep (334ft 7in x 65ft 7in x 6ft 6¹/₂in) was built by Christiani and Nielsen in Canada Dry Dock. The existing bridges were retained. Seacombe ferry was closed for three weeks in September 1999 while the bridges were supported, the old stage

removed and the new stage floated into position. The stage was subsequently slightly damaged in storms in early February 2000 forcing the closure of the terminal for several days. The superstructure containing a glass-walled waiting room area is distinguished by an unusual tubular A-frame structure which is clearly visible across the river. The stage was financed by Merseyside PTE with a contribution from 'New Wallasey', a government-sponsored urban renewal fund. It was officially opened on 7th April 2000 by Lord Macdonald, Minister for Transport.

Despite indifferent weather, 2000 was a good year for charters and cruising and, early in 2001, it was decided to have *Mountwood* refitted at Birkenhead by Wright and Beyer, a member of the Cammell Laird Group. On its return to service early in 2002 it was renamed *Royal Iris of the Mersey* although only *Royal Iris* appeared on the vessel. The three projects represented an investment in excess of £7.5 million and assured the future of the Mersey Ferries for many years to come.

Royal Daffodil, *formerly* Overchurch, *is seen moored at the Ferries' berth, on the East Float, adjoining Duke Street Bridge, Birkenhead. Note the removal of the forward gangway door and the much extended covered accommodation on the promenade deck.*

T. B. Maund

APPENDIX 1

BRAITHWAITE POOLE'S REPORT
TO COMMISSIONERS OF WALLASEY BOARD OF HEALTH
dated 5th December 1860

On the Mersey there are 30 ferry steamers viz:

Ferry	Miles	Total Boats	Daily in work	Trips Daily	Miles Daily	Average Daily Miles per boat
Eastham	6	2	2	12	144	72
Rock Ferry	2	5	3	31	124	41
Birkenhead*	$1.^1/_8$	6	3	57	128	43
Monks	1	2	2	13	26	13
Woodside	$^3/_4$	8	5	102	150	30
Seacombe	$^3/_4$	2	2	34	52	26
Egremont	$1^1/_2$	3	2	30	90	45
New Brighton	3	2	2	27	80	40
TOTAL		30	21	306	794	38

* including Tranmere, the two having been connected by a bridge.

Average of 9 boats out of service daily, either under repair, not wanted or on excursion trips.

In comparison with paddlers working on the Thames, each of which operated in excess of 100 miles a day, those on the Mersey averaged a paltry 38 miles a day largely due to their underpowered engines and unsuitability for cross-river traffic.

Seacombe, Egremont and New Brighton boats are timed to run in such an orbit as to work only one-third of their time and stand idle for two-thirds. Although a boat is under steam in summer for 15-18 hours per day, only five hours are spent in actually running.

Three or four boats ply half-hourly between Egremont, New Brighton and George's Landing Stage - 8 round trips, 3 miles each way; 6 x 8 = 48 miles, stopping only at those two ferries on each trip from 7.30am to 10.30pm, 15 hours. *Elizabeth* and *Tiger* run also half-hourly between Seacombe and George's Pier, a distance of c.1500 yds, 16-17 trips daily, 5.0am to 11.0pm, 18 hours. Therefore it takes one hour for 3,000 yds. Passengers can only cross the river every half-hour in daytime though at Woodside they can cross daily every 10 minutes and nightly every hour and on public holidays every 5-mins, which acceleration is soon to become their daily practice.

The running speed of the Wallasey boats may be taken as 10 mph with the tide and $3^1/_2$ mph in flood and ebb tides, stoppages included at the ferries and at the Landing Stage against an average of 18 miles and 9 miles respectively on the Thames. The passage across to Seacombe averages 10 minutes against the seven minutes to Woodside and duplicate boats are employed, as it would appear, unnecessarily in as much as the Egremont boats actually ferry over the same ground.

Most of the vessels, having been built as tugboats with $4^1/_2$-$6^1/_2$ft draught are unsuitable for ferry traffic. Their inferior accommodation for passengers is proverbial everywhere both on deck and below; their ill-ventilated cabins, want of retiring rooms for females and children, who are also exposed to much danger at low water by being transported in small, inconvenient boats, crowded to excess or carried by boatmen between the steamer and the stages; the general dirty condition of these boats, &c, &c are circumstances to be recorded as intolerable nuisances, in order to show hereafter that the Commissioners acted wisely from the beginning in their determination to build a better class of vessel and to remedy these evils.

VALUATIONS OF COULBORNS' FLEET

| Name | Year Built | Last New Boiler | Original Cost £ | Coulborn £ | Valuation by | | |
					Vernon £	Sanderson £	Kellock £
Elizabeth	1840	1853	300	900	800	600	400
Wallasey	1847	1857	2,500	2,350	1,800	1,600	1,250
Th. Wilson	1845	1854	1,500	900	1,500	1,000	1,400
J. Atherton	1846	1855	4,800	2,300	2,300	2,200	1,700
Fairy	1849	1860	5,200	2,500	2,000	2,000	1,400
Tiger	1853	1853	3,000	2,450	1,900	1,200	1,350
Liscard	1858	1858	5,200	5,000	3,800	3,000	2,000

The Birkenhead company carry the chief portion of the cattle traffic and merchandise across the river from the North Landing Stage to Tranmere where Messrs Willoughby employ three carts, three horses and 3 men in the delivery of goods. They pay to the Corporation of Liverpool £350 p.a. rent for Tranmere slip and goods warehouse and £150 for the passenger slip; total £500. Luggage boats are occupied 2 hours in performing round trip, loading and unloading and they run five times daily except Sundays.

At Rock Ferry, Mr Hetherington prosecutes a small goods traffic, there being a small goods shed and yard for its reception at the top of the slip but it is altogether only a trivial business. The passenger traffic is tolerably well conducted but it would be a great improvement to amalgamate the working of the three ferries – Eastham, Rock and Tranmere – as they would unitedly produce a decreased expenditure, greater accommodation, increased traffic and an increased revenue.

'...assuming that you may arrive at an apposite conclusion, the next point to determine will be the precise description of the boats that should be ordered to be built and it has just flashed across my mind that you will very naturally ask how it happens that I, as a Railway Traffic Manager, can possibly know anything about Ferries and Boat building. As such, I feel it necessary to explain that, Ferries being the natural barriers, obstructions and hindrances to Railways, I have had very much to do with their management and mismanagement, to work and consult thereon with my late brother officers, Robert Stephenson, Locke and Brunel; where scarcely an invention or scheme of any sort connected with any ferry ever escaped our observation. I have made tours of inspection with these gentlemen of several of the chief ferries in Europe: besides which I have recently had the greater advantage of an extensive tour of inspection of the rivers and ferries of America and am conversant with the building and sailing of all classes of vessels from a Canal Boat to a Line of Battle Ship......'

The Merchandise traffic would be carried, on completion of the piers, in a separate boat from Prince's LS. A population of 12,800 will ensure in fuel, food and raiment upward of 40,000 tons weight per annum. Very little of this goods traffic has ever been sought or developed at the Wallasey Ferries.

APPENDIX 2

WALLASEY FERRIES
PASSENGERS CARRIED & ORDINARY REVENUE

Year Ended	TOTAL PASSENGERS	REVENUE £	NOTES
25 Mar			
1862		10,732	
1863	3,001,518	18,495	
1864		20,196	
31 Dec			
1864 (9 months)		19,994	
1865		23,634	
1866		22,547	
1867		24,771	
1868		26,945	
1869		27,973	
1870		29,085	
1871		30,333	
1872	4,702,833	32,869	
1873	5,171,250	34,579	
1874	4,922,900	34,754	
1875	5,611,206	34,535	
1876	5,537,519	35,949	
1877	5,568,573	36,973	
1878	5,490,607	37,761	
31 Mar			
1879	5,430,218	35,527	
1880	5,635,588	37,101	
1881	5,965,998	40,137	
1882	6,544,172	44,020	
1883	6,722,819	46,560	
1884	7,145,279	48,294	
1885	7,684,742	49,395	
1886	7,758,322	47,342	
1887	8,211,462	49,734	
1888	8,064,642	44,974	
1889	8,244,927	44,204	
1890	9,090,867	49,453	
1891	9,565,739	54,956	
1892	9,671,172	51,259	
1893	10,191,151	53,520	
1894	10,758,307	51,442	
1895	10,692,054	54,659	
1896	11,538,064	59,225	
1897	12,200,306	60,576	
1898	13,130,281	67,079	
1899	14,626,608	75,383	
1900	15,087,680	79,142	
1901	15,468,110	82,351	
1902	16,631,753	83,391	
1903	16,658,091	76,024	
1904	17,209,537	77,652	
1905	17,931,936	78,428	
1906	17,996,349	77,983	
1907	18,746,025	81,172	
1908	7,576,735	81,899	

Year Ended	PASSENGERS SEACOMBE	EGREMONT	NEW BRIGHTON	TOTAL	REVENUE £	NOTES
1909	13,758,268	2,351,040	2,065,129	18,174,437	83,865	
1910	16,136,131	506,239	3,742,998	20,385,368	90,098	L
1911	16,766,493	2,306,716	2,987,963	22,061,172	88,678	
1912	18,224,361	2,986,369	3,578,586	24,789,316	98,765	
1913	15,742,729	2,694,182	4,100,998	22,537,909	99,365	
1914	17,191,154	2,987,871	4,033,870	24,212,895	107,772	
1915	17,012,176	2,779,890	3,647,141	23,439,207	103,386	
1916	16,260,800	2,258,033	2,695,751	21,211,584	107,835	
1917	20,041,715	2,869,992	4,881,678	27,793,385	115,419	
1918	20,175,413	4,670,395	6,951,463	31,797,271	126,902	
1919	19,831,352	3,103,639	5,598,192	28,533,183	180,787	
1920	21,906,821	3,597,368	6,529,211	32,033,300	202,852	
1921	21,932,176	3,316,650	5,592,662	30,841,488	233,038	
1922	19,788,619	3,978,770	3,366,026	27,133,415	255,459	
1923	18,507,980	3,203,084	4,038,391	25,749,455	246,240	
1924	19,749,783	3,097,342	3,938,825	26,785,951	235,355	
1925	19,901,677	3,078,606	4,016,582	26,996,865	234,021	
1926	20,321,760	3,149,278	4,162,973	27,634,011	238,109	
1927	20,227,392	2,567,394	3,387,590	26,182,376	221,222	
1928	20,433,943	2,628,159	3,472,437	26,534,539	227,061	
1929	20,424,789	2,651,175	3,559,979	26,635,943	235,294	
1930	20,638,482	2,568,658	3,706,441	26,903,581	231,405	
1931	20,341,460	2,355,564	3,401,430	26,098,454	213,204	
1932	20,238,969	2,246,238	3,304,034	25,789,341	204,897	
1933	21,389,296	275,106	4,043,575	25,707,977	202,816	A
1934	21,515,848	1,014,019	4,334,149	26,864,016	222,327	
1935	19,575,308	1,106,404	3,468,663	24,150,575	196,375	B
1936	18,261,611	958,687	3,013,404	22,233,702	189,093	
1937	17,760,435	454,900	2,511,816	20,727,151	178,420	C
1938	17,808,792	350,477	2,640,578	20,799,847	177,087	C
1939	16,372,471	301,865	2,421,537	19,095,843	164,793	D
1940	15,687,203	200,732	2,786,970	18,665,905	163,621	
1941	14,363,941		2,261,026	16,624,967	151,164	E
1942	13,912,350		1,600,259	15,512,609	152,104	F
1943	14,207,200		2,150,265	16,357,825	208,589	
1944	12,485,885		3,283,363	15,769,248	283,459	
1945	13,315,678		3,712,849	17,028,527	280,323	
1946	13,751,760		4,032,945	17,784,705	266,629	

Year Ended	PASSENGERS			TOTAL	REVENUE £	NOTES
	SEACOMBE	CRUISING	NEW BRIGHTON			
1947	14,688,297	92,203	3,584,831	18,365,331	237,024	
1948	16,744,401	170,320	4,299,193	21,213,914	281,065	
1949	15,757,515	195,888	3,135,462	19,088,965	249,616	
1950	15,926,297	199,739	3,907,824	20,033,860	260,210	
1951	14,825,050	175,390	2,710,149	17,710,589	236,727	
1952	14,924,248	326,750	2,234,447	17,485,445	296,780	
1953	13,395,301	251,744	2,796,020	16,443,065	314,175	
1954	10,706,657	241,086	2,907,166	13,854,909	318,890	G
1955	9,991,936	241,064	2,443,233	12,676,233	333,307	
1956	10,160,660	230,310	3,086,607	13,477,577	367,434	
1957	9,212,403	199,046	1,929,440	11,340,859	317,389	
1958	8,543,958	178,549	1,769,649	10,492,156	328,171	
1959	7,905,092	186,299	1,730,967	9,822,358	341,184	
1960	7,773,481	175,274	2,053,962	10,002,717	332,658	
1961	7,289,458	179,456	1,671,440	9,140,354	322,477	
1962	6,784,880	164,155	1,533,529	8,482,564	345,680	
1963	6,188,826	134,973	1,083,485	7,407,284	301,742	
1964	6,075,498	133,004	1,169,266	7,377,724	351,094	
1965	5,755,501	135,673	1,141,338	6,999,512	284,974	
1966	4,940,864	103,566	827,169	5,871,599	289,403	
1967	4,670,830	103,344	812,481	5,586,655	274,465	
1968	4,236,565	91,448	724,936	5,052,949	270,087	
1969	3,950,155	83,944	726,847	4,760,946	229,522	
1970	4,039,076	74,692	432,210	4,545,978	202,000	H
1971	3,047,398	63,235	292,756	3,403,389	n/a	
31 Dec						
1971	3,077,382	76,286	216,089	3,369,757	214,000	J
1972	2,709,929	91,210			2,801,139	K
1973	2,461,710	95,928			2,557,638	
1974	2,085,445	108,458			2,193,903	
1975	2,134,281	110,344			2,244,625	
1976	1,720,000	94,371			1,814,371	
1977	1,598,000	52,824			1,598,000	
1978	1,618,000	33,183			1,651,183	M

NOTES

A   1st Apr.-21st May 1932 only. Egremont closed due to damage by steamer.
B   First road tunnel opened 18th July 1934.
C   Egremont & New Brighton closed for winter from 1st October 1936.
D   Through electric train service Liverpool-New Brighton commenced 13th March 1938.
E   Egremont officially closed 13th May 1941.
F   No New Brighton contracts issued.
G   Basis of calculation of contractors' journeys changed.
H   Undertaking transferred to Merseyside PTE 1st December 1969. Data is for 13 months ending 31st December 1971.
J   Wallasey Tunnel first tube opened 28th June 1971.
K   New Brighton closed all summer. Decision to close permanently made 7th Nov.
L   Egremont closed for rebuilding.
M   From 1978 issue of multi-modal tickets makes actual passenger figures a matter of conjecture.

A pre-1914-18 view of Prince's Landing Stage, looking north, with the Cunard Aquitania embarking passengers for New York. The Woodside luggage boat, believed to be Oxton or Bebington is discharging its load while a number of mainly horse drawn vehicles wait to embark. This view clearly demonstrates the chaotic conditions on the stage before it was lengthened in 1921 to provide a third luggage boat berth.　　M. Jenkins collection

APPENDIX 3
LIVERPOOL LANDING STAGE

IN 1821 *Gore's Directory* listed a number of departure points for ferry vessels viz: North side of George's Dock Basin, Parade Slip on west side of George's Dock, Stairs on the west side of King's Dock, Stairs on the west side of Nos. 2 and 3 Graving Docks and the Basin and Slips at the west end of No. 1 Graving Dock. The vessels often fought for spaces at these quays but the gradual introduction of steam led each ferry operator to seek individual landing places. A 'running out stage' on the same basic principle as the later one at Egremont, was provided at the Parade Slip, probably during the extensive reconstruction of George's Dock in 1822-24.

In 1822, Thomas Parry's Seacombe steamers were advertised to depart from the Marine Parade along the west side of Prince's Dock but, in 1832, Parry rented a single vessel inlet built into the southern tip of Prince's Parade which became known as the Seacombe Ferry Basin. This gave Seacombe passengers the advantage of escaping the chaos of George's Ferry Basin and from 16th December 1842, the first floating stage to be employed on the river was launched at Cato's yard, Brunswick Dock and brought into use in the entrance to this inlet. Passengers could now embark at all states of the tide in relative comfort and safety. The Egremont boats originally started from North Pier, George's Dock but they soon joined the New Brighton vessels at the Marine Parade. The stage in the Seacombe Ferry Basin remained in use until 1857 when the inlet was filled in during preparations for the installation of the first Prince's Landing Stage. They were then obliged to join the Egremont and New Brighton boats at the north end of Cubitt's 1847 George's Landing Stage which was fully described in Volume 1.

When the first Prince's Landing Stage was opened on 1st September 1858, the luggage boats were transferred there from George's stage but the advent of larger steamers soon meant that the latter was as congested as ever. The ferry operators continuously pressed the Dock Board to improve landing facilities. A letter from Braithwaite Poole to the Mersey Docks & Harbour Board, dated 12th August 1863, read as follows:

'Gentlemen,

I am instructed by the Wallasey Local Board to ask your permission to erect a gangway on the verge of George's Landing Stage similar to the one erected by the Wirral Commissioners to facilitate the ingress and egress of passengers.

And at the same time, respectfully to call your attention to the inadequate accomodation (sic) at the stage now that the large new vessels, the *Cheshire* and the *Water Lily* are plying.

Hoping you will issue orders to lengthen the stage southward.'

After various alternative schemes had been considered, the fine new George's Landing Stage, joined at the north end to Prince's stage to create a floating structure 2,478ft long, was opened to the public on 27th July 1874. However, because of the carelessness of a gas fitter, it caught fire and was substantially destroyed on the following afternoon.

By 5.0pm that day, the Seacombe boats were departing from a temporary landing at Waterloo Steps but, within a few days, all ferry departures were transferred to a small portion of the northern stage which had survived. Eventually, George's stage was given a temporary plank floor and this limited accommodation was used until the rebuilt stage was towed back into position at the end of July 1875 but repair work was not fully completed until 8th April 1876. During this time, boats had to load alongside each other and it became necessary for orders to be given that the connecting gangplanks must not be uplifted until the main gangway had been raised to prevent passengers being stranded on the wrong boat.

Two berths of 150ft were allocated to Wallasey, one for Seacombe and the other for the northern ferries. The ferry operators were charged for the use of the stage, Wallasey's contribution being 16% of revenue derived from all traffic chargeable with tolls. Additional charges were ten shillings (50p) per year for two balanced gangways, £5 per year for stagemen's hut shared with Woodside and £150 per year for 'an office compartment' though they retained their old luggage office. In December 1876 lamps were attached to the gangways and a simple shelter was erected for waiting passengers. A shelter was provided for the Wallasey traffic in 1878.

The luggage boats were allocated berths at the northern end of the stage, Wallasey making use of the embayment which they had originally requested from 1st April 1880 to facilitate end loading. This embayment was opposed by Birkenhead who refused to use it because of the navigational difficulties of getting in and out of it and had advocated its elimination during the rebuilding after the fire. By 1882, Wallasey had had enough experience of using it to join with Birkenhead in advocating its removal. The Dock Board wanted to move the goods boats further north but the ferries opposed this and by 1888 had finally convinced the Board that the solution lay in removing the embayment. Birkenhead and Wallasey were persuaded to support the Dock Board's Bill for the extension of Prince's Landing Stage including the filling in of the embayment and final agreement was reached in May 1889 though it was 1894 before it went in conjunction with the replacement of Prince's Landing Stage which, when joined to George's stage, created a floating structure 2,478ft long – almost half a mile.

In 1897, the Dock Board reviewed the landing arrangements and increased the combined space allocated to the Woodside and Wallasey ferries by 40ft, of which Wallasey gained 30ft (20ft for passengers and 10ft for goods). Any gangway alterations were to be done by the Council. The following year the Board agreed to the installation of two 'overhead' gangways on the Liverpool stage giving direct access to the upper decks of steamers. These were located between the main deck gangways with a steep staircase approach and a sliding handrail was installed on each vessel to make a resting place for the gangways. A similar

gangway was installed at Seacombe and loading and unloading was greatly accelerated at the busy periods.

In the early years of the century, the use of 160ft long boats created berthing problems and Wallasey asked for an additional 20ft at the passenger berth. Birkenhead refused to co-operate and, in a compromise, the Dock Board gave Wallasey an additional 5ft and a gap of 10ft between the Seacombe and Woodside berths.

The passenger bridges at Liverpool were originally open to the elements but they were glazed and adorned with advertisements by the turn of the century. By 1910 the original narrow bridges were seriously congested and at peak times passengers had great difficulty making their way against the peak flow. Wallasey suggested the provision of a new bridge, placed conveniently to serve the Seacombe, Egremont and New Brighton traffic. Birkenhead agreed to participate financially, Wallasey paying £300 per year and Birkenhead £200 per year for 20 years. An Agreement was signed by the two Corporations and the Dock Board on 27th February 1911 whereby No. 2 bridge

A late 1930s picture of holiday crowds boarding the Woodside boat (left) and waiting for the Seacombe steamer Wallasey *to complete tying up at George's Landing Stage. On the right, eager passengers wait on the steps to the upper deck gangway.*
G. Parry collection

176

was to be moved 90ft south and a new 25ft wide bridge was to be positioned approximately in its former position. As a temporary safety measure, queue barriers, rather like cattle pens, were used on the landing stage from August 1911 to contain the huge crowds waiting for the New Brighton boats at busy weekends.

Wallasey proposed a bridge over which passengers could walk direct from the upper deck of the boats to the Pier Head without touching the main deck of the landing stage but did not think it should bear the whole cost. The Dock Board refused to move in the matter until Wallasey agreed to pay the whole of the expense. However, in March 1912, when Liverpool Corporation announced a Pier Head improvement scheme involving changes to the tramway termini, it was agreed that No. 2 bridge would be moved 69ft north and the new bridge (No.1A) was to be positioned 46ft south of the old No. 2 bridge. This was done on 8th July 1913; the bridge was roofed in and opened for traffic during the autumn, providing considerable relief at peak hours and summer weekends.

In 1921 George's stage was lengthened by 55ft at the south end by inserting a complete new section; Wallasey's two passenger berths were moved southwards and a second berth for the Birkenhead luggage boats was created which benefited Wallasey by eliminating encroachment on their berth. As the flow to the two Wallasey berths was greatly improved by their proximity to No. 1A bridge, Wallasey Corporation agreed to take over some of the bridge charges paid by Birkenhead Corporation and their annual contribution rose to £300.

The landing stage had now reached the form which became familiar to thousands of ferry passengers over several decades. By the time that the ferries passed into the ownership of the Merseyside PTE in 1969, the stage was in poor condition having been given only barely essential maintenance for many years. It was the privatisation of the Dock Board as the Mersey Docks and Harbour Company in 1972 that brought matters to a head as the obligation to provide landing facilities ceased. The full story was dealt with in Chapter 12 of Volume One augmented by additional material in Chapter 8 of this volume.

A 1957 view from the Dock Board offices across the river with either Wallasey *or* Marlowe *approaching the landing stage and her sister approaching Seacombe stage in the background. The Woodside boat (left centre) also approaches its berth.*
Medley & Bird

The crew of Daffodil on the occasion of the visit of King George V, who crossed the river in this vessel to lay the foundation stone of Wallasey Town Hall. The complement has obviously been augmented for the occasion. Seamen's jerseys emblazoned with 'Wallasey Ferries' were used until after the 1939-45 war; the inscription was then reduced to 'W C F' as an economy measure.

M. Jenkins collection

APPENDIX 4

THE FERRIES' STAFF

THE employees of the ferries undertaking were divided into two broad classifications – land-based and 'floating' – and the pay structure was usually framed so that the floating staff received higher pay in recognition of the dangers and hardships which they faced. As was normal for the times, discipline was strict – even harsh – in the 19th and early 20th centuries and pay for the less skilled men was barely above subsistence level. Hard economic times were often dealt with by reducing wages across the board and strikes brought a ruthless response from the employers. Nevertheless, for the times, Wallasey Council was an enlightened employer and jobs on the municipally owned ferries were eagerly sought. Employment ran in families and many men gave loyal service for over 50 years for, at a time when there were no pensions for manual workers, a man would continue working for as long as he was physically able or until his employer decided he was no longer fit. Working hours, originally 12 per day on six days a week, were gradually reduced during the 19th century until the eight-hour day was introduced in 1911 though it was difficult to apply this to all the floating staff. Paid holidays, sick pay and superannuation schemes were generous for the times.

Surprisingly, until 1923, even the Masters and Engineers were mostly unskilled workers. They joined as firemen or junior deckhands and worked their way up over very many years. Alternatively, they obtained experience on tugs or lighters on the river and sought more secure jobs on the ferries. The floating grades in the early municipal years were Masters, Mates, Engineers, 1st and 2nd class hands and 1st and 2nd class firemen (i.e. stokers). In later times, engineering staff were no longer termed 'floating' being grouped with the maintenance and repair staff ashore. Records of rates of pay are sketchy but a table of examples will be found at the end of this section.

Working Practices on the River

On paddle steamers, a typical crew consisted of 10 men and a boy – Master, Mate, Engineer, Assistant Engineer, two engine room hands, two firemen, two seamen and a deck boy. One of the seamen would act as helmsman, the helm being situated on deck, originally abaft the funnel so as to keep the linkages with the rudder as short as possible. In the early years of the twentieth century, the wheel was moved to a flying bridge but the earliest examples of these provided no protection from the weather. A seaman would be stationed as lookout in the bow. In very thick fog when the lookout was not visible from the bridge, another man would stand some yards behind him to act as a relay for any information and a third would man the steam whistle. In fog the luggage boat would follow the passenger boat across the river. Luggage boats were obliged at all times to give way to passenger boats and New Brighton boats to Seacombe boats.

The crew of Daisy *which was active from 1879 to 1910, The master is at rear centre and the others are (left to right) mate, chief engineer, three deckhands and two engine room staff.*
R. T. McMahon

On the Seacombe crossing, the ten-minute service demanded a three-minute turnround at each landing stage and the limited space available at the Liverpool stage with other boats mooring fore and aft demanded a considerable degree of skill from the Master. The mooring ropes were carried on each vessel, stowed on double bollards fore and aft. Seamen would throw a line to a stageman who would haul in the rope and secure it to the bollards on the stage while the men on board would judge when to tighten them round the bollards, figure eight fashion. Once the boat was secured, the seamen would open the sliding gangway door after ensuring that all disembarking passengers were behind the brass line on deck and then, in conjunction with a stageman, lower the gangways on to the deck. Standing orders demanded that both gangways were to be used except at night. When departure time approached, the bell would be rung from the bridge, the gangways raised and the doors closed. The stagemen would hurriedly loosen the mooring ropes and throw them back on board to be stowed by the deckhands as the vessel moved away. When the upper deck gangway was in use, the Mate would descend from the bridge, slide back a section of movable rail and capture a rope attached to the gangway with a special hook, bringing the gangway down on to the deck. As soon as the waiting passengers had embarked, this gangway would be raised.

The same routine was followed at all the ferry terminals though the urgency was not as great at New Brighton. The turnround on the Seacombe crossing was extremely slick and it was rare for a vessel to run late because of a poor turnround. Berthing was always done against the flow of the tide so that in one direction the boat described an S-shaped course and in the other, a direct course. At peak hours it was customary for regular travellers to take a constitutional by marching round the promenade deck in an anti-clockwise direction sometimes up to four or five abreast.

Deckhands swept the saloons and decks as necessary and all vessels were thoroughly cleaned overnight. This involved scrubbing the saloon floors and seats, flushing the decks and cleaning the windows. On the night boat, one saloon would be closed off while this was done and would not be reopened to allow the other to be cleaned until it was thoroughly dry.

All the boats were coaled at Seacombe at night, commencing with the first boat off the New Brighton service. The Foreman Coalheaver was responsible for arranging the order of coaling for the remainder. Coal was put into the bunkers through a circular hole near the engine room companionway and there were strict rules about ensuring that the grating protecting it was safely replaced. It was not possible for all the vessels to moor at the stage and coaling was done direct from *Emily* which moored alongside each in turn. When she was withdrawn, coal was loaded from bags which had been stacked on the south end of the stage. Vessels were moored abreast as necessary. Rules stated that ashes in bags must be unloaded at Seacombe daily at times least likely to cause annoyance to passengers; ashes were never thrown into the river.

Stagemen's duties varied between the different landing stages but all were responsible for lowering and raising gangways and assisting with mooring. At Seacombe one man was originally responsible for issuing tickets for bicycles and luggage but this became the responsibility of the ticket clerks when the new terminus was opened in 1933. They were responsible for cleaning the stage, bridges, waiting room and lavatories. At Egremont and New Brighton these duties extended to the full length of the pier, the terminal building and collectors' boxes which were dealt with at night when the service was not running. During fog, stagemen were required to ring the fog bell three times in rapid succession every minute; this function was eventually mechanised.

Luggage stagemen brought unaccompanied parcels ashore and stowed them in the shed provided; they were responsible for maintaining the chains, seeing to the lights and oiling the hinge pins on the floating roadway.

Maintenance of the oil-burning lights on the vessels and stages was the job of the Lamp Trimmer who also kept Seacombe ferry vestibule clean and washed out the collectors' boxes weekly. Deckhands on the luggage boats assisted the Mate in loading the vessel, operated the gangways and kept the decks clean, no sinecure when animals were carried. Roving collectors took cash from drivers and issued tickets.

There were frequent cases of seamen or stagehands diving into the river to rescue people who had fallen or jumped into the river. The boat would then be lowered to assist in the rescue. These efforts were always rewarded by the Council after the facts had been formally reported at a regular meeting; for many years the going rate was £1.

Bonuses

Various schemes for the payment of 'gratuities' (which would nowadays be called bonuses) to masters, mates and engineers in recognition of attaining certain levels of service, originated in 1867. They were originally paid to Masters for avoiding collisions and keeping the vessel clean and in good order. The rate in 1876 was £9 for six months. In 1870 a scheme based on coal economy was introduced for Engineers. A coal consumption norm for each vessel was determined and Engineers were paid two shillings (10p) for every ton of coal saved below this norm. By 1876 this had been changed, probably because every boat had a different norm which could vary depending on the origin and quality of the coal. The Engineers' bonus was then paid at the rate of £5 for six months for 'good conduct and management of engines and boilers, economy of stores and punctuality of trips'. Liverpool bye-laws prohibited making excessive smoke and there was a smoke bonus which was shared between the Master and the engine room staff and was forfeited if fines were levied. The fines were paid out of the smoke bonus fund and if there was insufficient left for a full distribution, all would suffer. In 1895 the smoke bonus for firemen, assistant firemen and trimmers was 6d ($2^1/_2$p) per week. In 1891, payments for good conduct etc. were increased from £5 to £10, a substantial sum in those days and a strong incentive to maintain high standards. Although regular travellers could cross the river for years without experiencing one, collisions involving ferry boats were not rare, especially when jockeying for position at Liverpool. Each incident would be carefully investigated and blame apportioned. In serious cases of negligence, not only would the bonus be lost but the culprit might

be disrated. There were occasional instances of a master being reduced to a mate or even a deckhand. For a time from 1927 bonuses were consolidated but eventually were separated once more, Safety and Qualification bonuses being paid into the PTE era. The frequency of minor bumps between Wallasey and Birkenhead boats at Liverpool was such that the two authorities had a knock for knock agreement to deal with these incidents.

Special bonuses were paid to all ratings in recognition of exceptional services during periods of very stormy or foggy weather.

Seasonal Work

From the winter of 1906-7, the seasonal men, engaged to handle the greatly increased summer traffic were not dismissed but were employed during the winter on maintenance tasks ashore which had hitherto been neglected or contracted out. These included repairs at terminals, renewal of pier decking and cleaning of mooring chains, machinery and pontoons. In the 1950s with New Brighton traffic declining, the extra crews for summer were to a large extent covered by regular staff on overtime. Mates were appointed as Acting Masters and seamen as Acting Mates for the full season and their jobs were covered by others

Part of a poster issued by Wallasey Ferries in the early 1920s to maximise the publicity value of the wartime exploits of Royal Iris *and* Royal Daffodil.
M. Jenkins collection

A 19th century picture of a master, recognisable by his distinctive headgear, standing in the 'cab' of the exposed bridge of his vessel.　　　　　E. J. MacWatt

working on their rest days. Seasonal workers, often retired people, were used as toll collectors and the like. The department deliberately carried a nucleus of surplus staff in the winter, employing them on cleaning and repair work. This fitted in with the practice of preparing the fleet for surveys at the quietest time of the year. In its second report in 1954 the Special Economy Committee criticised the practice of allowing staff to take their holidays in the summer season when the demand was greatest. However, by this time, staff were included in the national municipal grading scheme the rules of which laid down holiday entitlement.

In 1923 it had been recognised that the increased mechanical complexity of modern vessels demanded more skill in the engine room and the principal of appointing a nucleus of certificated engineers was adopted. These were designated Chief Engineers and allocated on the basis of one for each vessel. Their engagement was progressive over the next few years as older men, some with over 50 years service, retired. In 1960 'Ticket money' was introduced at varying rates between five shillings and £1 per week for Mates and First Seamen with Master's certificates and First Seamen with Mate's certificates.

The organisation of the undertaking in the post 1939-45 years provided for four sections:

1. Engineering and Repair Staff in charge of a Superintendent Engineer. This included the engine room staff afloat.
2. Floating Staff in charge of a Marine Superintendent; includes floating staff (except engine-room) and stage hands.
3. Collection and Inspection Staff in charge of a Superintendent.
4. Administration and Office Staff under the Assistant Manager; includes timekeeping and stores control staff.

In 1960 there were lengthy discussions about reducing the establishment. The number of Masters and Mates had been reduced from 12 at the turn of the century to 10 and the Corporation now wanted a reduction to eight. In those days redundancy of long-serving employees was not contemplated and the reduction was achieved by natural wastage over a period.

On 1st December 1969 the PTE took over 145 ferries personnel from Birkenhead and Wallasey Corporations but the need to supply services hitherto provided by other municipal departments resulted in the number of ferries' staff increasing to 245 at the end of 1972. The political decision not to make any employee redundant resulted in the number falling only to 210 by the end of March 1975. However, drastic cuts brought this down to 150 by 31st March 1977 at which level it remained for some years. The last coal fired boats carried a crew of 10 comprising two deck officers, two engineers, two firemen, three seamen and a boy but diesel and diesel-electric vessels with bridge control required fewer men and by the 1990s a crew comprised six men, two on the bridge, two in the engine room and two on deck. When *Mountwood* was recommissioned in 1999 and renamed *Royal Daffodil*, her crew was reduced to five with just one man in the engine room.

SPECIMEN WAGE RATES

Masters 1862 £1.17.0d (£1.85) per week; 1880 £2 pw; 1895 £2.5.0d (£2.25); 1919 £4.15.0d (£4.75) pw; 1927 £250-290 pa.
Senior Mates 1895 £1.13.0d (£1.65); 1919 £3.18.6d (£3.92) pw; 1927 £250-285; Oct. 1950 £6.7.4d (£6.37); Nov. 1955 £8.11.4d (£8.57).
Engineers without tickets, 1895 £2.4.0d (£2.20) pw; 1919 £4.12.6d (£4.62); 1927 £250-285 pa; Oct. 1950 £6.16.0d (£6.60) pw; 1955 £9.0.0d pw.
Seamen 1895 £1.6.6d-£1.7.6d (£1.32-£1.37) pw; 1919 £3.7.6d (£3.37) pw; 1950 £5.7.0d-£5.11.0d (£5.35-£5.55) pw; 1955 £7.10.0d-£7.14.0d (£7.50-£7.70) pw.
Firemen 1895 £1.9.6d (£1.47) pw; 1919 £3.10.6d (£3.52) pw; 1950 £5.16.2d (£5.81) pw; 1955 £7.14.2d (£7.71) pw.
Inspector 1919 £3.11.6d (£3.57) pw; 1950 £6.0.6d (£6.02) pw; 1955 £8.3.6d (£8.18) pw.
Lamp Trimmer 1919 £3.17.6d (£3.87) pw; 1950 £5.9.0d (£5.45) pw; 1955 £7.12.0d (£7.60) pw.

NOTE Because of deflation, 1919 rates were reduced in 1922 by an average of 15s. 0d (75p) per week in three three-monthly stages of 5/- (25p).

APPENDIX 5

CONTRACT TICKETS

ALL the Mersey ferries issued contracts (season tickets) which were available for unlimited travel for three, six and twelve months. These provided some working capital for the undertaking and had originally been issued to tie the passenger to a particular ferry though once the Wallasey ferries came under common ownership this was of no importance. However Wallasey had to do it because everyone else did it. One strange feature of ferry contracts was the issuing of an additional contract at a lower rate to any bona fide member of the same household except servants. The table of contract rates from 1st April 1869, shows that these tickets were veritable bargains (Table 1).

The contract system was designed for the use of the middle classes as no manual worker or clerk could find sufficient up front money as he often lacked job security. The number of contracts in use in September 1912 was as follows:

24-hour annual	56
Annual, first	3,322
Annual, additional	2,611
6-month	165
3-month	1,424
1-month	8,810
TOTAL	16,388

The number of contracts issued in the year ending 31st August 1914 was 146,776; as will be noted above, the introduction of the popular monthly ticket boosted sales enormously. There had been agitation for monthly tickets for some time but their introduction was a product of the fright felt by the ferries when faced with the railway extension to New Brighton which severely affected contract sales. Egremont, though not threatened by the railway, had to fall in line with New Brighton as the same boats served both. The reductions gave the management the excuse to rid themselves of the 'additional' tickets but they were only partly successful as a strong lobby managed to persuade the Council to retain the annual contracts. However, the differential between the first and additional tickets was now minimal. The Seacombe three-month additional contract was reinstated in 1915 at 6s.6d. (62p).

The price of contracts fell in 1881 (Seacombe only), 1884 (all), 1895 (New Brighton and Egremont), 1897 (some Egremont), 1907 (all), 1913 (Egremont and New Brighton) and 1914 when rates reached their lowest level as shown below (Table 2). The reduction of 29% for a Seacombe annual contractor compared with 1869 contrasts with no reduction at all for the ordinary fare passenger. The day and night contract was first issued in 1881 and was issued only for one year but was extended to all ferries in 1916 when it was increased to £2.2s.0d. (£2.10).

Table 1

	12 months		6 months		3 months	
Seacombe	£1.11.6d	(1.57)	19.0d	(95p)	12.6d	(62p)
Additional	15.0d	(75p)	9.0d	(45p)	6.6d	(32p)
Egremont	£2.12.6d	(2.62)	£1.11.6d	(1.57)	£1.0.0d	(1.05)
Additional	1. 1.0d	(1.05)	15.0d	(75p)	10.0d	(50p)
New Brighton	£3.13.6d	(3.67)	£2.12.6d	(2.62)	£1.11.6d	(1.57)
Additional	1.11.6d	(1.57)	1. 1.0d	(1.05)	15.0d	(75p)

Table 2

	12 months		6 months		3 months		1 month	
Seacombe	£1. 2 .6d	(1.12)	13.0d	(65p)	6.9d	(34p)	2.3d	(11p)
Additional	15.0d	(75p)						
Day & Night	1.11.6d	(1.57)						
Egremont	£1. 4.0d	(1.20)	13.0d	(65p)	7.0d	(35p)	2.6d	(12p)
Additional	1. 0.0d	(1.00)						
New Brighton	£1. 5.0d	(1.25)	13.6d	(67p)	7.0d	(35p)	smr3.6d	(17p)
Additional	1. 2.6d	(1.57)						wtr2.6d	(12p)

As indicated in Chapter 5, wartime inflation soon deprived commuters of these cheap rates, contracts reaching a new high level on 1st April 1921 as a result of which weekly (Monday to Saturday) contracts were issued for the first time at Seacombe 1s. 9d., Egremont 2s.0d and New Brighton (winter rate) 2s. 3d., bringing the system within the means of many more regular travellers. The restriction on the Sunday use of contracts was removed in 1925. Charges fell in 1923 and 1926 and there was a general reduction in fares, contracts and freight tolls on 1st April 1930. There was then a period of stability until the 1939-45 war re-ignited the inflationary spiral once more; by this time contracts were available only at Seacombe.

When bus and ferry contracts, which had been tried briefly in 1953, were again issued in 1959-60 (see Chapter 8) a new principle was introduced i.e. that contracts could be issued for either five days or seven days per week and this distinction was continued after 2nd October 1960 when the combined contracts ceased to be issued. The rates for a Seacombe contract in 1961-62 were 12 months £11. 13s.0d. (£11.65), one month £1. 4s. 0d. (£1.20), one month (junior) 14s. 0d. (70p), weekly (5-day) 5s. 0d. (25p), weekly 7-day 6s. 0d. (30p), weekly with cycle 5-day 7s. 6d. (37p), 7-day 8s. 6d. (43p), 7-day (24 hr) including car park, cars 13s. 0d. (65p), motor cycles 8s. 0d. (40p).

1

A selection of tickets from the Wallasey ferries.
1. *Seacombe contract issued by A. Parry & Sons valid 1845-46 (Courtesy G. H. Peers).*
2. *Egremont & Seacombe contract signed by ferry manager Braithwaite Poole and valid 1862-63 (Courtesy G. H. Peers).*
Opposite:
3. *Bus & Ferry ticket Moreton-Liverpool issued 5.4.54-27.11.55 at 1/- fare. There were two versions of this ticket, a red stripe for those issued on the buses and a green stripe for those issued at Seacombe ferry.*
4. *Last municipal issue of Bus & Ferry ticket Moreton-Liverpool, issued from 12.2.67 at 2/6d fare.*
5. *Combined Bus & Ferry contract. Issued between 31.5.59 & 2.10.60.*
6. *'Zone ticket' valid for 12 journeys between Seacombe & Liverpool.*
7. *Early morning return ticket Seacombe-Liverpool issued before 8.0am.*
8. *Weekly Contract for a lady expiring 10.4.48. Fare 1/9d. The overprints were allocated randomly to combat fraud.*
9. *Weekly Contract for a gentleman expiring 3.12.60. Fare 5/-.*

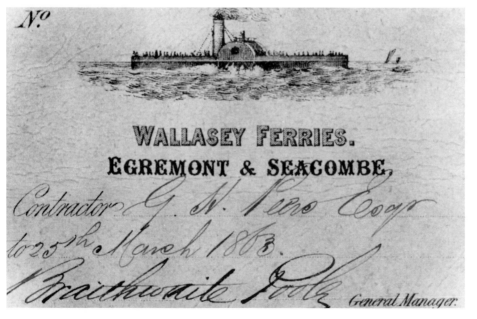

2

3

4

5

6

7

8

9

10

11

12

13

14

15

16

17

18

19

20

10 & 11. *Luggage boat tickets for passenger (4d) and Motor Car (1/-) issued on the last sailing on 31.3.47.*

12. *1/- Evening excursion return ticket Liverpool-New Brighton available after 5.0pm Mondays to Fridays.*

13. *Merseyside PTE Ultimate New Brighton-Liverpool 10p child return.*

14. *Merseyside PTE Ultimate 1¹/₂p ticket for dog, cycle, autocycle, excess luggage, truck or wheelbarrow on passenger boat.*

15 & 16. *Merseyside PTE Ultimate tickets for 2 adults @ 22p & 2 Children @ 11p.*

17. *British Railways excursion ticket for Liverpool & New Brighton issued in conjunction with rail ticket to Liverpool (Courtesy J. B. Horne).*

18. *Excursion ticket for Liverpool-New Brighton issued by Manchester South Junction & Altrincham Railway (Courtesy J. B. Horne).*

19. *Through LMS ticket from Brinscall (between Blackburn & Chorley) & New Brighton via Liverpool & ferry. (Courtesy J. B. Horne).*

20. *Through ticket from any Liverpool Overhead Railway station to Seacombe.*

APPENDIX 6

ADDENDUM TO VOLUME 1

The Railway Ferry

Much more information about the railway owned ferry at Monks Ferry has come to light since Volume 1 was published. It will be recalled that as a condition to their agreement to the Vesting Bill transferring the Chester-Birkenhead railway and its branches to the London & North Western and Great Western Railways jointly, the Birkenhead Commissioners required the railway companies to take back the Monks Ferry and cancel certain debts. The ferry was taken over by the railways on 1st January 1862 but as the railway companies owned no suitable vessels, they hired them from the Birkenhead Commissioners. This arrangement continued for more than five years but on 1st October 1867, the Commissioners gave six months' notice of withdrawal of their boats. The railways had insufficient statutory powers to run the ferry and clauses were hurriedly inserted in the LNWR (Additional Powers) Act, 1868.

The railway Joint Traffic Committee had considered alternative quotations for boat hire at their meeting on 13th December 1861 and these were as follows:

Birkenhead Commissioners, 2 boats @ £8 per day each at one month's notice.
Williams & Oulton, 3 boats @ £5,700 per annum.
W. & T. Jolliffe, 2 boats @ £8 per day each.
Robert Hetherington, 1 boat @ £9 per day.
Thomas Begbie, s.s.*Farm* £200 per annum and *Xanthe* at £70 per annum.

The staffing requirements were not discussed until the meeting on 10th January 1862 so presumably the Commissioners' staff carried on for another month or so. The railways engaged three men, a ticket collector and a toll collector at Monks Ferry and a man to meet the boats and attend the stage at Liverpool.

The question of acquiring their own boats was discussed several times particularly when there were complaints about the ferry. The Manchester, Sheffield and Lincolnshire Railway had two vessels for sale in 1865 but these were deemed to be unsuitable. Finally when the Commissioners drew up the drawbridge as it were in 1867, they appointed a sub-committee who turned to the LNW's Marine Superintendent at Holyhead, Capt. C. E. Dent, for assistance. He drew up a specification for three identical boats which unfortunately has not been traced and the order was placed with Bowdler, Chaffer & Co. at

Seacombe. The sub-committee received a report on the operating requirements on 30th April 1868 as follows:

Steamboat Dept.
Holyhead
20 April 1868

To the Manager of the Joint Committee,
Sir

In compliance of Minute 887 of the Joint Committee dated 30 March 1868, I beg to recommend the following arrangements for the Monks Ferry service:
A staff consisting of two masters, three mates, five seamen, three engineers and three firemen for the manning and working of the boats; this will supply two full crews with the necessary men on board the third boat to comply with the regulation of the Trustees of the Liverpool Docks with reference to the number that must be on board if a vessel is lying alongside a stage and also enable a third boat to be run in an emergency at short notice; a carpenter to undertake repairs necessary, he should also attend to the issue of coal and stores.

The boats should have two moorings and the reserve boat should lie at the jetty.

I have arranged with Capt. Barker, Superintendent of the Woodside ferry boats that the present moorings shall be lifted and brought on shore next month and that if the companies purchase them, they (the companies) will be at the expense of laying them down again.

The coal should be brought by rail and a reserve stock established on the jetty by the reserve berth which would also become the coaling berth. The coal should be put on board by a shoot or small crane, the latter preferable; there is ample space at this jetty for the erection of fitting or repairing sheds should such be hereafter considered desirable. The stores viz: tallow, soft soap, masts, brooms, emery cloth, paint, black varnish, rope etc. should be kept with the present stores of the companies and issued weekly to the boats, the issue being demanded and a book kept for the purpose in each vessel and signed for on receipt.

As the vessels are guaranteed for six months against faulty construction in hull and machinery, I do not think it will be advisable to go to the expense in providing repairing machinery etc. It will be preferable to leave it to whoever has the superintendence of the boats to suggest such improvements from time to time as would be found profitable from the practical experience of the working. I enclose an estimate of the probable cost of working these steamers on the plan laid down; the estimate is framed on a very liberal scale and I think under careful management a considerable reduction in the working expenses is possible.

2 masters at 39/- per week	£3.18.0d
3 mates at 30/6d per week	4.11.6
5 seamen at 28/6d per week	7. 2.6
3 engineers at 39/- per week	5.17.0
3 firemen at 28/6d per week	4. 5.6
1 carpenter at 40/- per week	2. 0.0
Depreciation & insurance	27. 0.0
*Coals 50 tons at 10/-p.w. delivered	25. 0.0
*Chandlery	2. 0.0
*Ordinary repairs	9. 0.0
*Discharging of coal – 8 wagons at 1/6d	12.0
*Board of Trade Certificates	2.13.6
TOTAL per week	£94. 0.0

* These are approximate, gathered from information obtained as to present consumption and the contract prices paid by the establishment for such articles. The present weekly allowance to such of the Woodside boats (about the size of the Monks Ferry boats) as tallow 14lb, waste 12lb, engine oil 7 pints, soft soap 2.1/2 lb., brooms 2 and emery cloth 3 sheets.

Faithfully yours
Charles E. Dent.

The three vessels were named *Thames, Mersey* and *Severn* and it soon became apparent that too little attention had been given to their design in relation to their working environment. The Joint Committee was told by Capt. Dent on 5th June that *Thames* and *Severn* had failed to reach their contract speed of 10 knots, but because of time restraints their slightly inferior performance had had to be accepted. All three were top heavy and the need for ballasting was being examined. The following month there were complaints about the 'crankiness' of the boats which had apparently been remedied. Dent recommended the removal of the ladies' cabins to give more deck space. It was decided to do one boat and, if satisfactory, to follow with the others. *Severn* was done in August and the others within the next two months. There was insufficient width for the luggage trucks to pass between the boiler casing and the paddle boxes and partitions had to be modified to provide additional width of 10 inches. £10 per boat was authorised for this work. Then it was found that more headroom was required between the paddle boxes and £8.15.0d (£8.75) per vessel was authorised for this to be done. A gridiron to enable the boats to be beached for repairs at Monks Ferry was completed by the end of August 1868.

There were many complaints about the ferry staff both as regards quality and quantity. A report in the Albion Newspaper for 9th July 1869 stated that only two men were acting as crew on one boat on 23rd June and the man in charge was intoxicated.

The Captain and mate were dismissed, the engineer fined 10s. (50p) and a junior seaman fined 2s.6d (12$\frac{1}{2}$p). In July 1869 new arrangements were proposed. Four additional men were appointed to superintend the luggage on the boats and stage and the Mersey Docks and Harbour Board was asked to provide waiting rooms at both ends of the Liverpool stage; this was done by the end of the year at a rental of £20 per room per annum. A covered way for passengers using the turnstile at the top of the slip at Monks Ferry was proposed.

In September 1872 revised temporary berthing arrangements were made with the Dock Board, the railway boats being given the former Tranmere berth at the south end of the stage as that ferry had closed on 29th June 1872. The railway boats could also use the berth on the inside of the south end of the stage. They later applied for the Rock Ferry berth and it is not clear what happened when Tranmere reopened in May 1873.

On the face of it, three boats were more than adequate to maintain the service and it seems likely the vessels were troublesome as records show boats being hired from both the Birkenhead Commissioners and the Wallasey Local Board at various dates.

After the ferry closed in 1878 there was a scheme to use it for the cattle trade but the parties could not afford the rent demanded by the railways or the cost of the necessary alterations.

WOODSIDE ANNUAL CONTRACT MEDALLIONS
(opposite)

On page 29 of Volume One reference is made to the changeover from card tickets for Woodside annual contracts to medallions to be worn on the watch-chain from 1861 and images of these for the years 1861-65 have recently become available. It will be noted that the shape was changed each year to reduce the risk of fraud. The 1861 issue appears to have been made in brass but the others are a dark bronze colour, similar to old copper coins. Most of the serial numbers are upright and accurately spaced suggesting that more than just a hammer and individual number punchs may have been used. However, the 1865 issue bears inaccuracies of spacing which suggest that individual punches were used or a less competent person used them. It is not known how long this practice was continued but there was eventually a reversion to card tickets.
Reproduced by courtesy of Mr Tim Ely.

		OBVERSE	REVERSE

	OBVERSE	REVERSE
	YEARLY CONTRACTOR 1861 WOODSIDE FERRY	NOT TRANSFERABLE Nº 2260 & TO BE SHEWN WHEN REQUIRED
 	1862 YEARLY CONTRACTOR BY WOODSIDE FERRY	NOT TRANSFERABLE & TO BE SHEWN WHEN REQUIRED Nº 375
 	1863 YEARLY CONTRACTOR WOODSIDE FERRY	NOT TRANSFERABLE AND TO BE SHEWN WHEN REQUIRED Nº 1995
 	YEARLY CONTRACTOR 1864 WOODSIDE FERRY	NOT TRANSFERABLE AND TO BE SHEWN WHEN REQUIRED Nº 2120
 	1865 YEARLY CONTRACTOR BY WOODSIDE FERRY	Nº 1941 NOT TRANSFERABLE & TO BE SHEWN WHEN REQUIRED

APPENDIX 7

THE ENGINE ROOM ROUTINE

THE following, contributed by Mr T. Morgan, a marine engineer of many years experience, describes, in graphic terms, the Engine Room routine prior to a steam-driven ferry vessel going into service and at the end of the day.

The steamer for the 6.0am service had lain alongside the landing stage all night. Everything was shut down and the six fires had been banked. The Chief Engineer goes down the ladder into the inky blackness of the unlit engine room, takes his torch from his pocket and switches it on. The shaft of light is reflected off the highly polished steel and brasswork and he makes his way into the Boiler Room. His fireman is already shaking the banked fires into life by the light of a paraffin lamp.

'Morning Jack'. 'Morning Joe, everything OK?' 'Yes' is Joe's reply. The Chief then blows the Water Gauge glasses to ascertain if there is sufficient water in the boilers and it is safe for the Fireman to bring steam pressure up to the full 180 lb/sq.in. The Fireman would do this himself before doing anything else but chances cannot be taken with high pressure steam and the Chief wants to see for himself that the Water Gauges are working properly. Having blown all four glasses through - two on each boiler - he opened each of the six furnace doors in turn and looks at the furnace crowns to see that there is no sign of overheating.

Finding about 60 or 70lbs. of steam on the pressure gauges, he very carefully eases the Auxiliary Steam and Dynamo Stop Valves on both boilers off their seats, just enough for s wisp of steam to hiss into the pipelines. Valves on steam lines must be opened very slowly when everything is cold because when steam enters an empty pipe it will immediately expand and condense. If the valve has been opened quickly, the condensed water will be driven with great force up to the next valve and possibly rupture the pipe with disastrous consequences so, until everything is warmed up, things must be taken very carefully.

After a few minutes he opens the valves a little more and, because it was a colleague and not himself who shut down the previous night, he goes back into the Engine Room and, with the aid of his torch, checks that all the drains on every piece of machinery are open and that all the exhaust changeover cocks are set to atmosphere. Drains must be opened to allow any water of condensation which has accumulated overnight to drain away into the bilges and to prevent any pipes from being under vacuum. Returning to the Stokehold, he slowly opens the Auxiliary Stop Valves. By this time the needles on the pressure gauges are climbing steadily towards 'the Blood' - the red line on the gauge dials indicating the working pressure. Going back to the Engine Room, he eases the Dynamo Engine stop valve off its seat and there is a hissing and spluttering as steam and water issue from the drain. After giving the engine some attention from his oilcan, the Chief bars the engine round by hand to just over the centre because, being a single cylinder machine, it won't start from any position. He then opens the valve a little more and the engine begins to turn. Giving it a few minutes to warm through, he then opens the stop valve fully. The voltmeter on the switchboard is showing 110 volts so he closes the Circuit Breaker and light floods the Engine Room. He closes the drain.

The next piece of equipment to claim his attention is the Boiler Feed Pump. The forward one was in use yesterday so he will use the aft one today. This is set away in the same careful manner as the Dynamo and he is careful to open the Discharge Valve to the boilers first. He sticks his head round the Boiler Room door. 'Feed pump's on, Joe.' The Fireman can regulate the flow of water into the boilers by means of the Feed Check Valves on the boiler fronts.

Jack now turns his attention to the Sea Water Circulating Pump for cooling the Condenser. This is treated in the same careful manner as the Dynamo and Feed Pump. Incidentally. the sea water discharge from the condenser could be seen as a continuous stream of water pouring from the ship's side, just aft of the starboard aft gangway. The Air Pump next receives his attention and is dealt with in the same meticulous way as everything else. This pump draws air and vapour and the water of condensation from the condenser. The air and vapour goes free to the atmosphere and the water is pumped to the feed tank where it is picked up by the feed pump and delivered back to the boilers again. Now that the condenser is available, the Chief goes round and changes all the exhaust switch cocks to condenser from atmosphere. up to now, all the exhaust steam has been discharged up the two waste steam pipes up the aft side of the funnel.

By this time the Second Engineer has come aboard and is setting away the Sanitary Pump to keep the toilet flush tanks full, checking the blocks of solid grease in the Plummer Blocks which lubricate the propeller shaft in their bearings, making sure there is plenty of oil in the Stern Tube oil tank; the Stern Tube is where the propeller shaft passes through the hull out into the water. He then starts the Main Engines. Besides the six oil boxes on the Main Bearings of the Crankshaft and the four for the Running Gear, there are over 90 oiling points on each engine to be attended to with the oil can. The Main Stop Valve on each boiler is now carefully eased open, waiting until the steam has had time to warm the pipes thoroughly before opening them fully. The Steering Engine is then dealt with in the same way. The warming through of the Main Engines can now start but first the Chief will notify the Master or Mate that he is going to move the engines under steam so that some one can be detailed to keep an eye on the mooring lines.

The Engine Manoeuvring Valves are now cracked open and, by constant manipulation of the Reversing Gear, the engines can be rotated two or three revolutions, first one way and then the other. A seaman makes his appearance and asks permission to try the whistle and the steering gear. On getting the affirmative answer,1 he disappears and, in a moment, there is a blast from the whistle and the chug-chug of the steering engine as it runs round from midships to hard-a-port, to hard-a-starboard and back to midships. At about 5.50am there is a sudden clamour of the Telegraph bells - 'Stand By'- followed by a few kicks of the engines and she is berthed and the gangways lowered for the first embarkation of the day.

What seems to be a long drawn out procedure in fact takes about an hour for, as one machine is warming through another is being prepared. The Main Engine Cylinder the Casing Drains will be left partially open until, perhaps, arrival at Liverpool on the first trip thus ensuring that everything is thoroughly warmed through; they will then be closed for the rest of the day.

Lubrication of all machinery is by hand oil can and is done about every half hour. At the same time the top an bottom ends of the connecting rods, the main bearings, valve gear eccentrics and piston rod guides are all felt by hand to ensure that everything is running cool.

The Chief and Second Engineer and their two firemen will be relieved and their colleagues will then take the vessel through to the last trip of the day. After disembarking her last passengers, she will move along the stage to her night berth. Fires have been cleaned during the day and there is a considerable amount of ash in the Ash Bunker. All this has to be shovelled into bags, hoisted up on to the deck through the Ash Scuttle and stacked on the stage ready for collection the following day. After this the coal bunkers have to be filled with fresh coal through similar scuttles, one on each side of the deck.

While this is going on the Chief and Second Engineer are shutting down. The two Main Stop Valves on the boilers are closed, the gauge glasses blown through and the water level brought up to about five eighths of a glass. All the exhaust changeover cocks are turned to atmosphere and the Air and Circulating Pumps are stopped and their drains opened. The Steering Engine and Feed Pumps are similarly dealt with and the Main Engine drains opened. Finally, after the Firemen have finished their work, the Dynamo is shut down and its drain opened and the two Auxiliary and Dynamo Stop Valves shut.

APPENDIX 8

NOTE: Owners of early vessels are shown under Name. Otherwise municipally owned.

Date built (Acquired)	Type	Name & Owner	Gross Tonnage	Dimensions (LxBxD) ft	Shipbuilders & Engine Bldrs
1822	Wood PS	Seacombe [1] PARRY	49	70x26.5x7	Mottershead & Hayes
1824	Wood PS	Alexander PARRY	40		Humble & Hurry
1824	Wood PS	Alice PARRY	50		Mottershead & Hayes
1826 (1834)	Wood PS	Sir John Moore ATHERTON	92	103.1x16.6x8.8	Land & Denny Eng: Murdoch & Cross
1829 (1830)	Wood PS	Loch Eck ASKEW	37	81.9x12.4x7.1	John Wood, Port Glasgow Eng: David Napier.
1831	Wood PS	John Rigby ASKEW	50	83.0x13.2x8.2	Humble & Hurry Eng: J. Rigby
1826 (1832)	Wood PS	Hero ASKEW	?	80.4x16.6x?	? (Tranmere) Eng: Foster & Gladstone
1830 (1835?)	Wood PS	Liverpool PARRY, PRESTOPINO	?		Mottershead & Hayes
1834 (1836)	Iron PS	Ennishowen EGREMONT SFCo.	70	91.6x15.4x8.0	? Dumbarton
1835	Wood PS	Admiral Lord Nelson (or Admiral) PARRY	?		
1836	Wood? PS	Seacombe [2] PARRY	50	77x14.9x7.0	
1837	Iron PS	Egremont [1] (later Jenny Lind) EGREMONT SF, PRESTOPINO, PARRY	68	87.7x17.4x8.2	Glasgow
1837	Iron PS	Thomas Royden EGREMONT SFCo.	108	90.7x15.1x7.4	Thos. Royden
1840	Iron PS	Elizabeth ATHERTON, COULBORN	51	88.6x15.3x7.8	Robt. Russell & Son, B'head
1845	Iron PS	Thomas Wilson PARRY	50	92.7x14.8x8.4	Thos. Wilson, B'head Eng: Fawcett & Wilson
1845	Iron PS	Queen of Beauty COULBORN	68	87 x 17 x 8	Thos. Vernon, L'pool ?
1834 (18??)	Wood PS	Sir Thomas Stanley PARRY	100	85.3x15.9x7.0	Thos. Wilson, B'head Eng: Wm. Fawcett
1846	Iron PS	James Atherton COULBORN	108	116.3x16.3x7.6	Thos. Pearson, L'pool Eng: J. Rigby
1839 (1846)	Iron PS	Duke SOTHERN, EGREMONT Co.	80	76 x 16 x ?	J. Sothern, Runcorn
1847	Wood PS	Wallasey [1] FLETCHER, COULBORN	119	109.8x16.6x9.0	J. Sothern, Egremont
(1849)	Iron PS	Invincible PARRY, PRESTOPINO	78	100x16.6x8.9	? (Clyde)
1849	Iron PS	Fairy COULBORN	75	118 x 16 x 7.5	Thos.Vernon, L'pool
1834 (1853)	Wood PS	Ramsgate Packet PARRY	107	94.5x14.9x9.8	? (Harwich)
1827 (1853)	Wood PS	Britannia PARRY, PRESTOPINO	80	67.7x14.8x6.2	Mottershead & Hayes
1853 (1857)	Iron PS	Tiger COULBORN	53	? x ? x6.3	Thos. Vernon & Sons
1862	Iron PS	Mayflower	182.8	135.6x20.1x8.1	H. M. Lawrence & Co.
1862	Iron PS	Waterlily	204	140x22.1x8.4	Jones, Quiggin & Co. Eng: G. Forrester
1862	Iron PS	Wild Rose	155	105.4x21.2x9.0	Jones, Quiggin & Co. Eng: G. Forrester
1858 (1864)	Iron PS	Gem (ex-Liscard) COULBORN	48 later 100	122x18x7.8 133.4x18.1x8.1	R. Napier, Govan Eng: G.Forrester

Machinery	nhp	Notes
Side lever 1-cyl	28	Sold by 1836 or rebuilt (see *Seacombe* [2])
Side lever 1-cyl	40	? sold 1829
Side lever 1-cyl	?50	? Burnt out 1825 & rebuilt. Sold 1833-39 Broken up between 1847-52
	50	
Side lever 1-cyl	30	Egremont steamer. Sold 1837 (?)
Side lever 1-cyl	40	Sold by 1853
Side lever 1-cyl	40	Built for Tranmere ferry. Sold 1835 or 1838 Also used on L'pool-Magazines-Hoylake ferry Sold 1853
	32	
Side lever 1-cyl		Destroyed in hurricane 6th Jan. 1839
	30	Probably a rebuild of Seacombe (1). Sold Feb. 1853
Side lever 1-cyl	70	Egremont steamer. Sold to Thos. Prestopino 6/1849. Renamed *Jenny Lind* & leased to J. R. Murphy 1850. Resumed original name & used at Seacombe 3-7/1853. Scrapped 1853.
Side lever 1-cyl	45	Egremont steamer. Sold 1853, probably to Bridgewater Trustees. Broken up after collision with *Water Lily* 1868.
Side lever 1-cyl	50	Cost £500. Bought as goods boat. 401 pass. New boiler 1853. Goods boat again 1862.
	47	442 pass. Cost £1,500. New boiler & to New Brighton 1854. Believed sunk 1858. Mainly luggage boat 11.1872-1877. Floating workshop during rebuilding of Seacombe ferry. Sold to W. E. Clayton (£152) 25.11.1878
	70	Ex-yacht. Still working 1.1856. Twin bulkheads; two compartments. Last Coulborn boat.
Side lever 1-cyl	45	Built entirely of oak for Eastham ferry. Offered for sale 1854. Registered in name of Thos. Doyle, Seacombe 1857. Broken up Apr. 1857.
Side lever 2-cyl 28in. 36in.	50	529 pass. Cost £4,800. New boiler 1855. Reboilered, engines repaired & hull altered 1864. Luggage boat 25.7.1878. Sold to R.Smith for £205 27.1.1881. Broken up 1884.
Side lever 1-cyl	30	Egremont steamer. Repossessed by Sothern 1847
Side lever 1-cyl	45	650 pass. Cost £2,500. Rebuilt by Coulbourns ?1857. 150 tons To Local Board £1,000 15.8.1861. Sunk 1.12.1867. Raised & sold 1.1868. Sold 1854 as passenger tender. Rebuilt 1861
Side lever 1-cyl	58	514 pass. Cost £5,200. New boiler & 60 hp 2-cyl oscillating engine 30in. 36in. 1860. Withdrawn 2/1862. Engine & boiler to *Wild Rose* & broken up 1862. Not used. Sold 1854. Sold by Thos. Prestopino 1866. Broken up at Tranmere 1868
Side lever 2-cyl	50	Built for Tranmere ferry. Several owners by 1853. Sold 1854.
Side lever 1-cyl	50	370 pass, Cost £1,500. To New Brighton 1859. Sold to Cato, Miller & Co. 4.8.1864 for £560.
2-cyl.oscillating Bore 34in. stroke 42in.	70	653 pass. (863 from 1877) Launched 14.5.62. In service 1.8.1862. Lengthened to 155ft 1877. New engines (Fawcett) 1877. Sold to Allsup 1885. To Rock Ferry Co. 1886. Renamed *Mayfly* 1888 Sold as hospital ship Dartmouth 1893.
2-cyl oscillating Bore 34in. Stroke 42in.	80	Launched 14.4.1862. Trials 1.8.62. Cost £5400 793 pass. First vessel with saloons. Gas lit. Forward saloons removed 1883 to accommodate carts. Scrapped by J. J. King, Garston 1892.
2-cyl oscillating Bore 30in. Stroke 36in.	60	Trials 30.9.1862. 503 pass. Sold 1883 T. Redhead as tug.
As rebuilt 2-cyl diag. 26in - 48in	40	417 pass. Cost £5,200. Sale by Coulbourns to foreign owners 1861 fell through. Renamed 1861 for service on Clyde. Bought from Mark Whitworth & Sons, Bristol 9.1864 £1,050. Major rebuild 12.1873-9.1874 by Allsups, Preston. Sold to Allsups 26.5.1881. Wrecked off Scilly Is. 26.11.1881 en route to Sierra Leone.

Date built (Acquired)	Type	Name & Owner	Gross Tonnage	Dimensions (LxBxD) ft	Shipbuilders & Engine Bldrs
1865	Iron PS	*Heatherbell*	205	159.8x21.2x9.0	Thos. Vernon & Sons Eng: John Jones & Co.
1867 (19.3.1874)	Wood SS	*Maggie*	119	87 x19.8 x9.7	Northwich
1869 (1872)	Iron PS	*Seymour*	110	121.6x18.0x7.8	Bowdler, Chaffer & Co. Eng: Fawcett
1852 (1872)	Iron PS	*Swallow*	93	131.7x15.1x7.3	A. Denny, Dumbarton
1864 (1876)	Iron Flat	*South End*	255	121.5x31.3x6.9	Bowdler, Chaffer & Co.
1879	Iron PS	*Sunflower*	345 later 242	140.2x26.2x9.6	T. B. Seath, Rutherglen Eng: D. Rowan & Co.
1879	Iron PS	*Daisy* 81303	285	150.2x25.3x10.3	T. B. Seath, Rutherglen Eng: D. Rowan & Co.
1879	Iron PS	*Primrose*	285	150.2x25.3x10.3	T. B. Seath, Rutherglen Eng: D. Rowan & Co.
1881	Iron DTSS	*Wallasey* [2] 84180	459	140 x 45 x 11	W. Allsup & Sons.
1883	Iron PS	*Violet*	273	150 x 26.1x10.2	W. Allsup & Sons
1884	Steel DTSS	*Crocus* 91174	301	130.9x35.1x10.9	W. Allsup & Sons
1884	Steel DTSS	*Snowdrop* [1]	300	130.9x35.2x10.9	W. Allsup & Sons
1891	Steel PS	*Thistle* 97858	301	150.0x26.2x10.5	J. Scott, Kinghorn
1865 (1891)	Iron PS	*Shamrock*	373	150.6x32.2x10.9	Scott & Co., Northfleet Engines C. J. Mare.
1895	Steel SS	*Emily* 105379	154	97.4x19.0x9.3	J. Scott, Kinghorn
1896	Steel PS	*Pansy* 106830	333	160.0x27.1x9.9	J. Scott, Kinghorn
1896	Steel PS	*John Herron* 106796	333	160.0x27.1x9.9	J. Scott, Kinghorn
1898	Iron/Steel SS	*Tulip* 109422	432	160.0x27.1x11.1	T. Walker. Sudbrooke, Mon. Eng: Plenty & Co.
1900	Steel TSS	*Rose* 113422	514	155.6x42.1x11.0	John Jones & Son, Liverpool
1900	Steel TSS	*Lily* 113451	514	155.6x42.1x11.0	John Jones & Son, Liverpool
1901	Steel DTSS	*Seacombe* [3] 115232	589	140.0x50.3x12.0	Cochran & Co., Annan
1906	Steel TSS	*Iris* 123971	465	152.0x40.6x11.2	R. Stephenson & Co. Eng: Rollo & Co.
1906	Steel TSS	*Daffodil* 123974	465	152.1x40.6x11.2	R. Stephenson & Co. Eng: Rollo & Co.
1910	Steel TSS	*Bluebell* renamed *John Joyce*	439	152.3x38.6x10.9	Cammell Laird & Co.
1910	Steel TSS	*Snowdrop*	439	152.3x38.6x10.9	Cammell Laird & Co.
1921	Steel DTSS	*Leasowe* [1]	734	146.3x50.1x14.0	J. I. Thornycroft & Co.
1921	Steel DTSS	*Liscard* [2]	734	146.3x50.1x14.0	J. I. Thornycroft & Co.
1922	Steel TSS	*Francis Storey*	464	150.0x40.1x11.0	Ailsa Shpbldg & Eng. Co.
1922	Steel TSS	*J. Farley*	464	150.0x40.1x11.0	Ailsa Shpbldg & Eng. Co.

Machinery	nhp	Notes
2-cyl. oscillating Bore 36in. Stroke 42in.	80	Launched 23.5.1865, del'd 11.8.65. Cost £7,500. 807 pass. (later 837). Sold £950 H. J. Ward, L'pool. 1891. Renamed *Erin's King*. St.George's Steam Tug Co. Dublin. Scrapped by King, Garston 1900.
2-cyl. simple	20	Coal barge. Cost £1,500 from West Hartlepool. Fitted with steam winch to lift $2^1/_2$t June 1874. Reboilered by G. Forrester 1.1883. Taken in part exchange by James Scott for *Emily* 18.12.1895 for £260.
Simple oscillating- 2-cyl. 33in.36in	60	543 pass. Ex-Tranmere Ferry Co.11.7.1872. £4,000. Sold to S. Davies, Tranmere 14.1.1886 £250. To J. Davies 1889.
? ex *Waterwitch*	30	Ex-Loch Lomond Steam Boat Co. Renamed from *Queen Victoria* 1868. Fitted with feathering floats. Purchased 14.5.1872 for £1,300. Into service 8.72. Sold to Thos. Seed 7.1882. Broken up 1883.
	-	Ex-Mersey River Steamboat Co. Landing stage. Sold 1883.
2-cyl. oscillating	60	Launched 13.8.1879. Cost £7,800. Pass. cert. 998. Built as luggage boat with railway track on deck. Rebuilt as passenger ship (951) 2.1882. Broken up by ferry staff end 1904.
2-cyl. oscillating 36in. - 66in.	90	Launched 13.8.1879. Cost £9,100. 965 pass. New boilers & saloon lengthened 1893. Sold to Hughes & Thomas £625 1910.
2-cyl.oscillating 36in. 66in.	90	Launched 5.7.1879. In service 2.10.1879. 965 pass. Sold 4.1906. To R. & D. Jones, L'pool for cruising 1908.
4-cyl. compound 30in. 35in. - 24in.	99	Luggage boat. Launched 10.9.1881 Into service 8.82. Cost £11,300. Based on Birkenhead steamer *Oxton*. Broken up 1925.
2-cyl. diag. oscill. 38in. 60in.	99	Launched 2.11.1883. Cost £10,250. 1,017 pass. Del'd 3.7.1884 Sold to J. J. King & Sons, Garston 6.1901 (£790) Broken up.
Compound 4-cyl. 18in. 37in.-24in.	113	Launched 23.8.1884, In service 26.1.1885. 1303 pass. Cost £12,250. Sold to Chester owners 1909 (£699)
Compound 4-cyl. 18in. 37in.-24in.	113	Launched 20.11.1884. In service 3.1885.Cost £12,250. Sold to Mersey Trading Co., L'pool for Rhyl-Llandudno service. Lost at sea off Rhyl 1908.
Compound 2-cyl. diag. 30in. 57in. 57in.	138	Cost £12,650. 1,200 pass. Withdrawn 1910. Sold (£750) to John Hughes & Co. 6.1911.
2-cyl. oscillating 34in. 48in.	154	Ex-Birkenhead Corporation. Cost £700. Renamed from *Woodside* 15.10.1891. Rebuilt as luggage boat & used as landing boat. The only two funnel luggage boat. Sold (£766) to J. J. King, Garston 11.3.1902
2-cyl. compound 12in. 20in. - 16in.	36	Coal barge. Launched 16.12.1895. Cost £2,041. Sold 9.1933 for scrap £550.
2 cyl. comp. diag 30in. 57in. - 57in.	204	1,240 pass. Sold 1916. Sank at Bull Bay, Anglesey 21.1.1917.
2-cyl. comp. diag 30in. 57in. - 57in.	164	1,240 pass. In service 21.7.1896. Requisitioned 1916. Sold to Soc. de Transbordment, Cherbourg as tender. Broken up 1925.
3-cyl. trip.expansion 13in. 23in. 34 - $22^1/_2$in.	60	Launched 28.9.1897. Suction dredger. Sold to Grayson, Rollo & Clover Docks 1934. Scrapped at Troon 1964.
8-cyl. trip.expansion 2x19in. 2x26in. 4x31-21in.	242	1,831 pass. Flying bridge added 1901. Sold to Palmer, Dublin and renamed *An Saorstat* 6.1927. Sold to British Iron & Steel Co. and renamed *Biscosalve* 1941. Broken up at Preston 1951.
ditto	242	1,831 pass. Sold to Palmer, Dublin & renamed *Failte* 6.1927. Sold to British & Irish SS Co. 1941. Wrecked & broken up at Passage West, Cork 1943.
6-cyl. trip.expansion 13in. 22in. 34 -$22^1/_2$in.	172	Luggage boat. Launched 28.9.1901. Cost £18,000. Sold 1929. Broken up.
6-cyl. trip. expansion 16in. 24in. 41in. 21in. stroke.	217	1,735 pass. Covered accommodation for steersman 3.1911. Requisitioned by Admiralty 1917. Extensive refit and renamed *Royal Iris* 1919. Cruise ship with grey hull 1923. Sold 12.10.1931 to Palmer, Dublin. To Cork Hbr Commrs. renamed *Blarney* 1946. Scrapped at Passage West 12.1961.
ditto	217	1,735 pass. Covered accommodation for steersman 3.1911. Requisitioned by Admiralty 1917. Extensive refit & renamed *Royal Daffodil* 1919. Cruise ship with grey hull 1932. Sold to New Medway Steam Packet Co. 1934. Sold for £1,000 and broken up at Ghent 1938.
ditto	207	1,563 pass. Sold to Palgrove, Murphy, Dublin for £2,450 3.11.1936. To Cork Harbour Commrs. and renamed *Shandon* 1946. Broken up at Passage West 1953.
ditto	207	1,563 passrs. Sold to LNE Rly. Co. for £2,350 12.10.1936 for Granton-Burntisland service. Renamed *Thane of Fife*. Tender service during 1939-45 war. Scrapped at Passage West ?.
6-cyl. trip.expansion $14^1/_2$in. $23^1/_2$in. 36in. -24in.	208	Luggage boat. Sold for £1,850 & broken up at Preston 9.8.1948. Other accounts say left Mersey 27.8.1948 for Troon.
ditto	208	Luggage boat. Requisitioned as floating crane 1941. Sold to Danish owners for c.£10,000 1946. Converted to salvage vessel and renamed *Lisca*.
8-cyl. trip. expansion 2x15in. 2x$23^1/_2$in. 4x25in.-21in.	187	1,629 pass. To Navy 1942 as Net defence vessel. Sold to Cork Harbour Commrs.8.2.1951 (£7,500). Renamed *Killarney*.
ditto	187	Launched 17.1.1922. 1,629 pass. Requisitioned 1943 as Net defence vessel. Reconditioned and converted to oil burning 1946. Wallsend Howsham pressure system. Sold 1952 £12,000.

Date built (Acquired)	Type	Name & Owner	Gross Tonnage	Dimensions (LxBxD) ft	Shipbuilders & Engine Bldrs
1927	Steel TSS	*Wallasey* [3]	606	151.4x48.1x14.5	Caledon Shpbld & Eng. Co., Dundee.
1927	Steel TSS	*Marlowe*	606	151.4x48.1x14.5	Caledon Shpbld & Eng. Co., Dundee.
1929	Steel DTSS	*Perch Rock*	766	144.6x50.1x15.4	Caledon Shpbld & Eng. Co., Dundee.
1932	Steel DTSS	*Royal Iris II*	607	151.0x48.1x13.0	Harland & Wolff, Govan Eng: D & W Henderson
1933	Steel SS	*Emily II*	284	121 x 24 x11	Cammell Laird & Co.
1934	Steel DTSS	*Royal Daffodil II* [1]	591	151.0x46.0x13.5	Cammell Laird & Co.
1944 (1949)	Wood TSMV	*Wallasey Belle*	125	108.3x17.8x10.1	Johnson & Jago, Leigh on Sea Eng: Gray Marine Motor Co.
1951	Steel TSMV	*Royal Iris* [3]	622	160.0x48.1x13.6	W. Denny & Sons Ltd. Eng: Ruston, Hornby, GE & Metro-Vickers
1951	Steel TSMV	*Leasowe* [2]	311	133.7x34.1x11.3	Philip & Son, Dartmouth Eng: Crossley Bros.
1951	Steel TSMV	*Egremont* [2]	311	133.7x34.1x11.3	Philip & Son, Dartmouth Eng: Crossley Bros.
1958	Steel TSMV	*Royal Daffodil II* [2]	609	143.1x46.1x12.0	Jas. Lamont & Co. Eng: Crossley Bros.
1960	Steel TSMV	*Mountwood*	464	152.3x40.5x12.5	Philip & Son, Dartmouth Eng: Crossley Bros. Ruston & Hornsby auxiliaries
1960	Steel TSMV	*Woodchurch*	464	152.3x40.5x12.5	Philip & Son, Dartmouth Eng: Crossley Bros. Ruston & Hornsby auxiliaries.
1962	Steel TSMV	*Overchurch*	468	152.5x40.6x12.5	Cammell Laird & Co. Eng: Crossley Bros. Ruston & Hornsby auxiliaries.

Machinery	nhp	Notes
6-cyl. vertical triple expansion 14^1/$_2$in. 23^1/$_2$in. 38-24in.	183	2,233 pass. In service 19.7.27. Cost £42,298. Reconditioned by Harland & Wolff 1958 (£62,401). Sold to Van Heyghen Frères, Antwerp (£5,150) 2.1964.
ditto	183	2,233 pass. In service 30.8.27. Cost £41,602. Converted to oil 1947. 2 oil fired Scotch boilers. Sold 23.2.1958 British Iron & Steel Corp. (£6,000). Broken up at Preston by Thos. Ward & Co.
ditto	185	Luggage boat. Launched 25.1.1929. Last vehicle ferry in service 31.3.1947. Fitted with twin Flettner rudders. Converted as relief passenger vessel 1947 (1,600 pass). Sold to Swedish owners 17.12.1953 (£8,800). Renamed *Betula* and converted into passenger and vehicle ferry.
6-cyl. vertical triple expansion 14in 23^1/$_2$in. 38-20in.	185	2,024 pass. In service 10.5.1932. Cost £43,290. Renamed *Royal Iris* 1.7.1947. Renamed *St. Hilary* 14.3.1950. Sold to Provinciale Waterstaat Zuid Holland 29.2.1956. (£12,000). Converted to car ferry & renamed *Haringvliet*.
2-cyl. comp. 13^1/$_2$in. 28^1/$_2$in.-18in.	53	Coal barge. Launched 26.6.33. In service 21.8.1933. Cost £9,690. Sold 1937.
Twin vertical triple expansion Cyl. 23^1/$_2$in. 38in. Stroke 24in	1,200 ihp	1,995 pass. (1955: 1,982 ferry service, 850 cruising). Cost £44,790. Sunk at Seacombe 8.5.1941. Raised 2.6.1942. Reconditioned by Grayson, Rollo & Clover & re-entered service 2.6.1943. Converted to oil 1947. Renamed *St. Hilary* 10.1957. Sold 24.8.1962 (£7,000).
2 SCSA 12-cyl. 4^1/$_2$in.-5in.	126	250 pass. Acquired as *Channel Belle* for £14,500. 11.1949. Renamed *Wallasey Belle* 1.4.1950. Laid up end 1950. Sold 9.53 (£1,250) to Martin, Torquay.
4 SCSA 6-cyl 10^1/$_2$in.-10^1/$_2$in. elec. generator	1,080 bhp	Launched 5.12.1950. In service 2.5.1951. 2,296 pass (ferry) 1,000 cruising. Cost £450,000. Refurbished 1972 (£68,000). Sold 1993 for use as a club at Cardiff. Moored, derelict, on Thames in 2002.
2 SCSA each 8 cyl. 10^1/$_2$in.-13^1/$_2$in.	1,280 bhp	Launched 18.5.1951 1,472 pass. ferry, 700 cruising. Cost £140,000. Sold 2.1974 to Greek owners & renamed *Naias II* (£3,400).
ditto	1,280 bhp	Launched 10.12.1951. 1472 pass. ferry, 700 cruising. Cost £140,000. Sold 3.8.1975 for use as a club at Salcombe, Devon.
Direct diesel propulsion	1,360 bhp	1,950 pass. Cost £225,000. Air brakes fitted 1963. Renamed *Royal Daffodil*. Sold to Greek owners (£55,000) 1977 & renamed *Ioulis Keas II*.
Direct diesel propulsion	1,360	1,200 pass. Bridge control. Automatic air brakes. Refitted 2001 by Wright & Beyer. Renamed *Royal Iris of the Mersey* 2002. ex-Birkenhead Corporation.
ditto	1,360 bhp	1,200 pass. Bridge control. Automatic air brakes. ex-Birkenhead Corporation.
ditto	1,360 bhp	1,200 pass. Bridge control. Automatic air brakes. ex-Birkenhead Corporation. Refitted 6.1999 by Wartsila NSD (UK) Ltd; Equipped with CW6L170 700kw engines. Through saloon on both decks. Forward gangway doors removed. Renamed *Royal Daffodil*.

INDEX

* denotes a photograph

3. Index of Shipbuilders, Shipowners & Other Maritime Firms

General Index